JOHN GAGE is the former Head of the Depart
at Cambridge University. He is an acknowledged
on the history of art and color and has written many books on the subject
including *Colour and Culture* and *Colour and Meaning*, both published by
Thames & Hudson.

WITHDRAWN

Thames & Hudson world of art

This famous series provides the widest available
range of illustrated books on art in all its aspects.

If you would like to receive a complete list
of titles in print please write to:

THAMES & HUDSON
181A High Holborn
London WC1V 7QX

In the United States please write to:

THAMES & HUDSON INC.
500 Fifth Avenue
New York, New York 10110

Printed in Singapore

John Gage

Color in Art

196 illustrations, 167 in color

Thames & Hudson world of art

For Paula

Who keeps the colours flying

FRONTISPIECE
1. **Ellsworth Kelly**, *Spectrum 1*, 1953.

© 2006 Thames & Hudson Ltd, London

First published in 2006 in paperback in the United States of America by Thames & Hudson Inc., 500 Fifth Avenue, New York, New York 10110

thamesandhudsonusa.com

Library of Congress Catalog Card Number 2006901312

ISBN-13: 978-0-500-20394-1
ISBN-10: 0-500-20394-6

Printed and bound in Singapore by CS Graphics

Contents

Introduction

Colour is implicated in physics, in chemistry, in physiology and psychology, as well as in language and philosophy; yet it is visual art alone that has engaged simultaneously with most or all of these branches of knowledge and experience. Thus, to know art goes a long way towards knowing colour and, whereas in my earlier studies, *Colour and Culture* (1993) and *Colour and Meaning* (1999), I gave some attention to the sciences of colour, in this book I approach these other topics largely through the thought and practice of artists. But, of course, this thought and these practices were, and are, inflected by the prevailing intellectual and social climate of the day, just as they in turn contribute to it. Some philosophers in the ancient Greek world appealed to the experience of the painters' use of pigments to explain their notions of the nature of colours and their mixture in matter; but, from Aristotle onwards, they were also very aware that the surface appearance of colours is very deceptive: 'We do not see colours as they really are', wrote the Peripatetic author of the only surviving early Greek treatise, *On Colours*, who knew that the surface appearance of colours is not to be trusted. This is an idea that means essentially that it is the context of colours as well as their immediate physical stimulus (the internal or surface structure of the objects that reflect some wavelengths of light and absorb others) that determine how they are seen. It is an idea which has continued to preoccupy artists, at least up to the Op Art of the 1960s, notably in Josef Albers's *Interaction of Color* (1963), where the proposition that 'In visual perception a color is almost never seen as it really is – as it physically is' was demonstrated in the most elegant and visually exciting way [2].

Presented in this rather bland verbal formula, it is, however, a scarcely plausible notion, for the 'physical' element in colour is simply a set of wavelengths that impinge on the eye and have, as yet, no identity as what we understand as 'colour'. This physical element is not 'colour', but variable types of radiant energy which are 'really' out there in the world, but invisible. Even the human visual system does not produce 'colour', since the mechanisms of the retina simply convert physical into electrochemical energy, which is fed into the nervous system, and ultimately into the cortex of the brain. One set of the retinal photoreceptors, called 'cones', is receptive to wavelengths of light around 420 nanometers (units of frequency); another, to wavelengths of around 530 nm; and a third, to frequencies of around 560 nm, corresponding roughly to our perceptions of blue, green and red. These are the 'primary' colours of light. Yellow, however, which appears at a wavelength of around 580 nm, and is usually regarded as an unmixed colour, is thought to result from the interaction of the 'red' and 'green' cones. The retina records and transmits sensation, not perception, and the recognition of even a single colour depends upon complicated cerebral processes, such as inference and memory. 'Colour' is thus, first and foremost, a question of psychology (see Chapter 2). The gap between colour sensation and colour perception can be illustrated by the fact that the human eye is capable of discriminating between many millions of colour stimuli (the fact that various researchers have put the number at between one and ten million suggests that these figures are not based on empirical studies, but are extrapolations from a limited database), but the brain chooses to perceive and record only a limited number. I shall have more to say on this in Chapter 5, on colour language.

The discovery in the early nineteenth century that there are as few as three different types of cone function in the retina depended on the much earlier reduction by painters of the distinct categories of colours to three 'primaries'. These were not the primary colours of light, red, green and blue [3], but red, blue and yellow, which, it was thought – with some justification – could generate the whole range of colours by mixing. Colour-mixing had been little practised in antiquity for largely ideological reasons: nature should not be interfered with by man; mixture produced change, which was a bad thing. But there were also good chemical reasons why it was risky, and it could produce unpleasant visual results. By the later Middle Ages, however, there were more examples of mixed colours – green from blue and yellow, for example – where specifically green pigments were rare and costly; and the tool for mixing, the painter's palette, begins to make its appearance in Europe around 1400. The development of oil painting in the early Renaissance hastened the extension of mixing by inhibiting undesirable chemical reactions between particles of pigment, which were now sheathed in a film of protective oil. The new Renaissance interest in naturalistic painting depended on the capacity to match the various colours of nature with pigment mixtures. But artists were also fascinated by the idea that, symbolically as well as practically, the three 'primary' or 'primitive' colours could encompass the whole world of colour, an idea which appears for the first time in treatises on art in the second half of the sixteenth century. Chapter 1 looks at how the primaries themselves became tinged with ideology.

It is sometimes said, especially by artists, that colour cannot be described or discussed in words. It is true that the recent attempts by ethnolinguists to identify a universal 'basic' colour vocabulary have met with well-founded criticisms, but it is also true that the love of colour among artists has led them to be far from reticent about it, and in this book I have drawn heavily on their views, which have an immediacy and often a poetry that work in the opposite direction to the urge for simplification characteristic of philosophy and the natural sciences. What I propose to show is that artists have a great diversity of views even about similar aspects of colour, and exemplify this diversity in their work. Experimental psychologists who, since the beginnings of their science in the mid-nineteenth century, have been concerned with human (and animal) responses to colour, have

3. **Wilhelm von Bezold**, *Colour Circle*, from *The Theory of Color in Relation to Art and Art-Industry*, 1876. Bezold was a Munich physicist and meteorologist, but his book is one of the earliest by a scientist to be directed specifically at artists. Unlike Moses Harris's symmetrical circle [29], von Bezold's circle is asymmetrical because it not only incorporates the newly identified light primaries, red, green and blue, and their complementaries, blue-green, purple and yellow, but also recognizes that, perceptually, the areas of each colour are not equal.

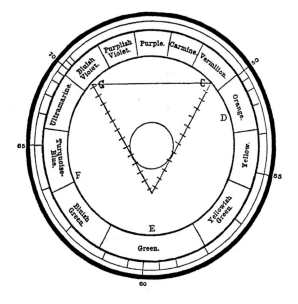

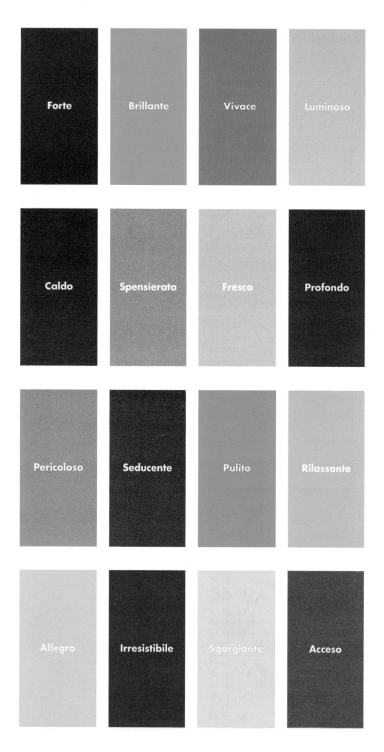

Forte

Brillante

Vivace

Luminoso

Caldo

Spensierato

Fresco

Profondo

Pericoloso

Seducente

Pulito

Rilassante

Allegro

Irresistibile

Sgargiante

Acceso

rarely drawn on the experiences of artists, as opposed to small samples of the 'general public' (often in fact university students) and, as a consequence, they have drawn many conclusions – for example, on the question of colour preferences, which have, for the most part, remained stranded in the circular arguments of opinion polls and market research [4]. In many parts of this book, but especially in Chapter 6, I look at the more open-ended treatment of colour meaning by artists.

Since many artists in the twentieth century, notably Matisse (1869–1954) [5] and Kandinsky (1866–1944) [6], at a time when the radical reshaping of modern art called for manifestos and extensive verbal commentary, have been remarkably articulate about their approaches to colour, I have drawn more heavily on them than on the pre-modern painters I looked at in my earlier books; and this means that I give here greater prominence to recent art than in those earlier studies. I have also extended the discussion into two new areas: to non-European art, where it seems to me that some colour issues are articulated more clearly than in the European tradition; and to media other than painting and sculpture – film, performance and other multi-media works – where there are new issues at stake and new ways of approaching the old ones. This book is concerned with the history of colour, but is not itself a history; rather, each chapter develops a theme from physics, or chemistry, or psychology, or linguistics, for example, which is intended to pinpoint that discipline's relationship with art. Although it begins with physics and chemistry, and works through physiology, colour is primarily a psychological phenomenon. Hence, the issues raised are unlikely to be resolved, but instead will be successively reinterpreted and exemplified through the creative ingenuity of artists. I hope by the end of this survey to have conveyed some sense of this endless creativity.

4. Hewlett-Packard advertisement, 2002. This chart, from an advertisement for computer printers, reflects the widespread belief that colours are closely related to feelings, and may be exploited in mass-marketing.

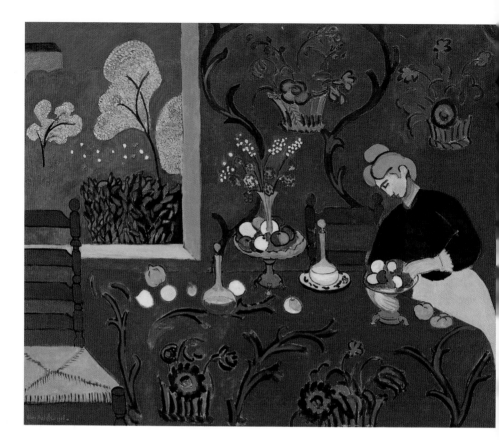

5. **Henri Matisse**, *Harmony in Red/La desserte*, 1908. The recent discovery of an early colour photograph of this painting shows that the red areas were originally green, and this is one of many examples of the radical revisions made by Matisse in the course of painting, revisions which he was one of the first to incorporate into a theory of process, discussed in his exactly contemporary *Notes of a Painter.*

6. **Wassily Kandinsky**, study for the cover of *The Blue Rider Almanac*, 1911. This is one of the earliest manifestations of Kandinsky's belief that blue was the colour most appropriate to round shapes (see Chapter 3); and in cocooning his rider in an aura of blue he was also alluding to the spirituality of this colour, an idea he shared with the spiritualist movement Theosophy.

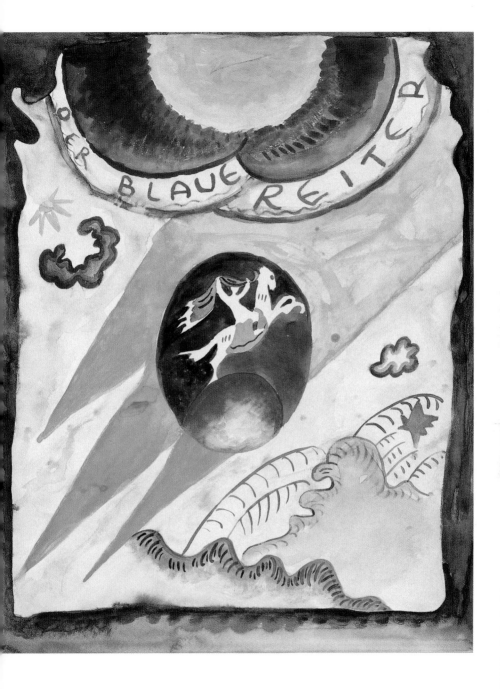

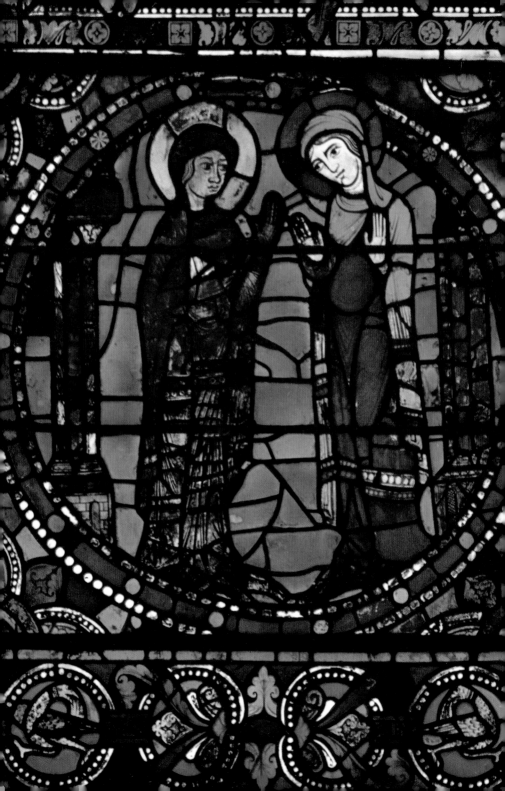

Chapter 1   Light from Colour – Colour from Light

Any European account of colour in art must begin with the belief, which dominated Western culture for many centuries, that light and colour are distinct entities, and that colours are themselves of two distinct types: those that are stable attributes of material substances, and those that are 'accidental', such as the evanescent colours of the rainbow [8] and the colours of some birds' feathers, which change according to the viewpoint of the spectator. The 'accidental' colours remained more or less mysterious until the close of the Middle Ages, and were not definitively united with light and with the colours of substances until the seventeenth century; but the colours of substances were much investigated and discussed, particularly because of their relevance to the practical activities of jewellers, dyers and painters.

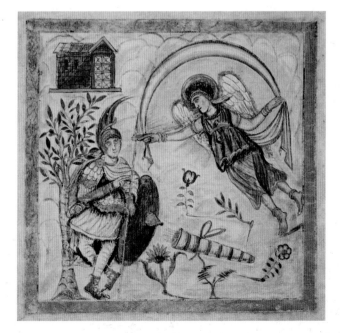

The Pre-Socratic philosopher Empedocles (fifth century BC), for example, compared the mixtures of the four elements, earth, air, fire and water, to the way painters achieved harmony by mixing colours. None of the recorded ancient Greek treatises on art has come down to us, but the single surviving Greek treatise on colour, by a follower of Aristotle (fourth century BC), on the other hand, specifically stated that colour should be studied 'not by blending pigments as painters do', which suggests that other philosophers besides Empedocles were still inclined to do just that. The Roman painters of Pompeii used coloured under-painting in a similar way to a technique that Aristotle had described several centuries earlier, where artists overlaid 'a less vivid upon a more vivid colour, as when they desire to represent an object appearing under water, or enveloped in a haze' [9]. In practice, however, the more vivid – and more expensive – pigments tended to be used for the top layer, and Aristotle may

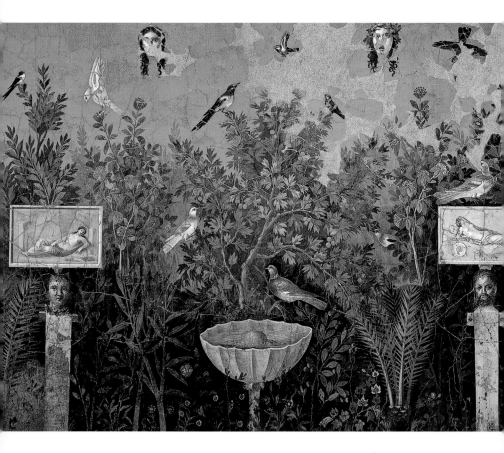

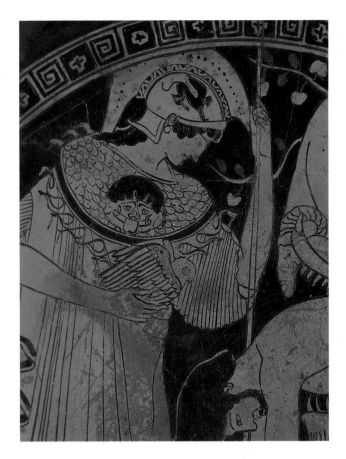

be thinking of lightness rather than saturation. He also argued that good drawing would give far more pleasure (in a portrait) than 'the most beautiful colours laid on confusedly', a point taken up by many ancient writers, who believed that colour was an aid to, but not the necessary condition of, realism. This idea was one of the most enduring aesthetic legacies of Greece to Renaissance and modern Europe, and will be discussed further in Chapter 3.

The historian of antiquity Pliny the Elder, whose discussion of art in the *Natural History* (first century AD) arose from his discussion of the materials of nature, drew attention to fourth-century Greek artists such as Parrhasios, who cultivated a pure outline [10] highly suggestive of three-dimensional form, and Apollodorus and Zeuxis, who developed techniques of chiaroscuro, both of which developments are reflected in surviving monuments of monochromatic painting, albeit later ones [11]. These techniques put a premium on the contrast of light

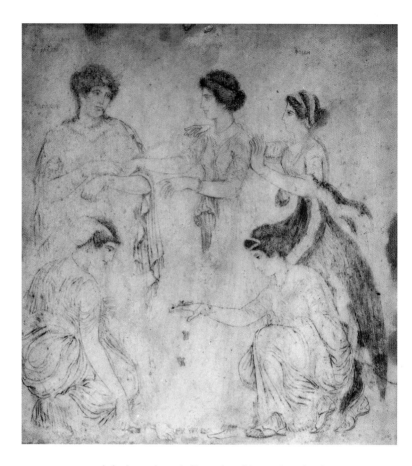

11. *Knuckle-Bone Players*, n.d. Monochrome is one of the earliest techniques to survive into modern times.

and shade, and we shall see that this continued to be a major – if not *the* major – preoccupation of painters until modern times. Even after Isaac Newton had united light and colour in the seventeenth century, for visual artists they were by no means the same thing. Newton demonstrated that colour was simply a manifestation of various wavelengths of light, but visual artists continued to think of it as far more complex than that. Colour had opacity as well as transparency, it could be shiny or matt, it had surface texture as well as hue, and, above all, it had an intrinsic tonal value (saturated yellow, for example, was lighter than saturated blue), and these were all vital components in structuring the visible world.

The greatest ancient virtuoso of line was the most famous of all Greek painters, Apelles, whose reported competition with Protogenes for the distinction of painting the finest line resulted in a panel on which their respective efforts were displayed, a panel

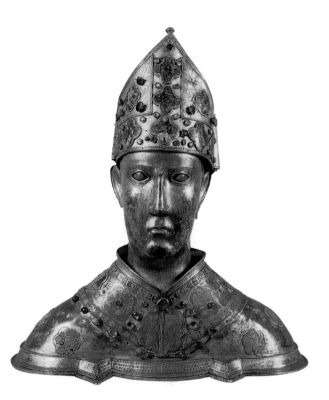

which, according to Pliny, bore nothing but these lines, and was taken to Rome, where it continued to be admired for several centuries, although it had disappeared by Pliny's day. But Apelles was also, according to Pliny, the inventor of a dark varnish which, spread thinly over his paintings, 'caused a radiance in the brightness of all the colours', while at the same time toning down those which seemed too bright. Most ancient wall-paintings and mosaic pavements were burnished and polished in a way which must have created a similar effect to this miraculous varnish by enhancing their light-reflecting capacities, as well as giving depth to the bright colours: the creation of light again took precedence even over the effect of hues themselves. This emphasis on light continued into the Middle Ages, whose most characteristic large-scale media for figurative decoration were glass mosaic and stained glass, and for smaller works, gilt-framed altarpieces and liturgical objects in gilt, gemstones and enamels [12].

The Primary Colours

Medieval thinking about light conceived of it as twofold: *lux*, the light source, and *lumen*, the light reflected from surfaces. And just as the 'accidental' colours were more highly valued than the colours inherent in materials, because they were more transparent and more inscrutable, so translucent or highly reflective substances, such as precious stones, metals and glass (often regarded as a stone), were most valuable, as appearing to embody or generate light itself. Medieval stained glass, so far as it has survived, seems to have passed through a number of colour phases: the early German glass at Augsburg, with its white backgrounds and strong red–green contrasts [13], and the slightly later glass of Chartres [7], and St Denis on the edge of Paris, which is dominated by blue. Blue was conceptually ranked as the darkest colour, next to black [14], and there is good reason to

13. *The Prophet Isaiah*, Augsburg Cathedral, *c.* 1130. This is some of the earliest surviving stained glass. The red and green glass was probably made from the same colouring ingredients, heated to different levels.

14. **French School**, *The Cruxifixion and the Ascension*, Poitiers Cathedral, 13th century. Here the close association of blue with black is clear in the blue hair and beard of Christ, and in this context blue may well have been seen as the luminous version of black.

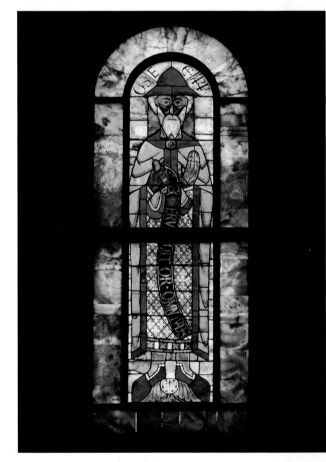

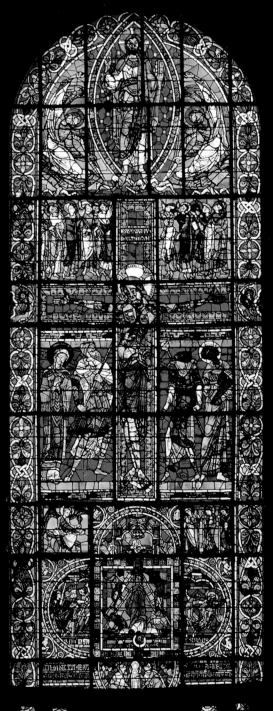

15. Medieval people in silver stain, from the Lady Chapel, Ely Cathedral, c. 1340–49. This panel is characteristic of the pale late-medieval stained glass, with its dominant yellows, created by a new ingredient, silver-stain, which permitted painting on the surface of the glass, rather than colouring it in the mass.

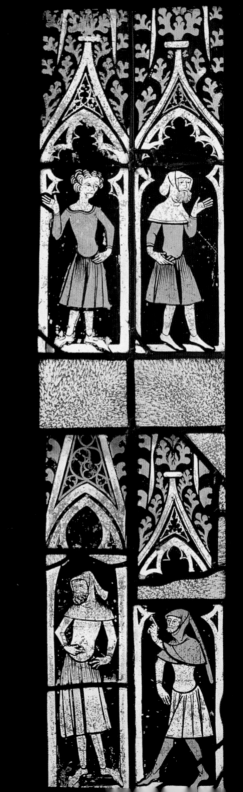

believe that this early French glass was designed to create an impenetrable, yet light-bearing darkness analogous to the unknowable God of early medieval theology. But from the thirteenth century onwards the more traditional belief in God as light again dominated theological attitudes in the West, and runs parallel to the increasing lightness of late-medieval glass, now painted with the newly invented silver-stain, which, when fired, produced a pale yellow [15].

Light itself was increasingly treated as a physical rather than a metaphysical phenomenon; shadow was no longer morally suspect, and cast shadows became increasingly interesting to painters, among whom was the early Renaissance master Masaccio (1401–28), who made the story of St Peter healing with his shadow one of the most striking episodes in his fresco-cycle in the Brancacci Chapel in Florence [16]. Light was now subject to

16. **Masaccio**, *The Shadow Healing*, 1425. This episode from the life of St Peter (Acts 5.15), is an eloquent, if oblique, testimony to the new importance of cast shadows in early Renaissance art. It shows the most active of the many cast shadows in the fresco cycle in this chapel.

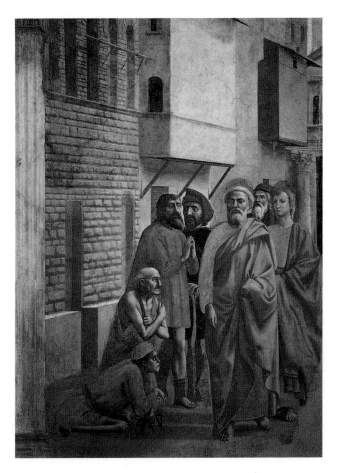

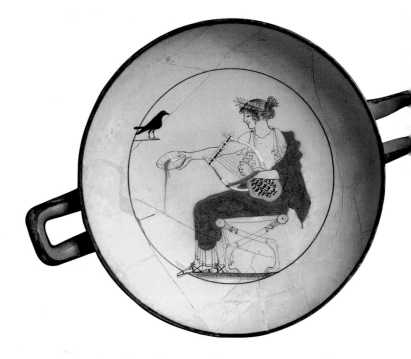

17. *Apollo Wreathed with Myrtle,*
white-ground kylix, 5th century BC.
This type of four-colour vase-
painting, with its palette of black
and white, red and yellow, is one of
the few surviving indications of the
palette of the 4th-century Greek
painters described by Pliny in his
polemic against the proliferation of
garish colours in modern Roman
painting (see p. 111).

analysis: the modern triangular prism seems to have been
developed as a tool specifically for studying the spectrum during
the sixteenth century, and in the seventeenth it was crucial to
Sir Isaac Newton's experiments, which demonstrated that all the
spectral colours are inherent in white light alone. No longer was
the intervention of any darkening medium required for colours
to be revealed, as Aristotle had supposed.

One of the late-sixteenth-century experimenters with the
triangular prism, the Neapolitan *magus* Giovanni Battista della
Porta (who also developed the *camera obscura*), could detect only
the three subtractive primary colours – red, yellow and blue – in
the spectrum it projected. Aristotle, following the fifth-century BC
poet Xenophanes, had recorded three colours in the rainbow –
red, green/yellow and purple – and della Porta probably had
Aristotle's rainbow spectrum in mind, since in his 'blue' he included
Aristotle's term for 'rainbow-purple' (*halourgon* in Greek, *halurgus*
in the Latin translations). Aristotle was still very much the leading
authority on all matters concerning the natural world in the late
sixteenth century. It may well be that his observations were also
much influenced by contemporary arguments in favour of this
fundamental primary triad, arguments for the most part based on
a new interpretation of Pliny's story of the four-colour palette used

by Apelles and other contemporary Greek painters [17]. In the light of the new freedom to mix colours encouraged by the technique of oil painting, from these colours – even as few as three – it was thought that all the others could be made.

However this came about, the red-yellow-blue triad had established itself as fundamental among artists all over Europe by the early seventeenth century. As the British artist Bridget Riley has observed, Rubens's copies of Titian's works are based far more on these three primaries than the Titians themselves, painted a century earlier. Bernardo Strozzi's Madonna in the *Adoration of the Shepherds* in Baltimore wears this trinity of colours almost like a badge [18]. It remained uppermost in the minds of painters, and in the early twentieth century found new ideological prominence in the arts of those early modern movements, loosely called Constructivist, which sought to identify and exploit the basic principles of design, notably in the

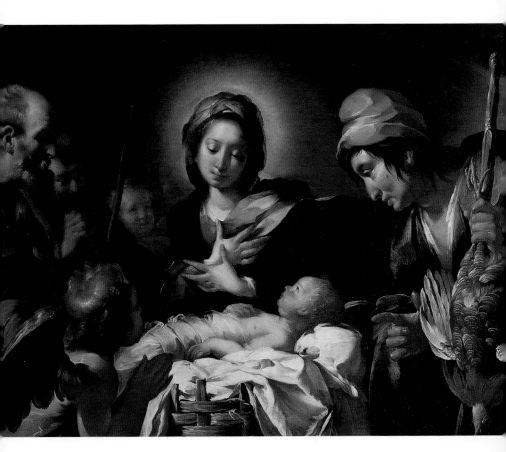

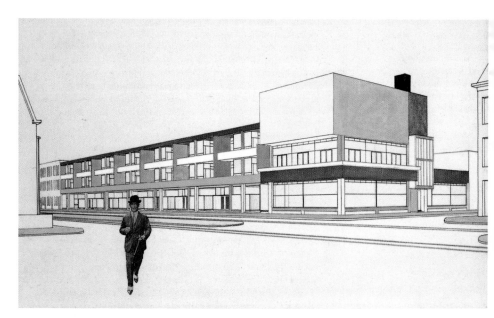

19. **Cornelis van Eesteren** with colour by **Theo van Doesburg**, *Axonometric from below, Winkelgalerij Shopping Mall, The Hague,* 1924. The primary-colour design here is by van Doesburg, the founding-father of De Stijl, who was always much involved in coloured architecture.

20. **Herbert Bayer**, *Design for a Newspaper Kiosk*, 1924. This design reflects the presence of van Doesburg at the Bauhaus, where Bayer was a student, two years earlier.

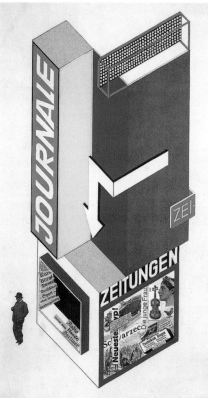

21. **Barnett Newman**, *Who's Afraid of Red, Yellow and Blue? I*, 1966. The large scale of Newman's series recalls De Stijl or Bauhaus architecture, but he was concerned to rescue the three primaries from design, and reinsert them into fine art.

Neo-Plasticism of the Dutch De Stijl movement [19], and at the German Bauhaus in the 1920s [20]. So prevalent was this triad, assumed to be the universal basis of colour, that in the 1960s the American colour-field painter Barnett Newman made a series of large works under the title *Who's Afraid of Red, Yellow and Blue?* [21]. As he wrote: 'Why give in to these purists and formalists who have put a mortgage on red, yellow and blue, transforming these colors into an idea that destroys them as colors?' Newman was concerned to make the triad 'expressive rather than didactic', although he omitted to suggest what, in his eyes, they were expressive of.

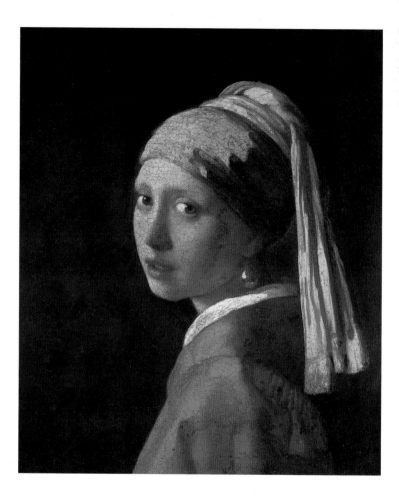

22. **Jan Vermeer**, *The Girl with a Pearl Earring, c.* 1665. Vermeer, who was unusually scrupulous about his expensive materials, such as ultramarine, often based his palette on blue and yellow at a time when his compatriot Christiaan Huyghens was arguing that these colours were the unique constituents of light.

The Newtonian Spectrum

In the second half of the seventeenth century new concepts of the colours of light began to establish themselves. One of these, proposed by the English scientist Robert Hooke and the Dutchman Christiaan Huyghens, that blue and yellow were the fundamental colours of light, offers a fascinating parallel to the contemporary painting of Jan Vermeer (1632–75), whose compositions are so often constructed around these two [22]. Blue and yellow, which were given new authority as the only primaries in the nineteenth century by the German poet Johann Wolfgang von Goethe on the one hand and the Scottish scientist James Clerk Maxwell on the other, also formed a dominant pair in the late cut-outs of Henri Matisse [23], and in the theory of Wassily Kandinsky (to be discussed later). The most widely influential

23. Henri Matisse, *Zulma*, 1950. Matisse, particularly in his late cut-paper compositions, also gave great prominence to blue and yellow, which 19th-century optical science had confirmed were the complementaries that could constitute white light.

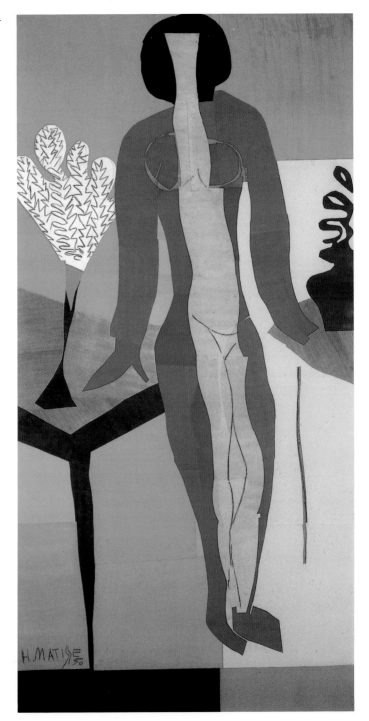

seventeenth-century theory of colour, however, arose from the spectral analysis of Newton, which, although it effectively demolished the notion of a limited set of primary colours (by showing that all colours were present individually in the spectrum of white light), was usually supposed, on the analogy with the seven tones of the diatonic musical scale, to show a sequence of seven basic colours: red, orange, yellow, green, blue, indigo and violet.

Very few artists before the twentieth century ventured to lay out their colour compositions in a spectral order, although in the 1750s Hogarth (1697–1764) devised a quasi-spectral palette (which he does not appear to have used himself) [24, 25], and at the end of that century the American painter Benjamin West (1738–1820), President of the London Royal Academy, proposed that the rainbow sequence should form the basis of the most harmonious compositions. West saw this arrangement first in Rubens and later in Raphael, but he failed to carry his academic colleagues with him, for they noted many exceptions to his rule among the Old Masters, and at least one spotted an anomaly in the President's perception of the rainbow, since, when recommending a weaker version of the spectral sequence in

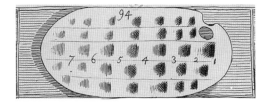

24. **William Hogarth**, diagram of palette, detail of an engraving from *The Analysis of Beauty*, 1753. Five 'bloom tints' are placed in the sequence, red, yellow, blue, green, purple, at No. 4 and are lightened towards No. 7 and darkened towards No. 1.

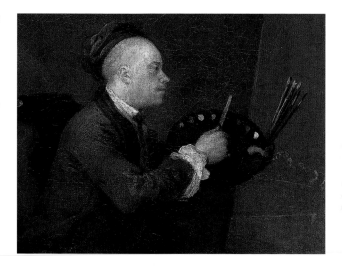

25. **William Hogarth**, *Self-Portrait Painting the Comic Muse* (detail), c. 1757. Here the practical Hogarth uses a more orthodox palette arrangement, running from light to dark.

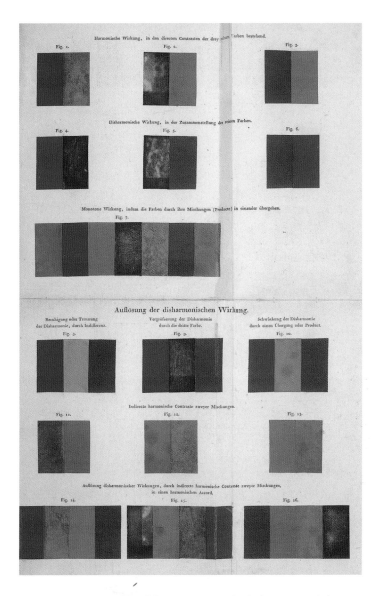

Harmonische Wirkung, in den directen Contrasten der drey reinen Farben bestehend.

Fig. 1. Fig. 2. Fig. 3.

Disharmonische Wirkung, in der Zusammenstellung der reinen Farben.

Fig. 4. Fig. 5. Fig. 6.

Monotone Wirkung, indem die Farben durch ihre Mischungen (Producte) in einander übergehen.

Fig. 7.

Auflösung der disharmonischen Wirkung.

Beruhigung oder Trennung der Disharmonie, durch Indifferenz. Vergrößerung der Disharmonie durch die dritte Farbe. Schwächung der Disharmonie durch einen Übergang oder Product.

Fig. 8. Fig. 9. Fig. 10.

Indirecte harmonische Contraste zweyer Mischungen.

Fig. 11. Fig. 12. Fig. 13.

Auflösung disharmonischer Wirkungen, durch indirecte harmonische Contraste zweyer Mischungen, in einen harmonischen Accord.

Fig. 14. Fig. 15. Fig. 16.

26. Philipp Otto Runge, *Colour Harmonies*, from *Farben-Kugel*, 1810. The figure reproduced here shows the 'monotonous effect' of five rainbow colours next to each other, where the middle colour is the product of the two flanking it.

subordinate parts of the composition, he had not noticed that the sequence of colours in the fainter secondary bow of a double rainbow is reversed. Although there are a few echoes of this theory in West's own work [27], he did not make a regular or particularly striking use of it. The German Romantic painter Philipp Otto Runge, too, in his *Farben-Kugel* or *Colour-Sphere* (1810) rejected the spectral arrangement of colours as too monotonous to be used in painting [26].

31

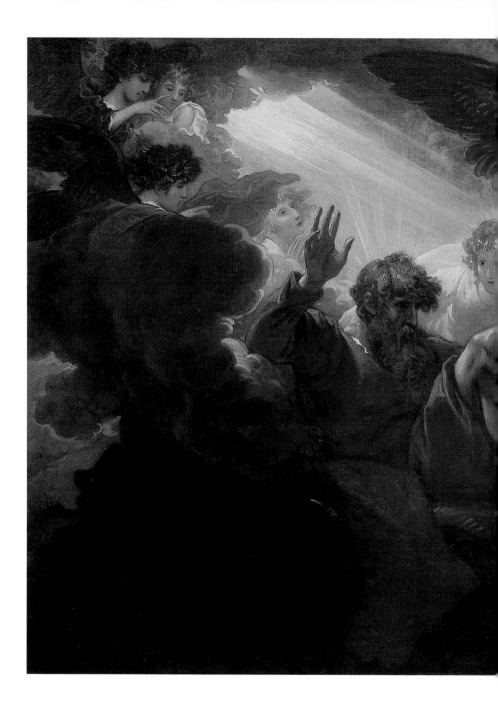

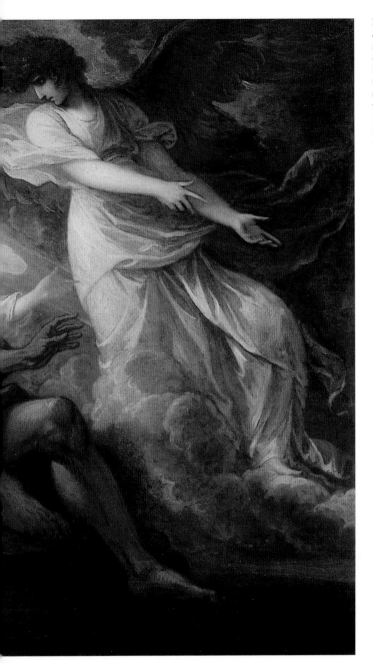

27. Benjamin West, *Moses Shown the Promised Land*, 1801. This is one of the few paintings to hint at West's theory that the most harmonious arrangement of colours was in the order of the rainbow-spectrum, warm colours on the left and cool to the right.

28. bottom left **Sir Isaac Newton**, *Colour Wheel*, from *Opticks*, 1704. Newton divided his circle, the first to be based on the spectrum, into the seven colours he had identified there, and placed white at the centre. Red is almost opposite green, blue opposite orange and yellow opposite violet, the pairs which came to be regarded as complementary to each other.

29. bottom right **Moses Harris**, *Prismatic Circle*, c. 1776, from T. Phillips, *Lectures on the History and Principles of Painting* (London, 1833). Although this book was dedicated to Sir Joshua Reynolds, President of the Royal Academy, Harris was an entomologist, anxious to find a system for classifying the colours of insects, and a version of this circle was published in his *Exposition of English Insects* in 1776. It may be the first symmetrical circle, with red opposite green, blue opposite orange and yellow opposite purple, and it also implies a black–white axis by the darkening of each colour towards the centre.

It was not until avant-garde painters in the early twentieth century began to explore the possibilities of abstraction that the Newtonian spectrum began to be deployed in its full range. In his *Opticks* of 1704 Newton had rolled his linear spectrum into a colour circle in order to plot mathematically the location of any mixture [28]. Newton's circle was asymmetrical because his divisions corresponded to the various proportions of the bands of colour he had located on his linear spectrum; but he had also noticed that a neutral, whiteish-grey could be mixed from only two colours opposite each other on the circle, so he placed 'white' in the centre. This suggested that there was something special about the opposite colours, and artists soon began to construct symmetrical circles, not only to locate maximal contrasts, but also to show that these contrasts comprehended the whole range of colour: red was opposite the secondary colour green, which was a mixture of the two remaining primaries, yellow and blue; blue was opposite orange, mixed from red and yellow, and so on. Moses Harris, who published what was probably the earliest symmetrical colour circle [29], called it 'The Natural System of Colours'.

Newton's was a mixture diagram, and the circle, or disc, painted with different-coloured segments and rotated rapidly had been used since antiquity to mix colours optically, through the effect of the persistence of vision. Ptolemy, who described this effect as early as the second century AD, compared it to looking at the potter's stained and spinning wheel. Newton does not seem to have spun his circle, but since all the spectral colours on it added up, in theory, to white, this would have been an interesting

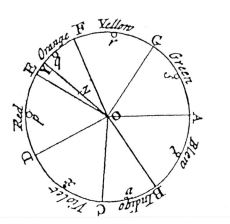

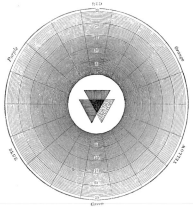

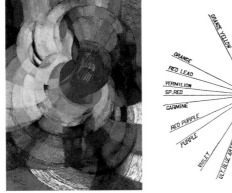

30. right **Frantisek Kupka**, *Study for Disks of Newton*, 1911–12. The colour divisions at the edges of Kupka's circles suggest that he was stimulated by the arrangement of a colour diagram, although the precise juxtapositions are closer to Rood's circle [31] than to Newton's. Kupka believed that Newton had used his circle to mix colours by spinning, which gave him a pretext for this dynamic composition.

31. far right **Ogden Rood**, *Contrast Diagram*, from *Modern Chromatics*, 1879. Rood established his contrasts by tabulating the colours which mixed to a neutral greyish-white on a spinning disc. He was also careful to specify pigments as well as abstract colours, which made his study particularly useful to painters.

32. below **Frantisek Kupka**, *Disks of Newton (Study for 'Fugue in Two Colours')*, 1911–12. This earlier version of the subject makes the Newtonian origin of the theme more evident, since the white and black circles are close together, and recall Newton's diagram of his 'Rings' [33], where, at the point of maximum pressure between the thin transparent plates, white is seen by transmitted light and black by reflected light.

possibility, and soon other researchers were trying the technique, notably the Austrian entomologist G. A. Scopoli in the 1760s, who used the technique to analyse the colours of insects. Disc-mixture became one of the principal methods of analysing the composition of white light in the nineteenth century [62], and when the Neo-Impressionist Georges Seurat referred to optical mixture by means of the persistence of vision, in his 1890 letter to Maurice Beaubourg (see Chapter 2), he was probably thinking of this method. In the twentieth century the idea formed the starting point for two very dynamic paintings with the title *Disks of Newton* (1911–12) [30, 32] by the Czech pioneer of abstraction Frantisek

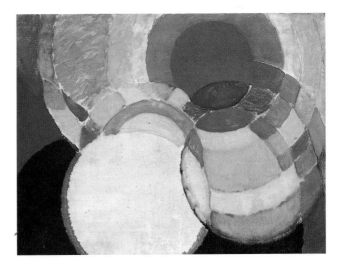

Kupka (1871–1957). It has, however, been shown that the large disc in *Study for Disks of Newton* [30] was based not on Newton, but on the more up-to-date circle published by the American physicist Ogden Rood in his *Modern Chromatics* (1879; French ed. 1881) [31]. Nevertheless, the black centre of Kupka's study now in Paris [32] suggests that he also had in mind Newton's diagram of the colours of thin plates, where 'Newton's Rings' circle out from the point of maximum pressure which, in reflected light, appears black, whereas in transmitted light it is white [33]. Kupka's subtitle, *Study for 'Fugue in Two Colours'*, makes this source more likely, since the fugal form in music makes much play with reversal, just as the colours of 'Newton's Rings' appear reversed (a phenomenon which led to the notion of complementarity).

Kupka made perhaps the most radically abstract use of the Newtonian spectrum in early Modernism, but he was not the only painter to deploy the full range of spectral colours in a circular form. Another artist who did so in a long series of paintings of the same period, Frenchman Robert Delaunay (1885–1941), disclaimed any scientific interest or capacity in a letter of 1913: 'None of the finite sciences have anything to do with my technique of moving towards light.' In another letter Delaunay claimed that it was only by the study of nature that he had discovered the laws of complementary and simultaneous contrast of colours, although he had long been familiar with the ideas of

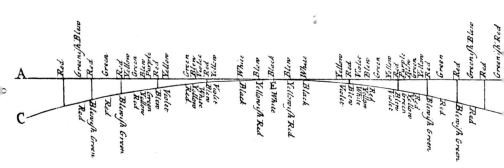

FIG. 3.

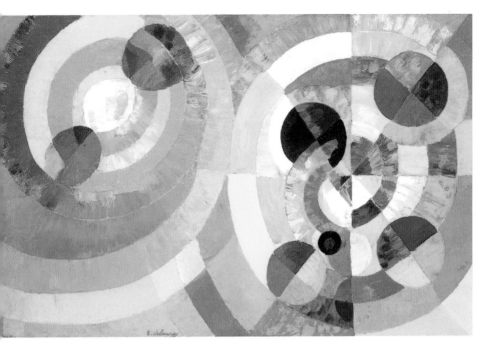

34. **Robert Delaunay**, *Formes circulaires (Circular Forms)*, 1930. Like Kupka, Delaunay started his series from the colour circle, but at this stage in his career he was still inclined to relate it to his studies of nature in the country.

the French chemist and colour theorist Michel-Eugène Chevreul, as well as with those of Rood, whose book had been much studied by French artists in the late nineteenth century, and which included a brief account of Newton's experiments. In an essay of 1912, 'On Light', Delaunay had already argued that 'light in nature creates movement of colours', and the creation of light and movement through colour was to be his prime objective as an artist. The following year he began a series of *Circular Forms*, to which he gave 'Sun' and 'Moon' titles when they were exhibited. Delaunay believed that colours close to each other on the by-now-standard circular diagram moved with a more rapid vibration than those more widely separated, such as complementary contrasts. In this 'Sun' painting [34] the primary disc has green and blue on the left of the circle and orange, red and brown on the right – all close tones which vibrate quickly. But within the circle these colours are juxtaposed with their complementaries, or near-complementaries – orange on the left and blue and green on the right – which set up much slower vibrations. Thus movements of great complexity are established by colour alone. As Delaunay wrote in April 1913, 'I am painting the sun, which is nothing but pure painting.'

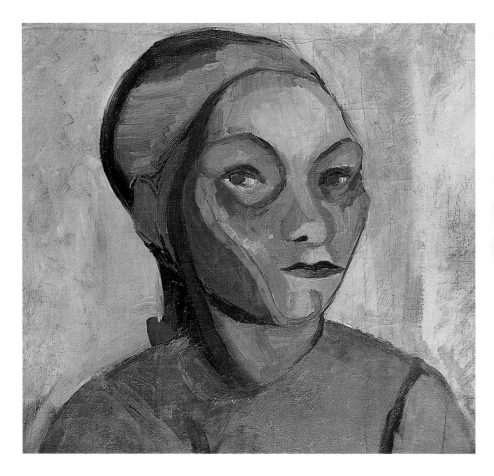

35. **Sonia Delaunay**, *Finlandaise*, 1908.

36. **Sonia Delaunay**, *Composition*, 1938. Sonia Delaunay's sense of vivid colour was stronger than that of her husband, Robert. She came from Fauvism [35], while he came from Neo-Impressionism, and was always more concerned with the creation of light and movement through colour, than with colour for its own sake, But her abstract formal vocabulary was always based on his.

Yet it is clear that Delaunay's particular interests were with light and transparency rather than with colour as hue. His early experiments with chromatics were certainly stimulated by his wife, Sonia Delaunay (1885–1979), a Russian painter and designer who had been trained in a Fauvist tradition [35] and had, from around 1911, been working with flat patchworks of coloured fabrics and papers. She declared later: 'In the matter of colours [Robert] had absolute confidence in me and always followed my suggestions.' Sonia, for her part, adopted a large part of Robert's formal vocabulary, which became much more hard-edged in the 1920s and thus more optically active [36], and she continued to work with it until her death in 1979.

Another early Modernist to use the full natural spectrum in the creation of light and movement was an associate of De Stijl, the Belgian artist Georges Vantongerloo (1886–1944),

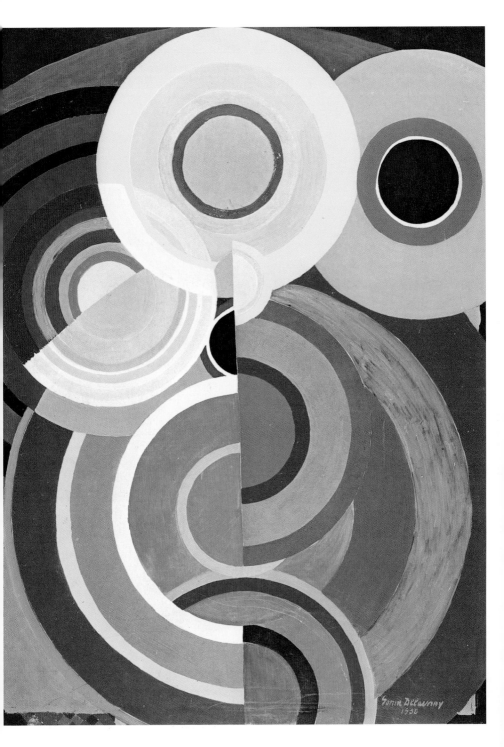

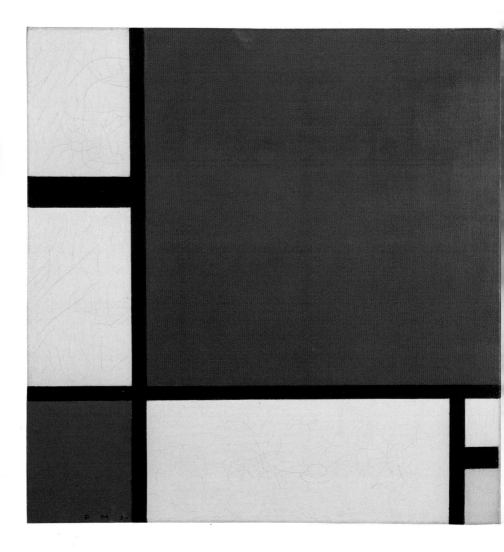

who, in the years around 1920, elaborated an aesthetic based on invisible vibrations, including colours, which were part of the 'absolute spectrum' extending to sound and heat and chemical 'rays'. Like the painter Piet Mondrian (1872–1944) [37], another member of the group, Vantongerloo had been much influenced by the theories of the Theosophist M. H. J. Schoenmaekers, whose *New Image of the World* (1915) had included a section on the theory of colours, in which blue, horizontal like the sky, and yellow, vertical like a ray of sunlight, were the fundamental colours, mixing to green, but also, according to a notion borrowed from Goethe's *Theory of Colours* (1810), transformed into red by a 'higher' process. Vantongerloo began his association with De Stijl in 1918, by using the three traditional primary colours, but soon scandalized Mondrian, the most doctrinaire painter in the group, by developing a spectral palette of what he called, in Newtonian vein, 'the seven colours of the rainbow'. Each colour was to be composed into a grid [38], whose precise areas were to be established by elaborate mathematical calculations, and by using those proportions of the primary colours that would mix on a spinning disc to a neutral grey. Mondrian at first thought that the theory might be workable at some future time, but later he wrote

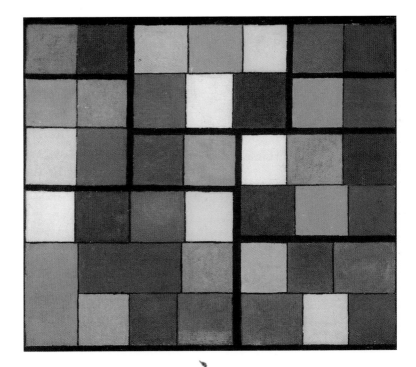

to the animator of the De Stijl movement, Theo van Doesburg, that Vantongerloo 'hasn't the faintest idea of the difference between the *manner of nature* and the *manner of art*'. Vantongerloo seems to have wanted to rebut these accusations in his essay 'Unity', of 1920, published in *Art and the Future* (1924): 'The formal means (*plastique*) of painting stays entirely in the domain of colour, without introducing anything at all of nature.' From this date he radically reduced his palette, although never again to the three primaries of red, yellow and blue alone.

The maturing Constructivism of the 1930s and 1940s shed the spiritual underpinning of the earlier movements, and replaced it with a more direct engagement with technology and society. The grids of up to 40,966 colours in a phase of the work of Gerhard Richter (b. 1932), beginning in the 1960s, seem to be a homage to the colour charts of house-paint manufacturers [39], and he explained their apparent randomness as a gesture, in the spirit of Pop Art, against the pious seriousness of the Neo-Constructivists, such as Albers [2, 91]. Yet the works had their own system, based on the three primaries plus grey. As Richter explained somewhat opaquely in 1974: 'The arrangement of colours on the squares was done by a random process, to obtain a diffuse, undifferentiated overall effect, combined with stimulating detail – the rigid grid precludes the generation of figurations, although without effort these can be detected.'

Randomness, chance, was also a very New York aesthetic strategy in the post-war years, but, in the wake of Surrealism, it

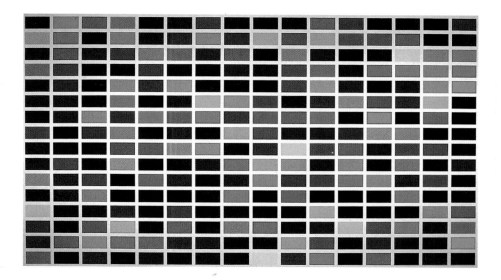

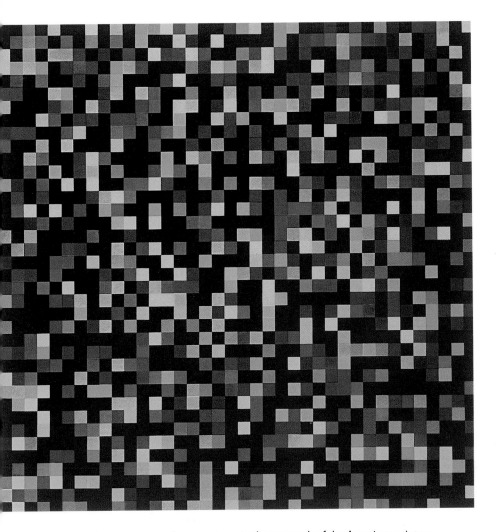

40. **Ellsworth Kelly**, *Spectrum Colors Arranged by Chance*, 1951–53. An American in Surrealist Paris, Kelly made much use of chance in his early work, and in his *Spectrum* series he made play with the idea that since all the spectral colours mix to white their sequence does not matter.

was also prominent in the approach of the American painter Ellsworth Kelly (b. 1923), working in Paris in the 1950s. Kelly's series *Spectrum Colors Arranged by Chance* [40] survives in eight versions, painted between 1951 and 1953, and it was succeeded by a series of equally random *Spectrums* into the late 1960s. In Kelly, Neo-Surrealist serendipity encountered the Neo-Constructivist grid in the most vivid way, and it could do so because of the systematic potential of spectral colour.

Another of the serious colour-Constructivists Richter almost certainly had in mind was the Swiss painter Richard Paul Lohse (1902–88), whose colour investigations deployed the full range of spectral colours in endlessly inventive series [41]. Where

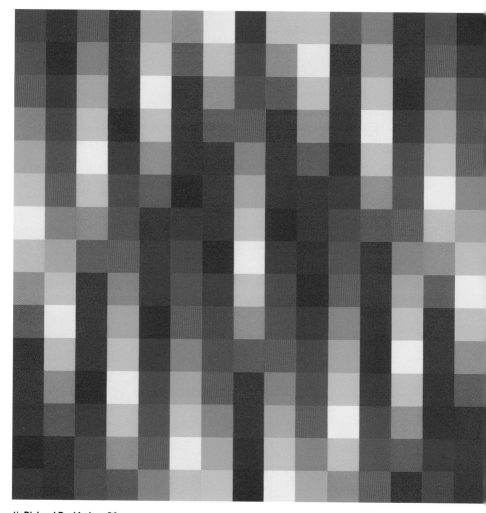

41. **Richard Paul Lohse**, *Fifteen Systematic Colour Series in a Circular Form*, 1952/83. Using as reference points his own constructed colour circles, Lohse deployed the full range of spectral colours to construct grids of striking luminosity.

Vantongerloo saw his colours as visible manifestations of the vibratory character of the created world, its invisible structure, Lohse's concern was largely topological. He usually started from the colour circle and, although he was interested in the circles of, for example, Goethe and the German chemist and colour theorist Wilhelm Ostwald, he usually constructed his own versions for each work. In this he fulfilled Mondrian's dream of work which was entirely in 'the manner of art'. Lohse's topological approach insisted that colours be seen individually:

> *Separation from the same colour and delimitation by other colours are the preliminary conditions of the homogeneity of the colour-square element. If a square structure is conceived in which the elements of one and the same colour touch at one or more corners, the integrity and the meaning of the colour square as an element and as a value factor of the system of co-ordinates are impaired, the sovereignty of the colour square and its constitution as an active individual are annulled.*

Lohse was also concerned that the area of each colour in each composition be equal. For him this had a social as well as an aesthetic meaning. As he wrote towards the end of his life: 'The crowd contains the possibility of the individual.' The perfect anonymity of his paint surfaces – as opposed to his highly personal sense of colour – was in tune with the technological world he admired: 'In no other form of art do the media and methods of a global technological strategy find a legitimate expression as they do in a constructive, logical, systematic or serial art, which is a sublimated and critical echo of the structures of civilisation.'

Art from Light
Late-twentieth-century technology also provided artists, in the form of the hologram, with a powerful new medium in light itself. The possibility of producing light of a single wavelength (coherent light) by means of the laser, developed in the 1960s, made it possible for the first time to produce on a flat surface images of considerable depth. Coherent light is, of course, monochromatic, and all early holograms were likewise monochromatic, usually recorded and replayed with light of the longer wavelengths, red or yellow. But in 1969 the American holographer Stephen Benton devised a method for recording all the spectral colours in a single hologram, which he called the 'Rainbow Hologram', and it is this type, which can only represent a relatively shallow space, that is

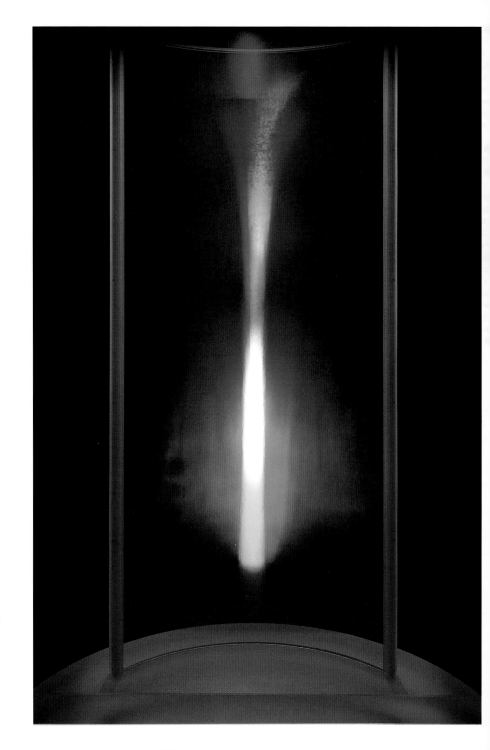

familiar to us from banknotes or credit cards. But artists have used this rainbow technology for larger purposes. The American sculptress Sally Weber's *Alignment* [42] creates three lines of red, green and blue (the additive primaries of light), which appear to hover six or eight feet in front of a curved acrylic screen, merge to make other colours, and finally white light, according to the position of the viewer. The work exemplifies what Weber (b. 1953) has called 'the natural integration of time, space and light', which differs only in its advanced technology from the light cultures in many ancient civilizations, from Egypt to the Americas. Here the 'accidental' colours at last harness their mystery for aesthetic ends.

Complementary Colours
The idea of most enduring concern to artists to come out of Newton's *Opticks* was complementarity, which, as we saw, emerged from his observation of the colours of thin plates [33]. At the end of the eighteenth century these polarities were linked to the new investigations of the sequence of coloured after-images seen when the eye is fatigued by a strong colour stimulus [43], and also to the contrasting colours of the shadows cast by the same object lit simultaneously by two lights. The powerful resources of modern light artists have made the production of after-images notably easier. Dan Flavin (1933–96), for example, has made a particularly striking use of them in a work such as *Untitled (to Pat and Bob Rohm)*, of 1969, when even a brief exposure to the intense yellow/green of the piece induces a strong purple/violet after-image suffusing the whole of the surrounding white gallery walls [44].

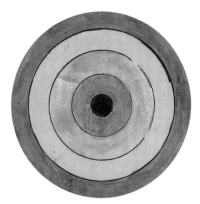

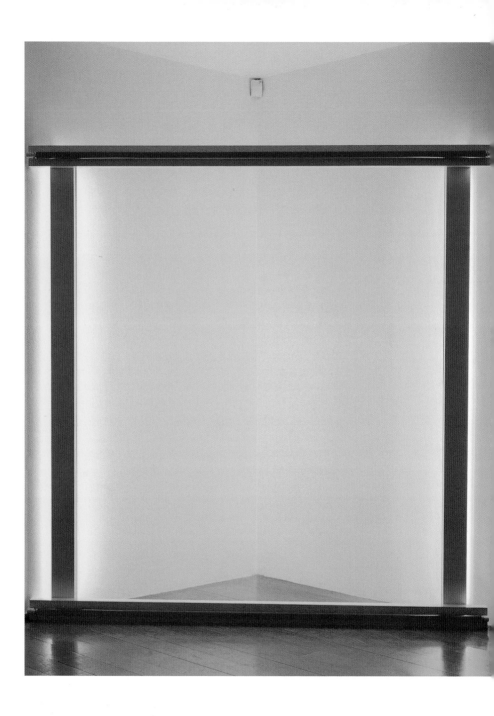

Around 1800 researchers in Germany and France described these involuntary pairs of contrasting colours as 'complementary', and throughout the nineteenth century complementary contrast was widely regarded as the most harmonious because it constituted a union of all three primary colours: red, for example, was opposite to green, which was an equal mixture of the two remaining primaries.

Maximal contrasts of this type had long been used by artists: highly saturated reds and greens were particularly favoured in late-medieval German painting, for example [45], and the new arguments for the importance of complementary, based on the physiological activity of the spectator's eye, were not entirely convincing, as we shall see in the next chapter. But in the context of the scientific positivism of the nineteenth century, complementary contrast was seen to be the *unique* key to colour harmony, which was given the force of law in an internationally influential book, *De la loi du contraste simultané des couleurs* (1839), by Michel-Eugène Chevreul. Although Chevreul had a conservative taste in painting, and was rather in favour of the subtler contrasts of similar hues, his large book, which was translated into English and German essentially as a guide to harmony, became a catechism of complementarity for many

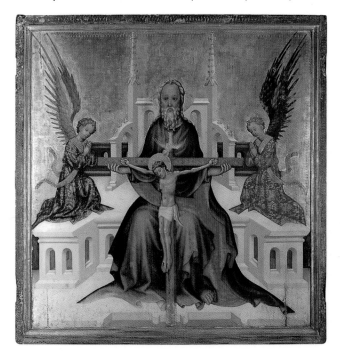

artists and theorists. The most significant theorist was certainly the French critic and historian Charles Blanc, whose *Grammaire des arts du dessin* (1867) was read by many of the major French avant-garde painters in the crucial decade of the 1880s. Blanc argued – tendentiously – that the greatest French colourist of the Romantic period, Eugène Delacroix (1798–1863), was a thoroughly scientific painter who had absorbed and used Chevreul's 'mathematical rules of colour'. It was almost certainly this imprimatur of a much-admired painter from the earlier part of the century that attracted the young artists to the complementary scheme, undoubtedly so in the case of the most uncompromising of them, Vincent van Gogh (1853–90).

In the early 1880s, van Gogh was teaching himself to be a painter in Holland, and, as he wrote to his brother Theo while he was reading Blanc's book in 1884: 'The *laws* of the colours are unutterably beautiful, just because they are *not accidental*' (Letter 371). And the following year he reported to Theo:

> I am completely absorbed in the laws of colours. If only they had taught us them in our youth! But it is the fate of most people that by a kind of fatality one has to seek for light a long time. For that the laws of colour which Delacroix was the first to formulate and to bring to light in connection and completeness for general use, like Newton did for gravitation, and like Stephenson did for steam – that those laws of colours are a ray of light – is absolutely certain. (Letter 430)

Van Gogh exploited his passion for the complementaries in many paintings from the mid-1880s onwards; but it was a far from exclusive passion, as he explained in another letter to Theo in 1885:

> These things concerning complementary colours, simultaneous contrast, and the neutralising of complementaries, this question is the first and principal one; the second is the mutual influence of two kindred colours, for instance carmine on a vermilion, a pink-violet on a blue-violet. The third question is the light blue against the same dark blue, a pink against a brown-red, a citron yellow against a chamois yellow, etc. But the first question is the most important. (Letter 428)

This precisely reverses the emphasis of Chevreul, but in one of his best-known paintings, *The Bedroom*, painted at Arles in October 1888 [46], Van Gogh showed that he was anxious and able to deploy the whole range of colour contrasts, analogous as well as

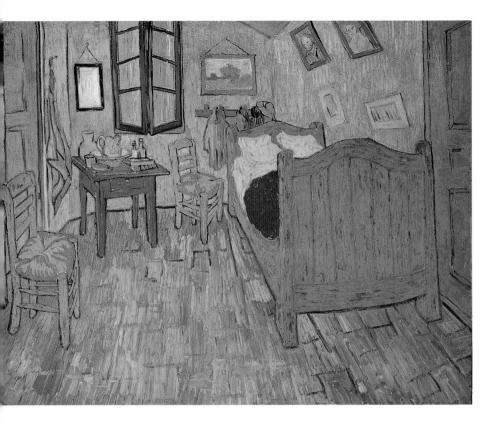

46. Vincent van Gogh,
Bedroom at Arles, 1888. This is
one of Vincent's first paintings
to be consciously structured
on complementary pairs.

complementary. Again, this most articulate of artists explained his idea in a letter to his brother. 'Colour', he said, 'is to do everything … [and] is to be suggestive here of *rest* or of *sleep* in general.'

> The walls are pale violet. The floor is of red tiles. The wood of the bed and chairs is the yellow of fresh butter, the sheets and pillows very light greenish-citron.
> The coverlet scarlet. The window green.
> The toilet table orange, the basin blue.
> The doors lilac.
> (Letter 554)

And from a letter (B.22) to Gauguin we learn not only that van Gogh had changed the 'real' white deal colour of the furniture to 'chrome yellow', clearly to create a 'kindred colour' to the sheets and pillows, just as the 'faded broken red' of the floor was allied to the 'blood red' counterpane, but also that the 'little note' of white in the mirror, with its black frame, was there 'in order to get

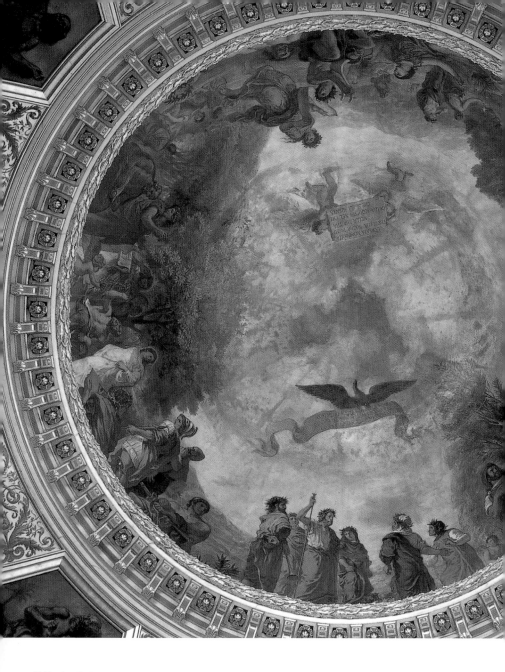

47. **Eugène Delacroix**, *Dante et les esprits des grands hommes*, 1841–45. For his large-scale architectural decorations (this cupola in the Palais du Luxembourg in Paris has a circumference of 20.40 m [67 ft]) Delacroix developed a technique of broad hatching in contrasting colours, which mixed optically at a distance and earned him the reputation of being a 'scientific' painter.

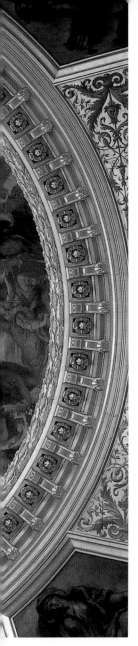

the fourth pair of complementaries into it'. We also notice the many kindred blues of door and glass, the green cement between the red tiles, and the red stripe on the green towel. This bedroom is a comprehensive array of colour contrasts which, van Gogh claimed, add up to 'absolute restfulness'. As he wrote to Theo: 'Looking at the picture ought to rest the brain, or rather, the imagination.'

Van Gogh's younger contemporary the Neo-Impressionist Georges Seurat (1859–91) also believed that art was essentially harmony, and that harmony was achieved by using similar elements as well as opposites. But unlike his friend and supporter, the one-time Impressionist Camille Pissarro (1830–1903), who, with Seurat, adopted the dotted, Neo-Impressionist technique, the younger painter was at first far more inclined to use high contrasts than close tones. He described himself in 1887 as an 'impressioniste-luministe', and it is clear that his chief objective as a painter was to reconstitute light by means of colour. Already in his schooldays he had had access to Chevreul's ideas through the writings of Blanc, who had illustrated a technique of optical mixing with small dots of colour, a method which came to be the chief characteristic of Neo-Impressionist handling. Seurat must have been impressed by Blanc's description of Delacroix's hatchings of pink and bright green in the flesh painting of the cupola at the Palais du Luxembourg in Paris [47], which created in that dark place 'an artificial light, by the play of colours'.

But since Chevreul's book of 1839 the study of the colours inherent in light, and the reconstruction of light through colour, had developed out of all recognition, principally in the hands of Hermann von Helmholtz in Germany and James Clerk Maxwell in Britain. Maxwell's work was known to Pissarro, and Seurat could have found his and Helmholtz's ideas on mixture in Rood's *Modern Chromatics*, from which he took notes. He also kept a copy of Rood's Helmholtzian colour circle [31]. The salient advances on Chevreul's more primitive and symmetrical complementary scheme were that a spectral red was now opposite a greenish cyan-blue, blue was opposite orange-yellow, and yellow opposite the reddish natural ultramarine. These more nuanced complementaries appear in a number of Seurat's paintings, notably *A Sunday on La Grande Jatte* [48], but they still coexist with the Chevreulian pairs; and until the end of his short life Seurat continued to conceive of the complementaries in terms of the now-superseded sets.

Even more significant, perhaps, the only surviving note taken by Seurat from Chevreul is from a passage not on hue but on

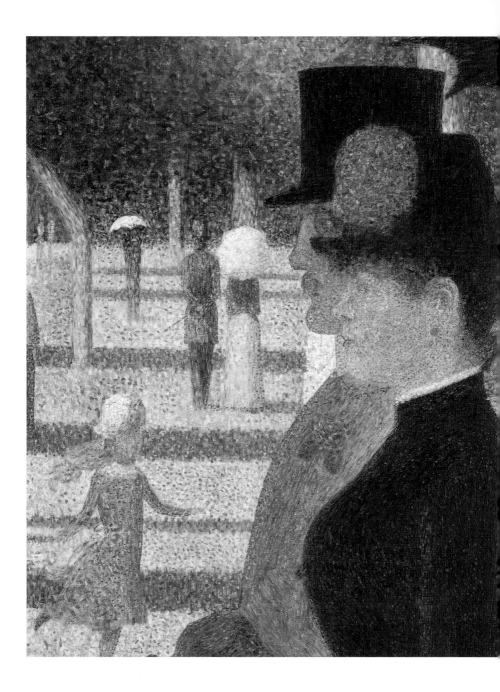

tone, or value: 'To put a dark colour near a different but lighter colour is to heighten the tone of the first and to lower that of the second, independently of the modification resulting from the mixture of complementaries.' It is clear from his many brilliant conté crayon drawings [49] that Seurat conceived of his compositions first of all in terms of light and shade; he had, after all, been trained at the École des Beaux-Arts, where the traditional values of chiaroscuro were still very much on the agenda. Charles Blanc, who was twice director of the École, included a substantial chapter on chiaroscuro in his *Grammaire* and concluded that colouring in painting was nothing but a more nuanced light and shade. Seurat's teacher at the École, Henri Lehmann, was himself a master of chiaroscuro and co-author of an article on the subject published by the school. As we shall see in a later chapter, darkness had always been a major element in the making of images. Leonardo da Vinci planned, but did not execute, a study of shadow in seven parts; and there was a

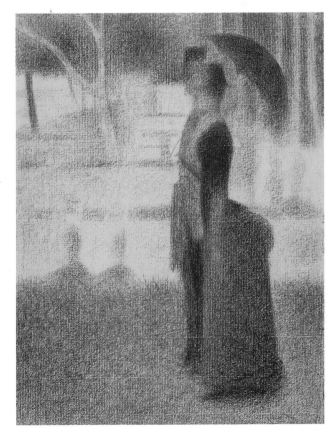

well-established tradition, even in Newton's day, that colour was inherent not in light, but in darkness, which was the sum of all colours. But, as we shall see in the next chapter, Seurat's approach to colour had far more to do with psychology than with the objective phenomena of light.

One of the optical effects most exploited by Seurat's dotted technique was 'lustre', which had been described by Rood in the context of optical mixture, where 'the colours are blended, though somewhat imperfectly, so that the surface seems to flicker or glimmer – an effect that no doubt arises from a faint perception from time to time of its constituents. This communicates a soft and peculiar brilliancy to the surface and gives a certain appearance of transparency; we seem to see into it and below it.' The phenomenology of lustre was explored most

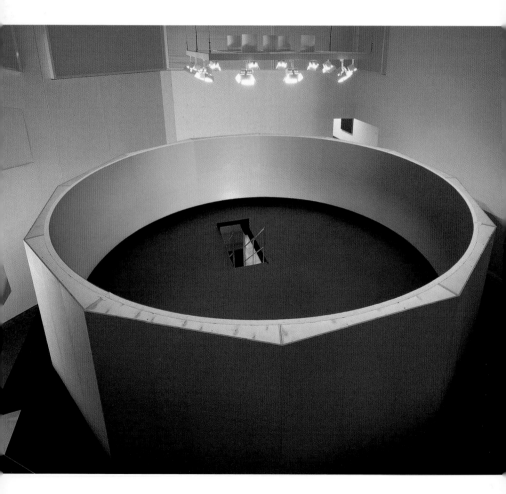

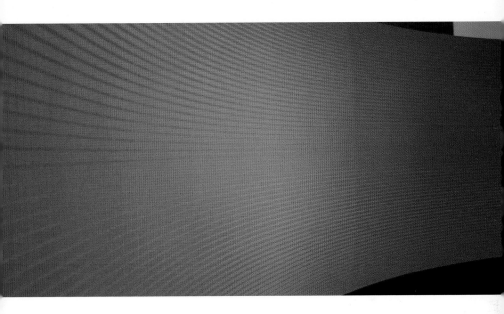

51. **Sanford Wurmfeld**, *Cyclorama* (detail), 2000. Starting from Seurat's optical mixing technique and inspired by 19th- and 20th-century circular panoramas, Wurmfeld has created a luminous painting from small painted squares arranged in spectral sequence round the inside of the drum. The optical effect is heightened by the sustained viewing encouraged by confining spectators to a small central platform, as in the traditional panorama.

OVERLEAF
52. **James Turrell**, *Night Passage*, 1987. Turrell's work depends on the behaviour of the human eye in extremes of light or darkness. Here the viewer is prepared for a wall of coloured light, by visual adaptation in a pitch-dark environment, on the way to the work itself.

intensively in the early twentieth century by the German psychologist David Katz, whose book in English, *The World of Colour* (1935), seems to have been of compelling interest to some New York painters: first Mark Rothko (1903–70) and now, much more clearly in the tradition of Seurat, Sanford Wurmfeld (b. 1942). Wurmfeld's 9-m (30-ft) diameter *Cyclorama 2000* [50, 51], shown in Germany, Hungary and Scotland in the early 2000s, envelops the viewer in light that is a function of the lustre, or 'film-colour' (Katz), created by the thousands of small squares on the immaculately painted surface, which covers twenty-four hues in a luminous circle. Like the traditional panorama, to which it is related, and like James Turrell's (b. 1943) light pieces [52], *Cyclorama 2000* confines the spectator to a limited viewing area, but unlike Turrell, this is to encourage the protracted viewing necessary to reveal the full effective interaction of surface and film colour. In Michael Fehr's words, the spectator is both a viewer of the painting and an 'observer' of the viewing self. What seems at first sight to be a particularly vast and remarkably beautiful Neo-Constructivist painting is in the end a wonderful vehicle of optical psychology.

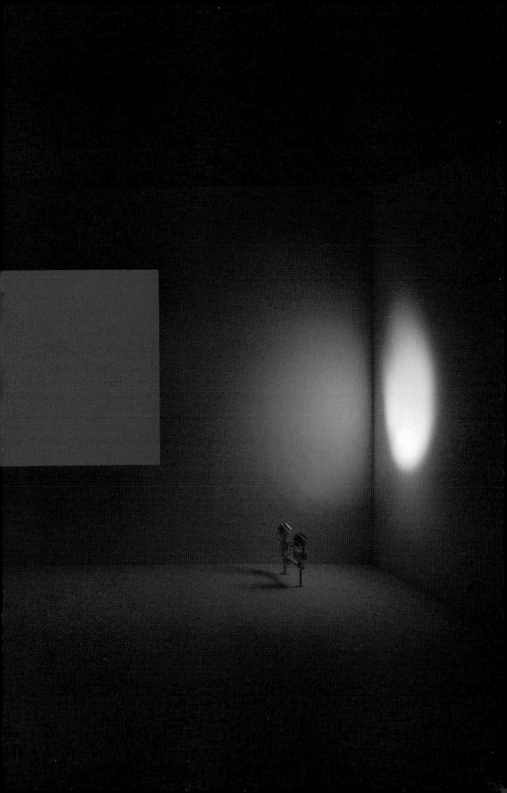

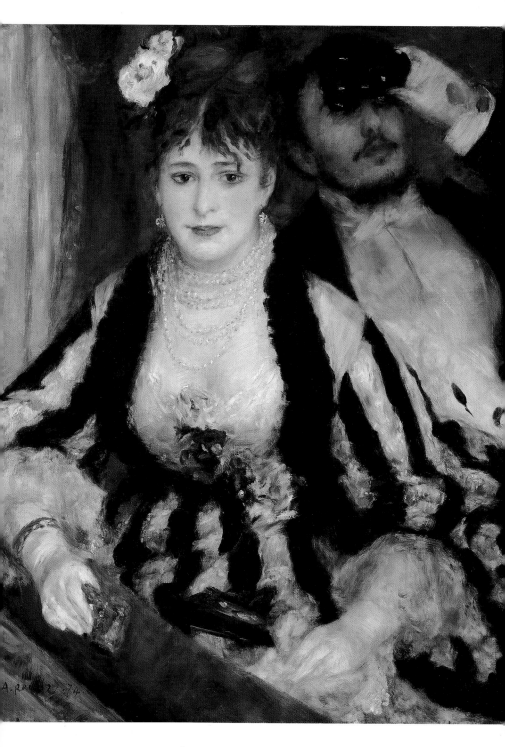

Chapter 2   A Psychology of Colour?

3. **Pierre-Auguste Renoir**, *a Loge*, 1874. Black dress had earlier been associated with sobriety, but its spread as a fashion colour in the 19th century, especially for evening dress, gave painters a new occasion to experiment with it. Renoir was one of the modern French painters whose handling of black was much admired.

We saw that darkness had been an important element in the perception of coloured structures, whether in the world or in painting, but it may seem paradoxical that it is a good starting-point for an investigation of colour in psychology at large. For in many parts of the world and at all times darkness, and in particular its principal representative colour, black, has been seen in, and as, a negative light. A survey of Mexican students in the 1960s, for example, showed that black was the colour most apt to generate subjective associations, and all of them were negative: death, depression and so on. This survey was typical of many investigations into colour preferences – important for the fashion and marketing industries – conducted by researchers in experimental psychology since the discipline's beginnings in the middle of the nineteenth century. But, with the exception of a wide-ranging but inconclusive study by the German psychologist G. J. von Allesch, based on experiments conducted in the early years of the twentieth century, artists have rarely been drawn into the discussion. In the context of the fascination with light among French painters around 1900, it is perhaps not surprising that, for masters of black such as Pierre-Auguste Renoir (1841–1919) [53], Édouard Manet (1832–1883) [54] and Henri Matisse [5], this colour could be given a positive twist only by being itself seen as a light. As Camille Pissarro once observed to Matisse that Manet 'made light with black'. This painterly interest is strikingly parallel to a contemporary phase in French physics, which was at this time much concerned with the non-visible areas of the spectrum, notably X-radiation, and in which 'black light' was a new concept – but one that was very soon abandoned by science. We saw in Delaunay, however, that the physical and optical sciences were not entirely congenial to all artists; and it is, indeed, to experimental psychology that we must turn for the closest analogies with artistic attitudes and practices, particularly in the matter of colour.

To begin at the beginning: developmental psychology has long used colour as an important index of the acquisition of knowledge

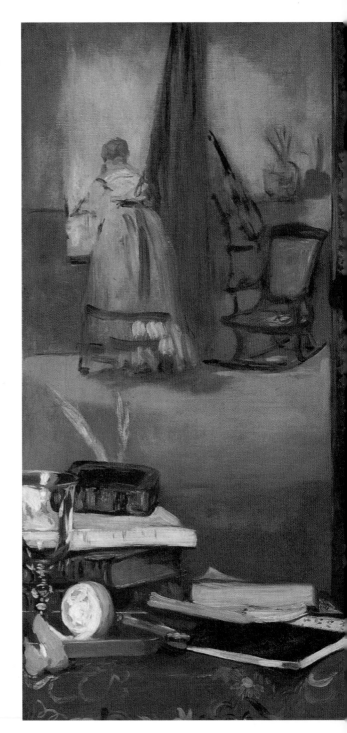

54. **Édouard Manet**, *Portrait of Zacharie Astruc*, 1866. Renoir and Manet were among those artists whom Matisse felt had made black not only into a colour, but also into a light.

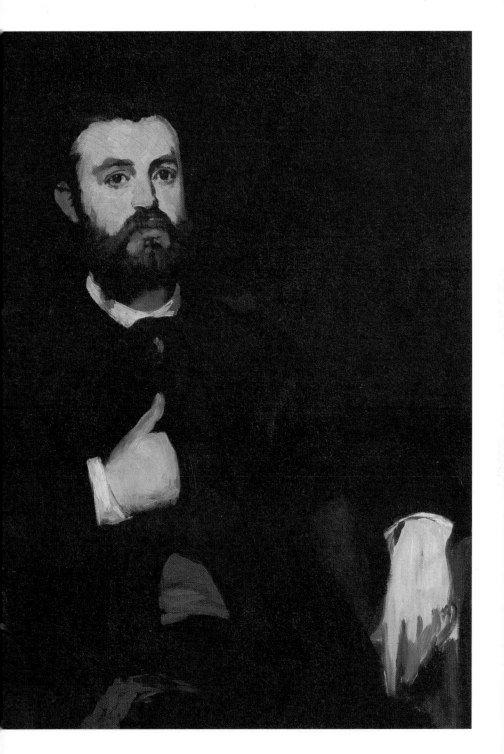

in infancy, and with the emergence of an ideal of a childlike apprehension of the world in Romanticism and early Modernism, this research soon fed into visual aesthetics. Friedrich Froebel (1782–1852), the Romantic Idealist educator, introduced into infant teaching his well-known 'gifts' – sets of nursery toys with abstract shapes and bright colours, some of which could be used as building bricks, and all of them designed to encourage creative play. The 'gifts' had a profound effect, for example, on the Modernist architecture of the American Frank Lloyd Wright (1869–1959), who was brought up on the Froebel system, and who proclaimed: 'Fortunately, human beings are really childlike in the best sense when appealed to by simple forms and pure, bright color.' Wright recalled in his autobiography that his games with these 'soft brilliant' Froebel colours and simple shapes were accompanied by visions of the fifteenth-century Florentine painter Fra Angelico's 'bright-robed angels, some in red, some in blue, others in green and one – the loveliest of all – in yellow, [who] would come and hover over the table'. Age, however, brought sobriety to Wright's colour sense; in his later buildings he used, and in his theory he recommended that colours be, the warm and soft and 'optimistic' colours of nature.

Late twentieth-century research into infant development supported Froebel's observation that colour discrimination precedes form discrimination in the youngest children, and that babies are able to distinguish red, blue, green and yellow many years before they have words to name them. Children, indeed, frequently make mistakes in colour-naming: Charles Darwin thought, quite mistakenly, that one of his children, aged seven, must be colour-blind because he habitually gave the wrong names to colours.

One of the most influential early twentieth-century art teachers and theorists of child art was Franz Cisek (1865–1946), who ran a private art school in Vienna around 1900, and later taught at the Craft School there. Cisek believed in the therapeutic value of music and colour, and argued that sick children would be helped by 'painting beautifully', by which he meant with 'pure' primary colours, of which red was 'the most beautiful colour on earth'. The 'cold' and mixed colours were a sign of weakness: 'weak generations love green, blue and mauve'. In the 1930s Mark Rothko came across Cisek's ideas in Wilhelm Viola's book *Child Art and Franz Cisek* (1936), which argued that the Viennese teacher 'was the first to discover that many children like to begin with colours without having made any previous drawing'; and in a notebook of that time Rothko wrote: 'Tradition of *starting with* drawing an academic notion. We may start with colour.' As we will see later, he took his own advice.

In an essay written towards the end of his life, the Russian Suprematist Kazimir Malevich (1878–1935) [55], who was also much involved with the reform of art teaching after the 1917 Revolution, and who introduced several experimental methods borrowed from modern psychology, argued:

> In childhood [a man] loves bright colours and perceives them in their pure form – yellow, red, green, blue. This … is characteristic for all children, both in the town and in the country: their consciousness seems to be on the same level. The only difference we may note is that town children more often use pure colour from the darker end of the spectrum than village children.

This last observation is a prelude to Malevich's remark that the clothes of the urban worker are dark and colourless except on

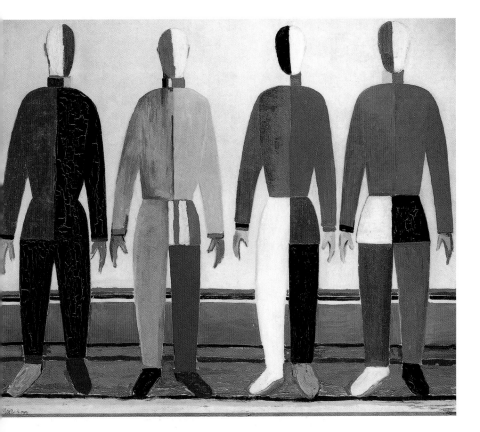

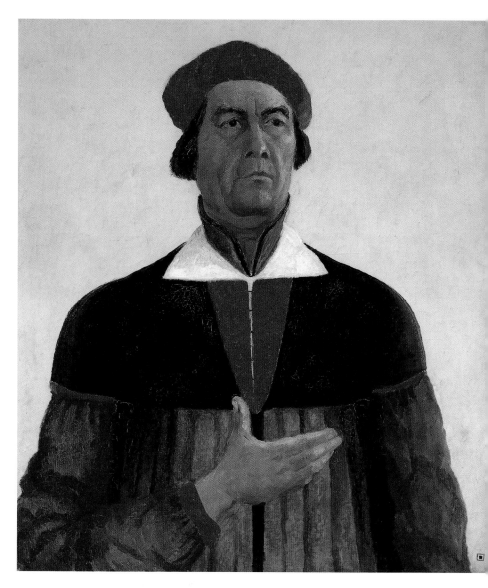

56. **Kazimir Malevich**, *The Artist (Self-Portrait)*, 1933. Malevich's bright costume, remarkable in an artist who had initiated the austerest phase of early abstraction [183], recalls the motley of the young Italian Renaissance dandies. Colour is used as a protest against the drabness of Soviet life.

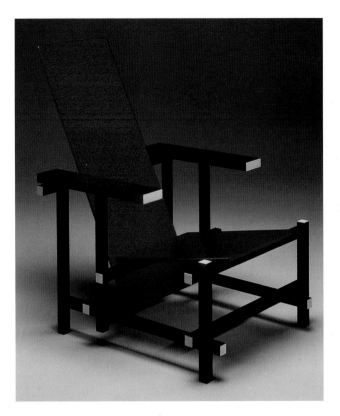

holidays, and that, although this festive dress may help town-planners to choose colours for the exteriors of buildings, the real energy of the town is in work, so that the scales of black and white '*belong to the highest point in the industrial developments of economic techniques*' (emphasis in original). Black or dark clothing had been regarded as the most appropriate dress for businessmen at least since the Italian Renaissance, and there must be some irony in the painter's representation of himself, harassed as he was in these years by the Soviet authorities, in what seems to be a colourful early Renaissance festival costume [56].

The taste for bright primary colour in Modernist art certainly began in the nursery. The colours (though not the form) of the De Stijl architect and designer Gerrit Rietveld's (1888–1964) iconic *Red-Blue Chair* [57] grew out of his work with nursery furniture; and at the the early Weimar Bauhaus, the German Modernist design school, the orthodox form coordinates (red square, blue circle, yellow triangle [see Chapter 3]) were embodied in the cradle which Peter Keler (1898–1982) made for the baby son of his teacher, the Swiss painter Johannes Itten [58]. At the early Bauhaus, too, the Furniture Workshop, lacking good raw materials during the economic depression after the First World War, was much employed in the production of brightly coloured children's toys [59].

The science of experimental psychology grew, especially in Germany, out of the closing section of Goethe's 1810 *Theory of Colours*, 'Effect of Colour with Reference to Moral Associations', in which the poet speculated, among other things, on a range of colour preferences. He already had views on children's tastes that may well have affected Froebel's teaching: speaking of an orange colour that he called 'yellow-red', he wrote that it was yellow 'in its highest energy': 'It is not to be wondered at that impetuous, robust, uneducated men should be especially pleased with this colour. Among savage nations the inclination for it has been universally remarked, and when children, left to themselves, begin to use tints, they never spare vermilion and minium [red lead].' Goethe was also much attracted to the colour preferences evident in female dress. Young women, he noted, are 'attached to rose-colour and sea-green, [but] in age to violet and dark green. The fair-haired prefer violet, as opposed to light yellow, brunettes blue, as opposed to orange, and all on good grounds.'

This type of thinking was fascinating to a group of young German revivalist artists known as the Nazarenes working in

58. **Peter Keler**, *Crib*, 1922. Keler's cradle, made for Itten's baby son, appropriately linked fundamental colours to fundamental forms, in a way that became standard at the Bauhaus, where Itten taught and Keler studied (see Chapter 3).

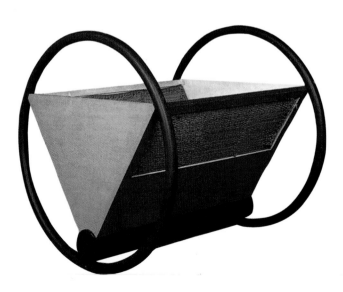

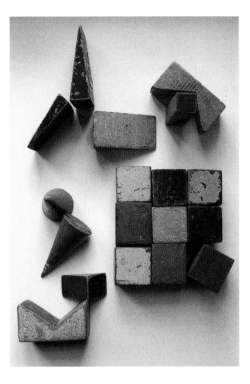

Rome in the early nineteenth century. In this period of growing nationalism, the psychological distinctions between northern and southern peoples became an important issue, and one that some thought might be visible in colour usage. Goethe himself had written that:

> Colours, as connected with particular frames of mind, are again a consequence of peculiar character and circumstances. Lively nations, the French for instance, love intense colours, especially on the active side; sedate nations, like the English and Germans, wear straw-coloured or leather-coloured yellow, accompanied with dark blue. Nations aiming at dignity of appearance, the Spaniards and Italians for instance, suffer the red colour of their mantles to incline to the passive [i.e., blue] side.

The leader of the Nazarene group, Friedrich Overbeck (1789–1869), wrote in 1808 that blonde hair and grey and crimson dress expressed 'feminine gentleness and amiability', 'true femininity'. Twenty years later, however, he dressed his blonde Germania [60] in pink, green, pale blue and a hint of yellow.

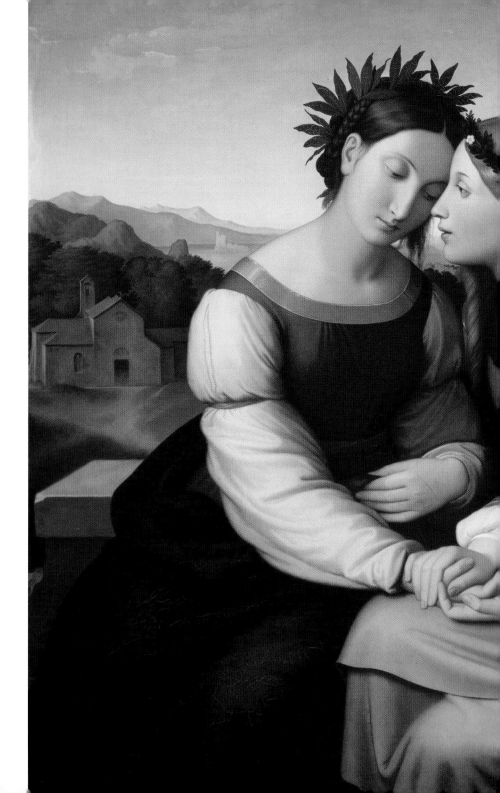

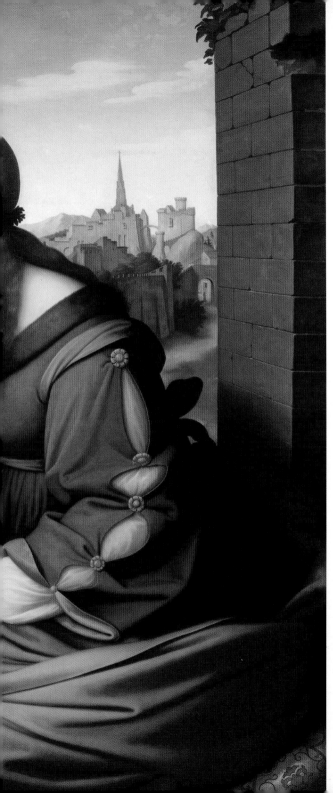

60. Friedrich Overbeck, *Italia and Germania*, 1828. Overbeck, the leader of the German revivalist painters in Rome, the Nazarenes, takes up the Romantic theme of friendship between nations, underlining the contrast of personalities by the contrasting colours of hair and dress.

61. Georges Seurat, *The Side Show (Parade)*, 1888. In his later work Seurat put as much emphasis on the directional lines and colour temperature of his compositions as on the reconstitution of light through the dotted technique. Here, although we are out of doors on a cool evening, the temperature is predominantly warm.

It is the brunette, Italia, who wears bright red. Dress, as always, was subject to changing fashion.

Neo-Impressionism: The Psychological Style
Nothing shows more clearly that nineteenth-century artists had absorbed the dominant culture of positivism than the development in France in the 1880s of a radically new technique of painting: those small units of pure spectral colour representing the division of light [48]. It might well be thought that a discussion of these *impressionistes-luministes* belongs entirely in our first chapter: Seurat did after all write that the '*purity of the spectral element*' was the '*keystone*' (emphases in original) of his technique. This was in a letter to the critic Félix Fénéon, who had, as Seurat admitted, long been the most influential interpreter of his quasi-scientific method. Yet in the same year, 1890, Seurat wrote of his 'Aesthetic' in a rather different vein to another journalist, Maurice Beaubourg:

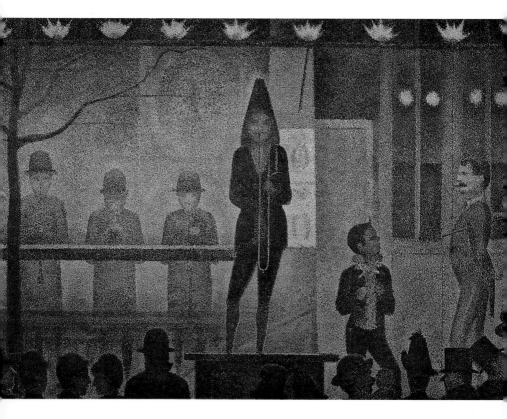

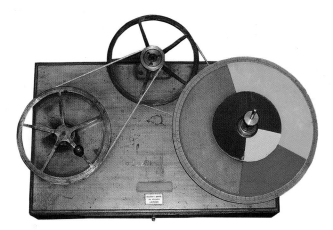

62. James Clerk Maxwell, *Maxwell's Discs*, c. 1855. Optical colour mixing on a spinning disc had been described by Ptolemy as early as the 2nd century AD, and had been practised occasionally in the Middle Ages and the 18th century. But it was not until it was realized around 1800 that the primaries of light are not red, yellow and blue that the spinning colour-top could become a precision tool for measuring the coloured components of white light. Maxwell used red, green and blue primaries to match the light grey in the centre of his disc. All the proportions could be altered to obtain exact matches.

Art is Harmony. Harmony is the analogy of opposites, the analogy of similarities of tone, of tint, of line … in combinations that are gay, calm or sad.… Gaiety of tone is the luminous dominant, of tint the warm dominant, of line, lines above the horizontal. Calmness of tone is the equality of dark and light; of tint, of warm and cool, and the horizontal for line. Sadness of tone is the dark dominant; of tint the cool dominant, and of line, downward directions [emphases in original].

These associations of tone or value, of hue and line are wholly psychological, and were probably brought to Seurat's notice by his friend, the mathematician and positivist aesthetician Charles Henry. The subjective effects of colour contrast, although they had been appreciated since Aristotle, were given renewed prominence, as we saw in Chapter 1, by Michel-Eugène Chevreul. Seurat went on in this letter to list his techniques: optical mixture, based on the phenomenon of the persistence of vision, which had, again, been fully discussed in antiquity by Ptolemy and, in the form of parti-coloured spinning discs, had been used in the eighteenth and nineteenth centuries for judging the components of mixtures [62]. Another type of optical mixture, with juxtaposed coloured dots, had been used by earlier painters, especially miniaturists, and had been discussed in the literature of optics, of miniature painting and theatre-painting, as well as of painting more generally, since the seventeenth century. But never before the Neo-Impressionists had these methods been used to reconstitute light.

It is clear from this aesthetic statement that Seurat, at least at the end of his life, was concerned above all with the expressive

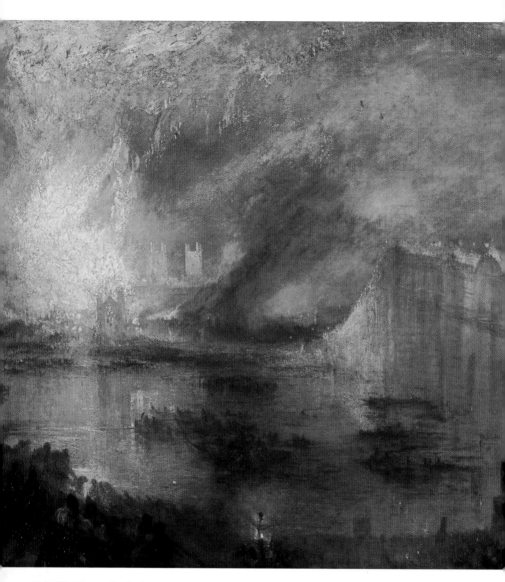

64. **J. M. W. Turner**, *The Burning of the Houses of Lords and Commons, October 16th, 1834*, 1834. Turner was the most radical painter to abandon the old belief that pictures should have a predominantly warm tonality (often the result of old yellowing varnish). Here he gave a particularly elemental thrust to his 'principle' of cool coloration, by using it for a subject of fire and water.

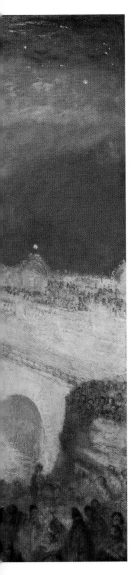

values of colour. Here he draws on a relatively recent, but widely accepted, notion that colours have temperature [61]. The ancient doctrine of the colours of the four elements had produced no unified view of which these colours actually were, and it was in the context of the theory of painting that the idea of warm and cool colours gained ground in the early eighteenth century. It was an idea closely dependent on the doctrine of the three primaries, for the belief that two of the primaries were warm and only one cool came (in the thinking of the English painter and first President of London's Royal Academy Sir Joshua Reynolds, for example) to underpin a rule that the colour of paintings, in accordance with 'nature', should be predominantly warm. This rule of thumb was generally abandoned by the Romantics, notably Joseph Mallord William Turner (1775–1851), who in the 1830s exhibited a number of largely 'cool' paintings [63], so that another painter, Frank Howard (1805–66), in his handbook *Colour as a Means of Art* (1838), could point to 'Turner's Principle': 'Turner has controverted the old doctrine of the balance of colours by showing that a picture may be made up of delicately graduated blues and white supported by pale cool green and enlivened by a point of rich brownish crimson' [64].

The most influential nineteenth-century British critic, John Ruskin (1819–1900), accepted the idea of colour temperature, but argued that any colour could be made warm or cool by changing

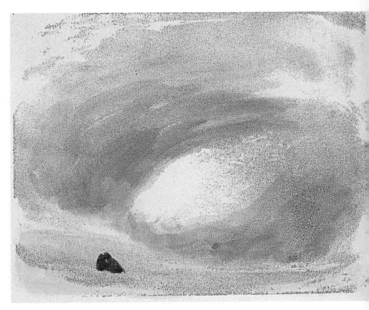

65. **Frank Howard**, *Turner's Principle*, from *Colour as a Means of Art*, 1838.

65. **Wassily Kandinsky**,
*Farbstudien mit Angaben zur
Maltechnik (Colour Studies with
Notes on Technique)*, 1913. Warm
and cool are prominent among the
contrasts noted on this sheet.

its context. The major modern proponent of colour relativity,
Josef Albers (see Introduction), recalled that when he was a young
painter in the Munich studio of Franz von Stueck, around 1920,
there were many 'fruitless controversies' about the spatial effects
of warm and cool colours. Kandinsky, too, in the early years of his
non-representational style, was much interested in colour
temperature, and devised colour relationships based entirely on
this type of contrast [65]. Yet, as he wrote in *On the Spiritual in Art*
(1911) in the context of red: 'Every colour can be warm or cold.'

Since warmth and coolness are themselves entirely relative
concepts, there is a continuous scale of degrees between them.
This scale is unlike the scale of the colour spectrum, in which each
step represents a change of hue; but it is analogous to the grey
scale between black and white, where there is no change of
colour identity between the steps. The Australian painter Wayne
Roberts (b. 1958) explored the relationship between the colour
scale and the grey scale in the 1990s, and concluded, paradoxically,
that the dark end of the grey scale corresponded to the red, least
energetic but 'warm' end of the spectrum, and the light end to the

66. **Wayne Roberts**, *Low Tide, Cancale*, 1995. Warm and cool colours are here given tonal functions: dark colours are warm and light colours cool.

most energetic but 'cool' extreme. *Low Tide, Cancale* [66] of 1995 is, according to Roberts, 'a colour-modulation representation of light', in which light areas are painted with blue-violet colours, and dark areas with red-yellow or green colours, according to their relative brightness. This, as Roberts said, gives the painting a strong sense not only of energy, 'but of light itself'; and it is a powerful demonstration of the unfamiliar truth that the 'warm' colours are indeed cool, and the 'cool' warm.

The Swiss chemist Heinrich Zollinger (b. 1919) has given a physical and physiological explanation of this striking paradox:

As we know, the wavelengths of light in the visible range of the spectrum vary from 400 to 700 nm, and the wavelength of electromagnetic radiation is inversely proportional to its energy.

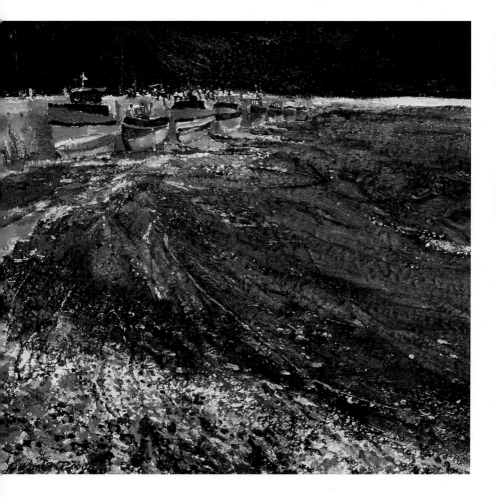

The violet and blue colors have wavelengths near 400 nm, and so are higher in energy than those at the long-wavelength end of the visible spectrum. The 'warm' colors red, orange, and yellow, however, are not at the high-energy end, but on the low-energy side of the spectrum.... The apparent contradiction is ... understandable on the basis of molecular motion and the wave/particle complementarity of light. If ultraviolet light is absorbed by molecules, its (high) energy results in the cleaving of chemical bonds and the destruction of molecules, or in the promoting of certain electrons to higher energy levels. This irreversible bond cleavage is well known from sunburn in places where levels of ultraviolet light are intense, such as on high mountains. Visible light is energetically too weak for most bond cleavages, but not for elevating electrons to higher energy levels.... In the long-wavelength part of the visible spectrum, another type of electromagnetic absorption must be considered in addition to the promotion of electrons to excited states as the physical cause of color.... Long-wavelength visible light and, even more so, near-infrared light is transformed into stretching, rotational, and bending vibrations of chemical bonds between particular atoms in a molecule. We sense these vibrations physiologically as heat. Therefore, an infrared lamp makes us feel warm, while an ultraviolet lamp does not.

Today, notions of warmth and coolness are still very much at the root of the idea of colour feelings, expressed most concretely in the practice of colour therapy. Belief in the healing power of colour has a long history; modern practitioners trace it to ancient Egypt, Persia, China and India, and to medieval European practices using precious stones. But, as we might expect, it was largely in the context of nineteenth-century psychology that it gained wider currency and became interesting to artists. Here, the concepts of polarity and complementarity became crucial. Goethe's argument that the eye, overstimulated by one colour, 'demanded' its complement, was extended to the whole of the human organism: an imbalance in an organ identified with one colour (kidneys, for example, in the Indian tradition were seen to be indigo, and the stomach, rather confusingly, dark blue; whereas in China the kidneys were orange and the stomach yellow) is treated by exposure to light of the complementary hue. In chromotherapy blue is usually regarded as complementary to red, as it is in the 1906 handbook by Arthur Osborne Eaves consulted by Kandinsky, and which he acknowledged in *On the Spiritual in Art*:

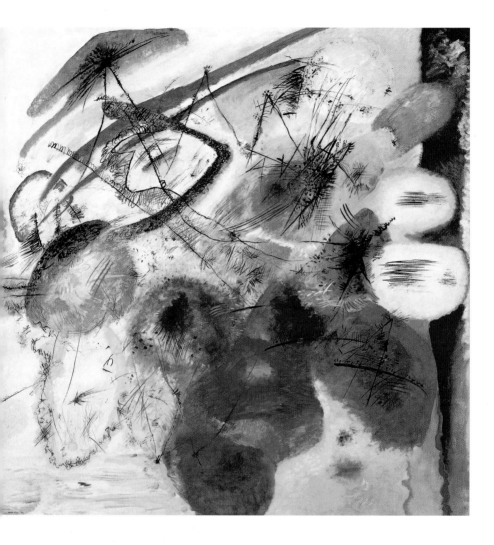

7. **Wassily Kandinsky**, *Black ?nes*, 1913. This is among the ?arliest of Kandinsky's paintings ? be completely free of subject ?eferences: colour and line are ?e sole means of expression.

Anyone who has heard of colour therapy knows that coloured light can have a particular effect upon the entire body. Various attempts to exploit this power of colour [Eaves's book was entitled Die Kraefte der Farben *or* The Powers of Colours*] and apply it to different nervous disorders have again noted that red light has an enlivening and stimulating effect upon the heart, while blue, on the other hand, can lead to temporary paralysis.*

At this time, Kandinsky was moving rapidly towards non-representational painting [67], and colour, if it was free of cultural associations and spoke directly to the 'soul' of the beholder, could be of major importance in this endeavour. Whether colours worked directly on the human organism, or only by association, was a significant debating point in German psychology at this time, and Kandinsky aligned himself clearly with the non-associationists: 'If this sort of effect [of red and blue light] can be observed in the case of animals, and even plants, then any explanation in terms of association completely falls down. These facts in any case prove that colour contains within itself a little studied but enormous power, which can influence the entire human body as a physical organism.'

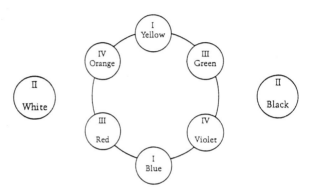

68. **Wassily Kandinsky**, *Colour System*, 1911, Figure III from *On the Spiritual in Art*. Here the contrasts of yellow and blue have priority even over white and black as the fundamental colours.

But in his own colour system [68] Kandinsky substituted yellow for red, following Goethe and the scientists who had, as we saw, made blue and yellow the primary colours of light. Chromotherapy depended on the fact that colours are variable vibrations of light. Colours could affect the body even if they were not seen; the French psychologist Gaston Déribéré found that even blind subjects could detect differences in the effects of red and blue; and research is currently in hand to open the world of colour to blind people by linking colours to a scale of audible pitches. As we saw earlier, it is a continuing paradox that the high-energy, short-wave colours (e.g., blue) should excite the organism less than the low-energy long waves of red, and it is also surprising that chromotherapists familiar with Goethe's *Theory* and concerned with the colours and chemistry of foods should have regarded blue as an acid colour and yellow as alkaline, when Goethe had proposed precisely the opposite. Well might Paul Gauguin (1848–1903) in the 1890s regard the treatment of mental disorders with colours as an example of colour's illogicality, which at least offered him an essential ingredient of mystery in his art [69].

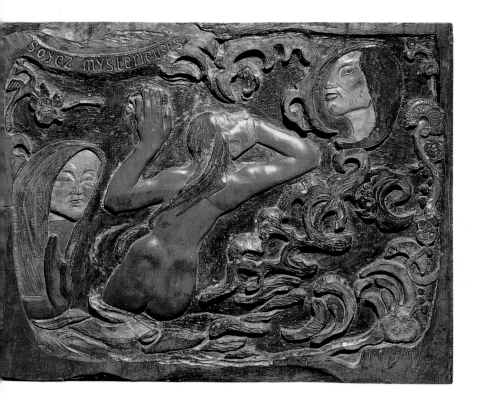

He wrote of colour's 'inner power, its mystery, its enigma' so that we 'cannot logically employ it except enigmatically', to call up immediate sensations, like music.

The belief in a physiological basis for colour therapy has hardly survived in mainstream psychology, but associationism has been far more durable, and has fed into many areas of commercial life [4]. Even at the height of the chromotherapy movement around the time of the First World War, the paint manufacturer that supplied colours for the decoration of shellshock wards in English hospitals, for therapeutic purposes, called them 'Firmament Blue', 'Sunlight Yellow' and 'Spring Green'. Associations are, of course, functions of particular cultures, and the ideal of transcultural meanings for colours, which was so much a feature of early Modernism, no longer convinces, although we shall find in Chapter 5 that there are some consistencies in the development of colour vocabularies. Von Allesch in the early twentieth century was able to find no consistent pattern of affective responses to colours among his many subjects. As his American follower A. R. Chandler wrote in the 1930s: 'The human organism is not

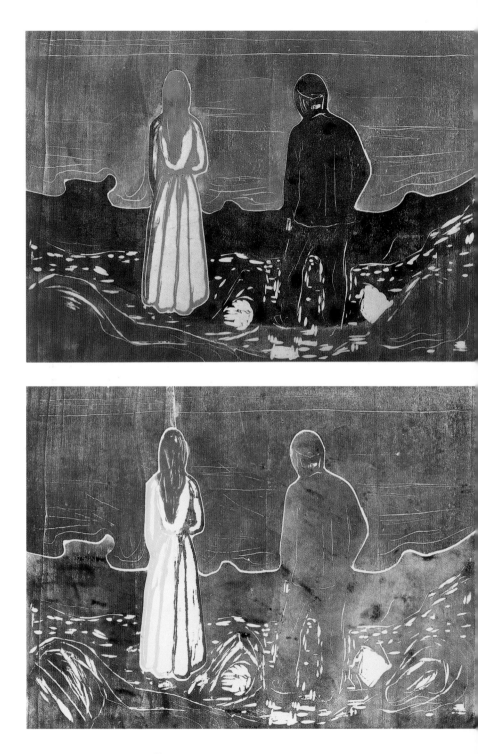

70. **Edvard Munch**, *The Lonely Ones (Two Human Beings)*, 1899.

71. **Edvard Munch**, *The Lonely Ones (Two Human Beings)*, 1899. Munch is regarded, with Van Gogh, as the father of Expressionism, but the very different coloured impressions of his woodcut designs suggest that he gave no particular significance to each colour.

so constituted as to react in a definite way to each color or each combination of colors. No color is invariably and unconditionally pleasant or unpleasant, exciting or soothing, dignified or tawdry.'

Yet it is precisely the uncertainties and instability in the interpretation of the effects of colours that fit them especially for the expression of unstable emotions. A programmatic art expressive of emotions did not emerge until the first decade of the twentieth century in Germany, but it had, of course, already been very much part of the aesthetic of Van Gogh, and of his younger Norwegian contemporary Edvard Munch (1863–1944), both of whom had been exposed to the new psychologically inflected aesthetics in Paris. We saw how Van Gogh articulated his feelings about colour most of all by reference to the quasi-objective theory of complementarity. Munch was far less systematic. As his friend the poet Sigbjørn Obstfelder wrote in 1893: 'His use of colour is above all lyrical. He feels colours and he reveals his feelings through colours; he does not see them in isolation. He does not just see yellow, red and blue and violet; he sees sorrow and screaming and melancholy and decay.'

Munch internalized his colours to the highest degree. We have an eyewitness account of his shouting to his printer, with eyes closed, the sequence of colours that were to make up his woodcuts, for him a major medium of expression. These magnificent and highly original prints are in some ways Munch's finest aesthetic statements. Many of his best-known paintings, such as *The Scream* (one version of which was stolen in 2004 from the Munch Museum in Oslo), were translated immediately into print form. Yet there is, nevertheless, something very puzzling about the handling of colour in these works. The woodcuts, especially, do not employ the same palette as the paintings, as we should expect them to do if they are to carry the same emotional charge. Even more remarkably, different impressions of the woodcuts differ substantially in coloration among themselves [70, 71], so that, far from expressing 'melancholy and decay', they seem to be part of some joyful aesthetic game. As we shall see so often in this book, it is the forms rather than the colours that convey the original or essential meaning of the work.

72. **Anish Kapoor**, *Mother as a Mountain*, 1985. Kapoor's raw pigments fall into a few, easily recognized colour categories, but his shapes are often impossible to describe.

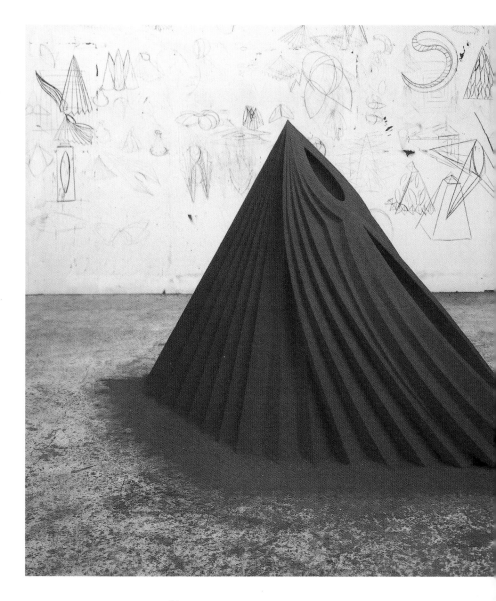

Chapter 3   The Shape of Colour

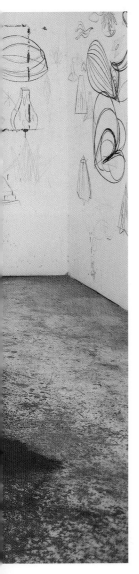

In the early 1980s the British sculptor Anish Kapoor (b. 1954) produced a series of bizarrely shaped coloured works tha illustrated his belief that shapes have a close affinity with colours [72]. What is particularly remarkable about these highly original pieces is that, while the shapes are wildly eccentric, the colours have no such complexity but rather have the strong, rich, raw-pigment coloration that has been the trademark of this Indian-born artist's work. There is a distinct asymmetry here between the roles of colour and form; and this has been so in many phases of the history of art, where they have often been seen as fighting one another for supremacy.

The existence of some intrinsic relationship between specific forms and specific colours has been a recurrent dream among philosophers and artists. An ancient Greek theory of colour already supposed that colours themselves had forms, since they resulted from particular conformations of atoms. Thus the Peripatetic philosopher Theophrastus questioned the notion of the Pre-Socratic philosopher Democritus that red and pale green (*chloron*, an imprecise term, which may mean simply 'damp') were opposites. This could not be the case, he said, since they do not have opposite 'shapes'. Early Modernism was also intensely engaged with the problem of fitting colours to shapes; the idea of primary colours gave it some sort of a rationale, and the development of abstraction in the 1910s and 1920s sometimes seemed to depend on it. Kandinsky was already thinking along these lines during his period in Munich, where the influential teacher Adolf Hoelzel had mooted the circularity of red, the rectangularity of blue and the triangularity of yellow. In his manifesto *On the Spiritual in Art*, Kandinsky shared Hoelzel's feeling about yellow, but reversed his other correspondences, since he regarded blue as round and centripetal, and red as a stable intermediate colour.

But it was in his native Russia, where Kandinsky's treatise became available in a 1914 translation prefaced by a diagram of the

73. **Wassily Kandinsky**, the jacket of a 1980 edition of *On the Spiritual in Art* based on the design of the original 1914 Russian edition. It was the first clear formulation of the idea of specific colour–form coordinates.

74. **Ivan Kliun**, *Forms and Colours*, c. 1931.

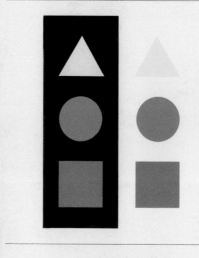

ORP Russian Biography Series, No. 4

THE LIFE OF VASILII KANDINSKY IN RUSSIAN ART
A STUDY OF
ON THE SPIRITUAL IN ART

Introduced and Edited by John E. Bowlt and Rose-Carol Washton Long. Translation by John E. Bowlt

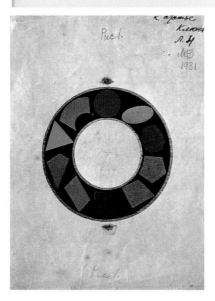

yellow triangle, the red square and the blue circle [73], that the investigation of colour–form coordinates became something of an obsession in the years following the Revolution of 1917 and the subsequent restructuring of art schools into aesthetic research laboratories [74]. In his essay 'An Attempt to Determine the Relation between Colour and Form in Painting' (c. 1930), Malevich described how he and his teaching colleagues examined the way in which, in the minds of some artists, forms evoked colour associations, and vice versa:

> With this aim each artist was individually shown a simplified geometrical drawing, in order that it might evoke colour associations in him. The experiments, made with several artists, gave approximately the same colouring associations. Thus we have some basis for saying that every form has its relatively characteristic, but not supplementary, colouring. Examining the differences between associations from the same form of the drawing we noted that they diverged only in the transition of related tones and their intensity, but that they remained basically similar.

Malevich insisted that this study was purely psychological, and depended on 'the creative imagination of the artist'. He concluded: '*Colour and form can be examined as separate elements in physics, but in artistic creation they cannot be examined as two different elements with the help of which sensation is determined*, since colour and form are the result of the same single sensation [emphasis in original].'

Kandinsky arranged a similar survey – though with a far larger sample of subjects – when he moved from Russia to the Weimar Bauhaus in the early 1920s, and concluded that the results confirmed his own feelings about the yellow triangle, red square and blue circle, feelings that were universally shared. But whereas Malevich's experiment began with forms, Kandinsky's began with colours, for not only was it his vivid response to colours in the Munich period that had stimulated this line of thinking, but the arbitrary limitation of the geometrical forms to three in his Bauhaus questionnaire of 1923 presupposed that only the three subtractive primary colours would be in play. Primary colours had to find equivalents in primary forms. And in the several schemes of colour–form correspondences that extended their range to the secondary colours, the forms attributed to these were far from uniform, and often

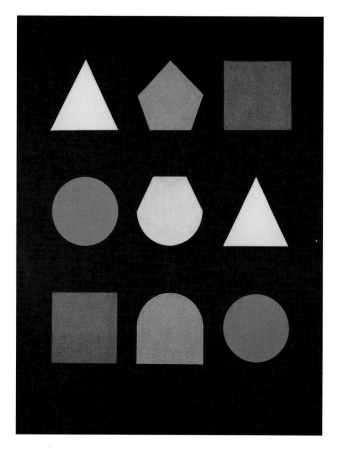

75. **Eugen Batz**, *Colours and Forms*, 1929–30. The teaching of colour and form in the Russian post-Revolutionary art schools and in the German Bauhaus ran on similar lines, but the solutions were very different, particularly for secondary colours and 'secondary' forms.

bizarre [75], for there is no universal geometrical concept of 'secondary shapes'.

A late arrival on the scene of Swiss Neo-Constructivism, the artist and designer Karl Gerstner, argued as early as 1957 that the work of Richard Paul Lohse [41] and two other contemporary Swiss artists, Max Bill (1908–1994) and Camille Graeser (1892–1980), showed 'a major contradiction between the conclusive concept of formal structure made by these artists, and their more or less arbitrary use of colors'. To address this problem, Gerstner, starting from Kandinsky's colour–form coordinates, made a series of works in the 1970s that matched colours and forms, using a computer to generate the intermediate shapes. 'My basic goal', he wrote, 'was to relate colors in an absolute and distinctive way to a formal structure. Only if this were possible would I be able to reach the goal I was after: making pictures that existed as undeniable truths in themselves.'

Gerstner believed that Kandinsky's linking of blue with the circle was 'undisputed' – which was far from being the case – but he felt that, from a psychological point of view, the radiance of yellow linked it more plausibly with a dynamic star-shape, and he felt obliged to stand the red square on a corner 'so as to express the main characteristic of red – the ambivalence of dynamism and strength'. Unlike Kandinsky, too, Gerstner accepted the standard psychological view that green was a fourth primary, and he devised an unusual shape, rather like a four-leaf clover, which he called the *sinuon*, because it was made up of sine curves passing through the right angles of the square as arcs [76]. And, just as Ostwald's twenty-four-colour circle [77], used by Gerstner,

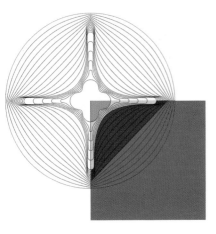

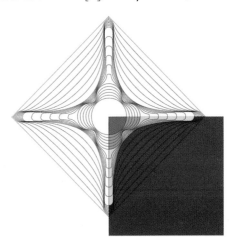

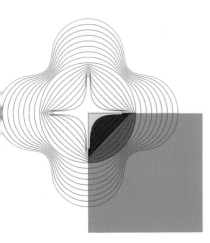

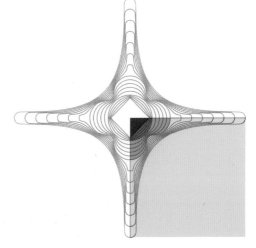

77. **Wilhelm Ostwald**, *Colour-Circle*, from *Die Farbenfibel*, 1916.

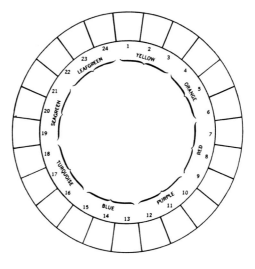

introduced an unusually large number of steps into the blue-green area, so Gerstner found that, although there were no intermediates between the triangle and the square, there was an infinite number between the square and the circle (the pentagon, hexagon, octagon, etc.), and he cited the German Renaissance philosopher Nicholas of Cusa to the effect that the circle was an infinite polygon. But the logic of form and the logic of colour were two quite independent systems, and although the formal element in *Colour Form Objects* [78] was computer-generated, he was unable

78. **Karl Gerstner**, *Colour Form Objects, Diversion Cycle*, 1970–75/82. Gerstner's colour–form coordinates began as revisions of Kandinsky's [73], but under the influence of Ostwald [77], whose colour circle has many greens, he gave considerable attention to green.

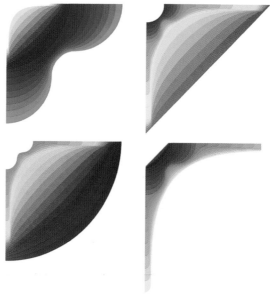

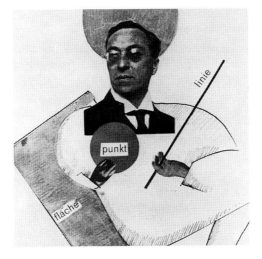

to use the same method with colour. He was even uncertain which reds, blues, etc, were 'primary': 'It would have been consistent with the idea also to produce the colors – or at least to have them calculated – by computer, but so far there is no instrumentation which is more precise than sensation.'

Unlike Gerstner, Kandinsky's Bauhaus colleagues did not always support his colour–form equivalents. The sculptor Oskar Schlemmer (1888–1943), for example, who had been a pupil of Hoelzel's, agreed with his teacher that red, not blue, was characteristic of the circle, since in nature (sun, fruit) it was an active colour, whereas blue was appropriate to the abstract, metaphysical square, a form that did not exist in nature at all [79]. Kandinsky was almost the only painter to use this repertory of 'primary' shapes in the 1920s, and since this was a visual language as flexible and ambiguous as any verbal language, it is not surprising that we find these precise colour equivalents only occasionally in his work [80].

Even in Latin Europe, where very similar correspondences were mooted, the equivalents were predictably various. In a series of compositions of 1913–14 entitled *Contrast of Forms* [81] French artist Fernand Léger (1881–1955) set red rectangles against rounded blue forms in the interest of contrast, which he saw as a quintessentially modern dissonance. But with Léger, a true heir to Cubism, these forms did not arise from geometry and abstract chromatics, but from the observation of the outdoor, albeit urban, scene. As he explained in an essay of 1914, they had their origins in 'the visual effect of round curls of smoke rising between buildings':

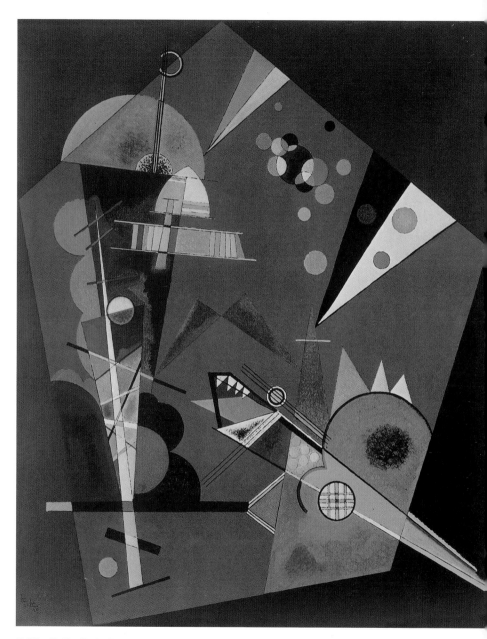

80. **Wassily Kandinsky**, *Tension in Red*, 1926.

81. **Fernand Léger**, *Contrast of Forms (Contraste de formes)*, 1913. Léger's choice of three near-primary colours to articulate the contrasts of his round and rectangular forms suggests he was well abreast of contemporary thinking.

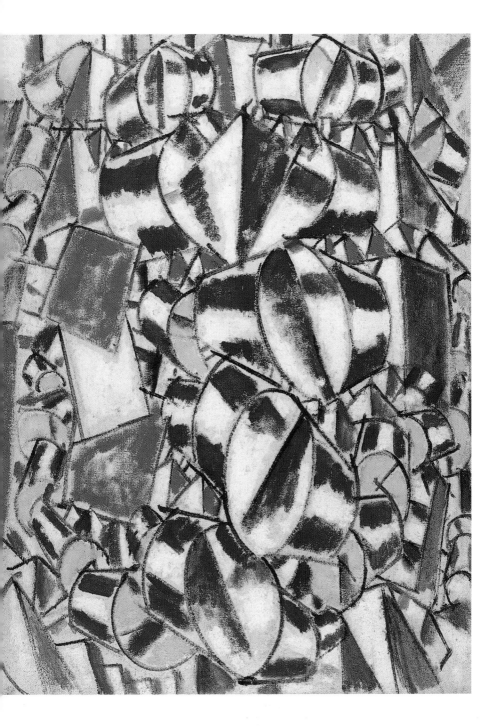

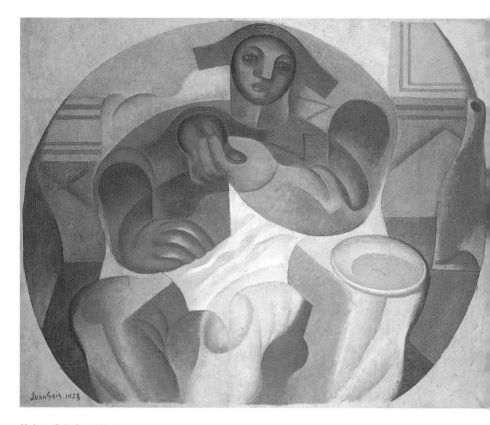

82. **Juan Gris**, *Seated Harlequin*, 1923. Although he never abandoned figuration for pure abstraction, Gris in the early 1920s spoke of the contrast of round and angular forms as analogous to the lightest and darkest colours, a view opposite to that of Kandinsky.

Here you have an excellent practical example on which to put into practice the results of this research into multiple contrasts of intensity. Concentrate your curves with the greatest variety possible, short of disuniting them; frame them by means of the hard, dry relationship of the surfaces of the houses – 'dead' surfaces which will acquire mobility by the fact that they will be coloured contrarily to the central mass, and that they are juxtaposed with 'live' forms; and you will get a maximum effect.

Here red is associated with the dead, and grey-blue with the alive: precisely the opposite values to those of the more exclusively non-representational artists.

    Closer to their abstract concerns, but also with a Cubist background, the Spanish painter Juan Gris (1887–1927), lecturing in Paris in 1924, proclaimed what he termed 'a sort of painter's mathematics', where the primary formal polarity was between the circle and the triangle [82]. For Gris the circle was the most expansive form, and thus corresponded to the brightest tones on the palette, the triangle the most concentrated, and thus appropriate to the darkest – clearly, in an abbreviated form, the opposite formula to Kandinsky's. A replay of the latter's 1923 Bauhaus experiment carried out with a handful of American graphic designers around 1990 also contested his values, giving red to the circle and blue to the square; and, as if to demonstrate the implausibility of the whole scheme, two subjects put all three colours, separate or mixed, in each of the three shapes. Shades of Barnett Newman [21], or of the Marxist architect Hannes Mayer, director of the Bauhaus in the late 1920s, who looked on these exercises as nothing but an idle academic game!

Yet this justifiable scepticism about the intrinsic relationships of specific colours to specific shapes should not blind us to the fact that they have nonetheless been a recurrent concern among artists for many centuries. The modern scientific view that the rod system of human vision – which processes light levels but not wavelength – is older than the cone system – which processes wavelength (i.e., hue) – seems to be strikingly anticipated in Pliny's account of the historical development of ancient Greek painting, which started with pure line, moved on to chiaroscuro, and only later began to use colour. In medieval times painting in monochrome, often in imitation of sculpture – although medieval, like ancient, sculpture was often coloured – continued this early practice, and the fifteenth-century development of monochrome engraving, which is the prelude to the nineteenth-century graphic art of photography, which was able only much later to find intrinsically photographic means of introducing colour, suggests that monochromatic images have usually been more or less adequate to satisfy our curiosity about the look of the world.

'Disegno' and 'Colore'

Just as the Modernist attempt to coordinate colours and forms was promoted largely in the context of teaching (Juan Gris's 1924 lecture was given at the Sorbonne), so it was in the early art academies of the sixteenth and seventeenth centuries that the most significant phases of the debate unfurled between the supporters of form and those of colour, between the Florentine emphasis on drawing as the fundamental basis of painting and the freer technique of improvising on the canvas directly with paint, characteristic of painters in Venice, such as Titian (c. 1487/90–1576). In seventeenth-century France this debate was continued by the supporters of Nicolas Poussin (1594–1665), who laid

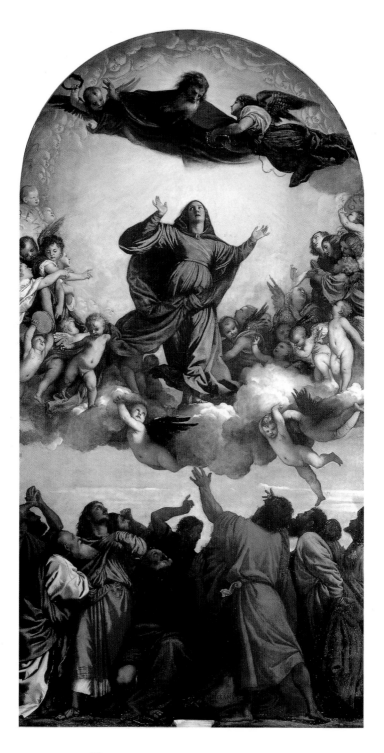

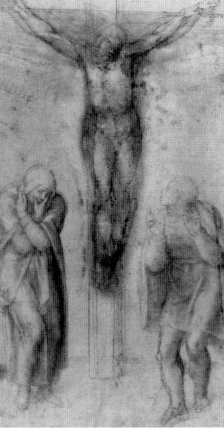

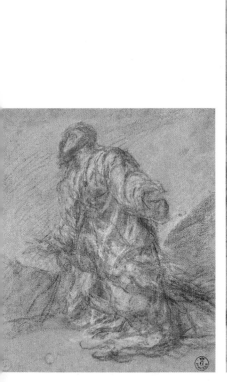

83. opposite **Titian**, *The Assumption*, 1516–18.

84. above **Titian**, *Study for 'Christ in the Garden'*, c. 1559–63.

85. above right **Michelangelo Buonarotti**, *Christ on the Cross between the Virgin and St John*, c. 1562. These two highly painterly drawings, with many changes of mind, one Venetian, the other Florentine, suggest that, at least at the end of their careers, Titian and Michelangelo had reached very similar views about the functions of drawing.

greater emphasis on design, and those of the Fleming Peter Paul Rubens (1577–1640), who continued the painterly emphasis of Venice. The French example, enshrined in the earliest national art academy (founded 1648), established attitudes that affected art education and criticism in Europe for more than two centuries. The debate now seems to be about nothing very significant. The meanings of *disegno* (which covers both 'drawing' and 'design') and *colore* (which includes pictorial colouring, painterly handling and the pigments and media that create it) were never clearly defined. Moreover, just as Venetian painters such as Titian were both outstanding draughtsmen [83, 84] and were happy to join the Florentine Accademia del Disegno, founded in 1563, so artists trained in Florence, such as Michelangelo [85], were not only brilliant colourists but, as the Sistine Chapel frescoes now reveal [86], could also handle pigments in a free and painterly way. There are many Renaissance examples of both painterly drawings

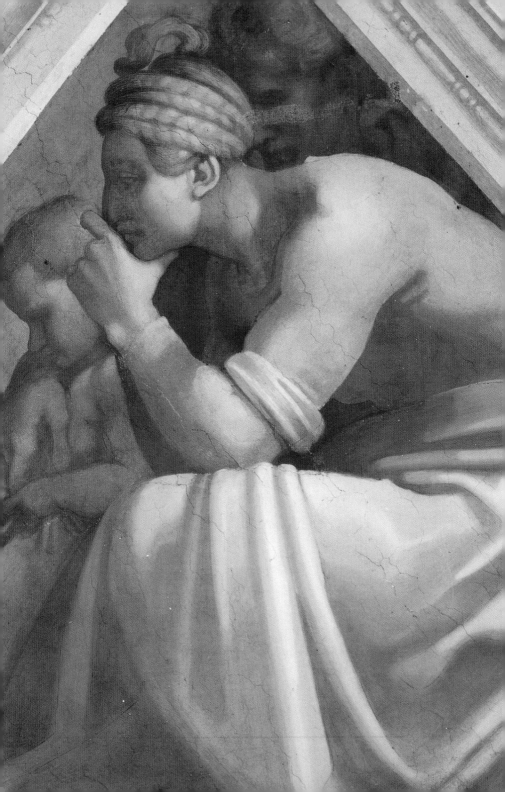

and linear paintings; and analyses made in the course of conservation have shown that the habit of improvisation in the course of executing a painting was far from being a purely Venetian practice. As in the later disputes between Delacroix and Ingres or between the Salon painters and the Impressionists in France, we are dealing as much as anything with local rivalries and art politics, rather than with substantial aesthetic issues. When, in the early seventeenth century, El Greco (1541–1614), who had begun his career as an icon painter in Crete but had subsequently developed his technique in Venice, made the unusual claim that colouring was more difficult than drawing, he was thinking not of the highly contrasted and saturated colours characteristic of his mature style [87], and which are evidence of the continuing influence of Byzantium, but rather of the problem of identifying and representing the colours of nature. As so often in this period, colour was understood, as it had been in Italian theory, as primarily a matter of truth to appearances.

There are, however, very substantial differences between painterly styles, between an emphasis on the integrity of local colours – for instance, Rosso Fiorentino (1495–1540) [88] – and

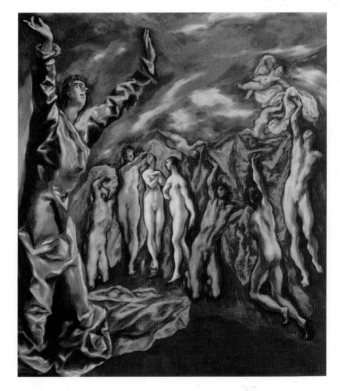

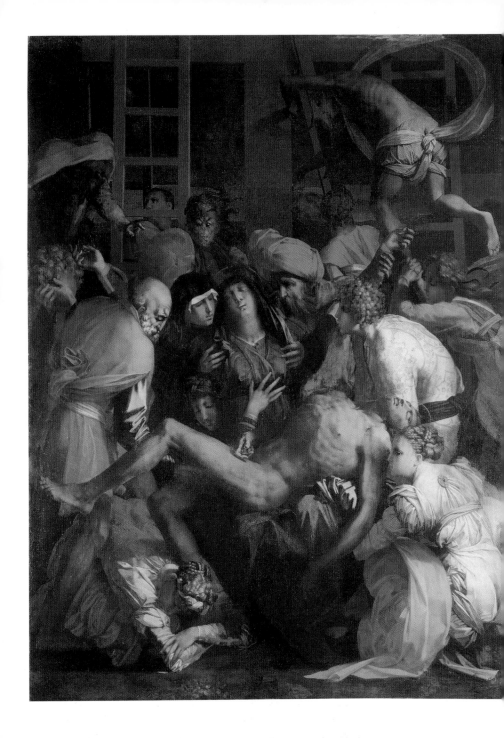

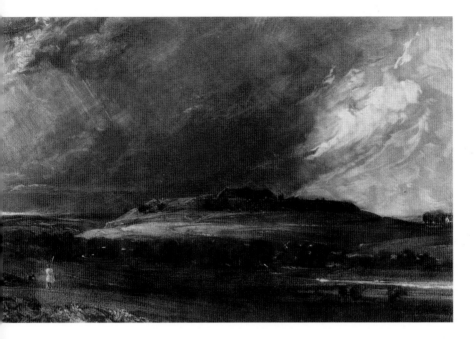

88. **Rosso Fiorentino**, *Deposition from the Cross*, 1528. Rosso's sombre subject is lit by intense flashes of contrasting local colour.

89. **David Lucas** after John Constable, *Old Sarum*, 1830. Constable believed that nature had its own chiaroscuro, and he worked with Lucas to illustrate this in a brilliantly original series of prints.

an emphasis on the liaison between colours, the linking of colour areas by evident brushwork as well as by the regulation of tone and the repetition of specific hues. It is the second of these approaches that is generally called colouristic, and it is something of a paradox that John Constable (1776–1837), a great colourist who was, indeed, partly responsible for deflecting the mainstream of nineteenth-century French painting towards colourism, should have aspired to render what he called 'the chiaroscuro of nature' [89]. But the idea of 'colour' had long included the management of light and shade, and we have seen what an important element this was in, for example, Seurat's picture-making.

What radically changed the relationship of form and colour was the arrival, in the early twentieth century, of non-representational painting. As Kandinsky recognized, the removal of traditional subject matter raised the question of what was to replace it. One answer – and perhaps the most important one – was 'colour'. Colour became a subject; it was what viewers looked for in painting, but, contrary to what is sometimes said about abstraction, it did not upstage form. Forms, whether the soft forms of a Rothko [90] or the hard forms of an Albers [91], are intrinsic to the look of their colours. As Bridget Riley (b. 1931) noted in 1978: 'One cannot tackle the instability and infinite variety of colour relationships without relying on some formal backbone.

90. **Mark Rothko**, *Orange and Yellow*, 1956.

91. **Josef Albers**, *Homage to the Square*, 1950. Rothko achieved interaction of colours with scale, layering and soft edges; Albers, with a subtle manipulation of tone.

You can see in Matisse just how essential drawing is if one is going to be involved with colour.'

But the reconciliation of form and colour was never easy. Riley spoke of a crisis in her own move from black and white to full colour in the late 1960s, a move which was prepared over many years but constantly delayed. The more or less geometric forms in her earlier work could easily be identified, she said, 'but if you say red, yellow or blue, you do not know at all what shade of colour you will be looking at.... The reasoning of my black and white work could not be extended into colour because it depended on a contradiction between stability and disruption … [but] I saw that the basis of colour is its instability.' On another occasion Riley recalled the transition to colour in terms of the search for simpler forms as vehicles for colour energies, which 'need a virtually neutral vehicle if they are to develop uninhibitedly. The repeated stripe seems to meet these conditions' [92].

Stripe painting was very widespread in England and the United States in the 1960s, and 'neutrality' of form an aspiration of many colour painters. Riley, who had long been a close student of Seurat, wanted to create supplementary colours in front of the canvas surface by means of simultaneous contrast, an effect only available through protracted viewing by the spectator. These powerful optical effects created by Riley in studies before she launched definitively into colour were described by one of her earliest supporters and critics, the psychologist Anton Ehrenzweig:

> Bridget Riley conducted experiments by adding colour to her dazzling optical painting [in black and white]. In one of her studies alternative [sc. alternate] bands of orange and blue gradually contract towards a critical area where the surfaces shrink into thin lines and assume a dazzling effect. Bridget Riley commented that it seemed difficult to judge which of the two colours – orange and blue – was deeper in tone. This was indeed so in the area of the broader bands. The vehement colour interaction between these bands done in complementary colours of almost equal tone prevented the onlooker from making a proper comparison. But in the critical area where the surface contracted to thin dazzling lines it became quite clear that the orange was in fact darker than the blue. The linear shape of the coloured surfaces had destroyed colour interaction and replaced it by a 'spreading' effect. The orange and blue tended to spread into each other and mix into a green.

Form is a decisive element in the creation of effects of contrast and assimilation: the stripes of Riley and the squares of Albers are far from being 'neutral'. Even the single zip of a Barnett Newman sets up an optical vibration when encountered on a vast canvas where, as Riley also noted of her own large, later canvases, the viewer's eye remains unfocused. A sequence of vertical or horizontal stripes sets up a powerful rhythm which may, or may not, inhibit the release of colour energies. Everything depends upon the viewer's inclination and ability to stick around.

Riley, who began her career making optically highly active monochromatic works, was also concerned in her colour paintings to create optical movement, and the appearance of new colours in new spaces through the activity of the viewer's eye [93]. In the late 1960s she preferred non-primary colours – orange, green, violet, cerise, turquoise, olive – which are more labile and readier to shift and join with other colour perceptions. But other hard-edge colourists have sought to achieve precisely the opposite effect. In the 1960s one of the earliest hard-edge American colour-field painters, Ellsworth Kelly, whose coloured

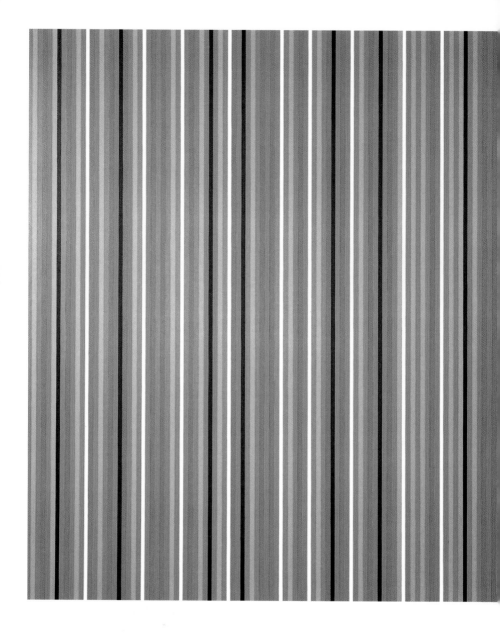

surfaces, unlike Riley's, used large units of form, aimed at making his edges inert: 'the edges happen', he claimed in 1963, 'because the forms get as quiet as they can be'. He saw himself engaged in 'a struggle to get figure and ground separated, to get shape to stand alone and edges to become as quiet as they need be'. Kelly achieved this by making his shapes more interesting, and by the very large scale of his works, which inhibits the switch between figure and ground, a phenomenon much studied by Gestalt psychologists from the early years of the century.

Riley, like Sanford Wurmfeld [50, 51], showed that the high activity of hard edges and repeated shapes could create a film of transformed colour which seems to hover in front of the canvas. But soft edges, with a minimum of interactivity, suggest a film within the plane of the picture, and painters such as Mark Rothko [90], who were concerned to create an inner light, exploited the effects of soft contours and many layers of coloured glazes, the latter a traditional technique used by Titian, Rembrandt and Turner, artists whose work Rothko particularly admired. Rothko also made much play with the juxtaposition of close tones, which, as in the work of his contemporary Ad Reinhardt [182], and sometimes of Albers, induces the viewer to search out the edges and takes them again beyond the surface.

This chapter began with coloured sculpture, the medium in which an emphasis on form is inescapable; and it closes with the work of a modern sculptor in which colour and form, reflectivity and transparency, are united in the highest degree. Donald Judd (1928–94) came to sculpture from painting, into which, in the 1960s, he began to introduce three-dimensional elements. He was very conscious of the effects of colour on shape, particularly on the crisp edges that were his particular contribution to the repertory of sculptural forms. 'Cadmium Red Light' was his favourite colour, he explained, because he thought 'it had the light value for a three-dimensional object. If you paint something black or any dark color, you can't tell what its edges are like. If you paint it white, it seems small and purist. And the red, other than a gray of that value, seems to be the only color that really makes an object sharp and defines its contours and angles' [94].

So even a supremely colouristic artist was concerned to adjust colour to fit form, in order to stabilize it; and where Riley found that 'what you focus upon is not what you see, at least not in terms of colour', Judd was apt to repeat the Minimalist slogan: 'You see what you see'. In his later multicoloured wall-sculptures [95] he minimized interaction by enclosing each hue in a compartment, so it is perhaps surprising that he became more and more impressed with the work of the greatest exponent of colour interaction, Josef Albers. Judd had reviewed *Interaction of Color* rather coolly in 1963, although he gave Albers credit for having put art in the forefront of colour practice and for teaching by experiment. But he began to collect Albers's work, and in 1991 wrote warmly of him in the catalogue of an Albers exhibition he arranged at his own art foundation in Texas.

In *Interaction of Color*, Albers, as we saw, restated the ancient Greek idea that we never see colours as they really are, but he amplified the 'objective' explanation of this fact – that it was due to mixture and lighting – with the more recently investigated subjective phenomena of the transforming effects of colour contrast and the tendency for colours in certain surface quantities to seem to spread beyond their actual boundaries. He and his Yale students devised some particularly elegant demonstrations of

94. Donald Judd, *Untitled*, 1973.

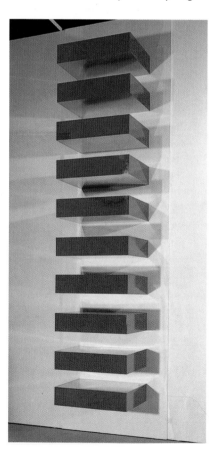

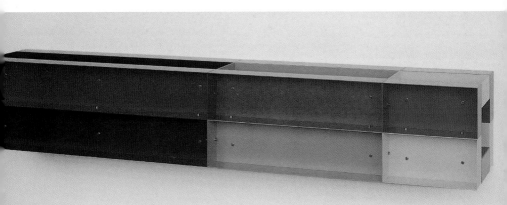

5. **Donald Judd**, *Untitled*, 1984. Judd saw sculpture as a type of painting; his earlier work made much play with internal reflections from painted surfaces, bright metals and transparent coloured Plexiglas. Later he used painted metal, but inhibited colour interaction by framing each coloured area in a three-dimensional grid.

contrast effects [2], and even before stripe painting became fashionable he had investigated the phenomenology of the stripe. Yet we cannot, strictly speaking, distinguish objective from subjective colour. All colour is subjective; the only distinction is that sometimes the stimuli are modified, by changes in lighting, texture, etc., before they reach the visual system, and sometimes, as is the case with contrast effects, colours originate within this system. Riley and Albers were particularly concerned to exploit the latter circumstances in their art; Judd, the former, since it is the ambient situation of three-dimensional work that creates the sense of movement and life. Judd made the crucial observation that, for the artist, colour is akin to a material: 'Color, like material, is what art is made of. It alone is not art... Other than the spectrum, there is no pure color. It always occurs on a surface which has no texture or which has a texture or which is beneath a transparent surface.'

Leaving aside the new-media art, such as holography [42], which is made from light itself, Judd was substantially right. He echoes the Renaissance reservations articulated by Leonardo da Vinci, that the beauty of colours 'is not to the credit of the painter, but of him who has made them'. Colour is inseparable from the surface that bears it, and from its material substance. How artists such as Anish Kapoor have prized the materials of colour, and have thought particularly deeply about them, is the subject of the next chapter.

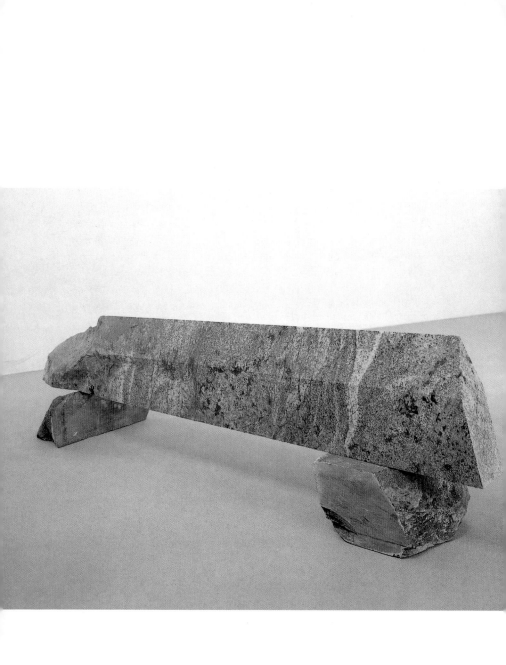

Chapter 4   The Health of Colours

In addition to a physics and a chemistry, colour has a geography.
Its sources were always of importance to artists and often
contributed significantly to its meaning. In his attack on garish
Roman taste, Pliny the Elder was careful to specify the origins
of most of those four colours used by the best Greek painters:
white from the Greek island of Milos, *sil* from Attica (yellow, or
possibly blue), red from Sinope on the Black Sea. Among the
tawdry modern colours he listed, the 'ooze from Indian rivers'
probably refers to indigo, a vegetable dye which, because of its
marketing in compressed blocks, was thought in the West to
be a mineral. Indigo is a particularly telling example of colour
geography, because although European knowledge of the Orient
was very vague in the Middle Ages, in many documents the best
variety was said to come, not from India, but specifically from
Baghdad, in modern Iraq.

The reputation of pigments and dyes depended first of all
on their stability, and then on their rarity, and hence their cost.
The blue that is still the most expensive natural pigment is
manufactured from the hard semi-precious stone lapis lazuli, until
recently mined only in Afghanistan; and it is still generally called by
the name given to it in late-medieval France and Italy, ultramarine,
because it came to western Europe from 'beyond the sea'.
Ultramarine was also extremely costly because of its laborious
and protracted method of preparation. Only in its raw form has
it been possible to use lapis lazuli in quantity, for architectural or
decorative inlays, or for sculpture, such as Tony Cragg's (b. 1949)
Hassocks of 1986, where a large block is combined with another
semi-precious stone, serpentine [96]. Grinding the hard stone
might take several days, and its processing many days more. The
late-fourteenth-century Florentine painter Cennino Cennini
devoted the longest chapter of his handbook on art to the
subject, where he advised: 'keep it to yourself, for it is an unusual
ability to know how to make it properly. And know that making it
is an occupation for pretty girls rather than for men; for they are

always at home, and reliable, and they have more dainty hands. Just beware of old women.'

In sixteenth-century Venice ultramarine was so valuable that it seems to have been employed by wealthy merchants as a sort of currency. Sometimes patrons would supply the most precious pigments to their artists themselves, as a sort of guarantee against fraud; but this is also an indication that the yen for conspicuous display was as much patron- as artist-driven, if not more [97]. This was a practice that had been noted in ancient Rome, and continued there well into the nineteenth century; and there is a curious echo of it in 1950s New York, where the newly successful Abstract Expressionist Franz Kline was persuaded by his fashionable dealer to switch to better-quality materials, and to charge the gallery for them.

The closest rival to ultramarine was azurite, another mineral blue, which came to Italy from beyond the Alps and was thus known as 'German Blue'. Another German blue, one of the first modern synthetic colours, was developed in the early eighteenth century, and first called Berlin Blue, but soon given its still-current name, Prussian Blue. Place names have become rather less common in modern colour usage: of the 125 English and French trade names for a single variety of blue published by Patricia Sloane in 1989, only four were the names of places. And in Arman's (b. 1928) series of the 1960s, which plays with the purely material character of painting [98], the paints that spurt from his tubes, unlike Anish Kapoor's powders or Arman's friend Yves Klein's customized pigment [103], have only an obvious commercial origin.

It was not only the source of the best raw materials of colour that was particularly valued by artists, but also their place of manufacture. Venice, which had specialist colour suppliers from the late fifteenth century, probably had the most developed colour trade in Europe in the sixteenth. Antwerp also had

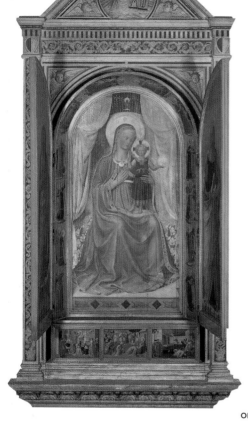

97. **Fra Angelico da Fiesole**, *Linaiuoli Tabernacle*, 1433. The Fiorentine Linen Guild stipulated that this altarpiece should be painted with the 'best gold blue and silver'. But the 'best' blue, ultramarine, was confined to the smaller image of the Virgin in the predella at the foot of the main panel.

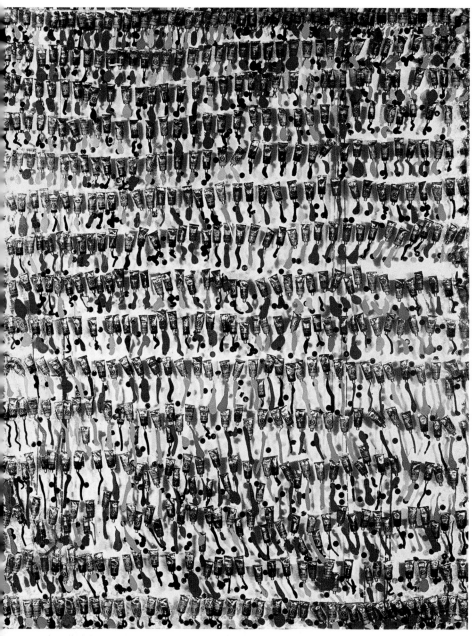

3. **Arman**, *La Vie dans le ville pour l'oeil
ife in the Town for the Eye)*, 1965. Here
rocessed and packaged paints are
ade into art.

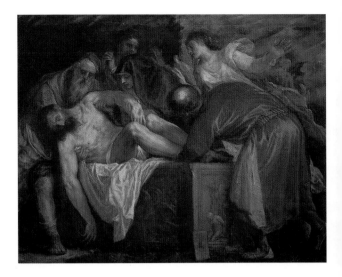

99. **Titian**, *The Entombment of Christ*, 1559. In his late work Titian used a broad and dense impasto, which became extremely influential in later centuries, One of its crucial ingredients was lead white.

specialist colour dealers and produced a famous blue, still called Antwerp Blue.

Venice was also known for the production of a number of colours, notably an especially fine lead white, in England called Venice Ceruse. Venetian colours were so fine and so famous that even Tuscan artists went, or were sent, there by their patrons for these materials, although fine blues were also made at a convent in Florence. The white was especially significant because, as a fast-drying oil paint with great body, it was important in the development of the brushy and impasto style of painting that was the most influential Venetian technical innovation in the sixteenth century.

It is thus no accident that what is surely the earliest detailed account (albeit from the mid-seventeenth century) of a sixteenth-century Venetian painter at work, Palma Giovane's description of Titian's last practice, focuses on the handling of colour [99]. Palma, who finished off Titian's great *Pietà*, now in the Accademia in Venice, just after his master's death, reported that the old painter used to begin his pictures 'with bold strokes made with brushes laden with colours, sometimes of a pure earth, which he used … for a middle tone, and at other times of white lead; and with the same brush tinted with red, black or yellow he formed a highlight'. After leaving these beginnings propped up facing the wall for up to several months, said Palma, the painter returned to them and brought them to a finished state, often using his fingers, as Leonardo had done before him.

Manufacturing Pigments

The profession of colour-maker and colour-merchant which began in earnest in sixteenth-century Venice became an even more important factor in nineteenth-century painting when, for example, the Parisian retailer Haro mixed paints of an unusually fluid consistency for Delacroix; and Père Tanguy was not only a major supplier to the Impressionists and van Gogh, but also sat to the latter as a model [100]. A whole range of prominent English artists, including Turner, endorsed the mysterious 'Van Eyck Glass Medium' produced in the 1840s and 1850s by the colour manufacturer Thomas Miller [101]; and others later mourned the passing of the colourman and theorist George Field (1777–1854), whose brilliant and high-quality pigments may well have made possible the unprecedentedly bright palette of the Pre-Raphaelite

100. **Vincent van Gogh**, *Portrait of Père Tanguy*, 1887–88. It would be pleasant to think that this sympathetic image of a colour-merchant was painted with his own materials, but the poverty-stricken van Gogh also bought from cheaper suppliers.

101. Advertisement for Thomas Miller's 'Van Eyck Glass Medium' for oil painting, from *The Art Union*, 1841. This novel medium (despite its brand name!) seems to have been based on borax, and Miller claimed it could be used for oil or watercolour painting. The list of testimonials shows it was tried by many well-known English artists.

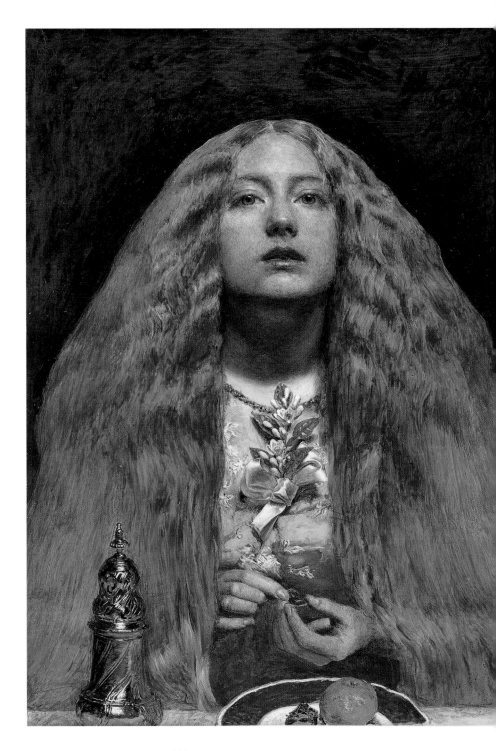

Brotherhood [102]. By the close of the century it had become usual for manufacturers of particular artists' products to be mentioned by name in the many practical handbooks now being published, often by the manufacturers themselves. One that has had an unusually long life is *The Science of Painting* (1891), by the French genre painter J.-G. Vibert, who had a close association with the Paris firm of Lefranc & Cie. We also know something of the particular brands of painting materials used by the Impressionists and Seurat (Edouard), by Cézanne (Sennelier) and by Matisse (Blockx), and rather more about the New York painters' frequenting an innovative colour-maker, Leonard Bocour, in the 1950s and 1960s. In 1960 Bocour was supplying a specially thinned version of his acrylic paint Magna to the Washington colour-field painters Morris Louis [105] and Kenneth Noland, who found that even with dilution it retained its intensity.

New York was perhaps the last important centre for new materials in Western art. Although the French artist Yves Klein (1928–62) had already commissioned a customized blue paint, IKB (International Klein Blue), for his small monochromes and sculptures, this remained very much his own personal material [103], and it was to New York that European as well as American artists turned for the new synthetic paints that had been being developed for industrial purposes in the United States since the 1930s. Synthetics were, of course, not new in themselves. One of the earliest recorded synthetic colours, also a blue, was the Egyptian Blue in use from before 2000 BC and invented, according to an ancient Greek source, by no less than an (unnamed) king. Reds made from heated yellow ochres have an even longer

history in cave painting; in the Middle Ages vermilion was synthesized from sulphur and mercury; and in the eighteenth and nineteenth centuries the research programmes of modern chemistry produced first blues, again, then a range of greens, violets and yellows. Many of these proved to be thoroughly unstable, and in the second half of the nineteenth century there was much debate about the permanence of colours, and several art academies introduced lectures on chemistry or even, as at the École des Beaux-Arts in Paris, a laboratory to test new products.

Stylistic and technical innovations did not always go hand in hand. The Impressionists were in general hostile to the modern mass-produced, machine-ground paints. Van Gogh sometimes ground his own paints – and his Paris supplier Tanguy ground by hand – although this was probably largely for reasons of economy. Seurat and the Neo-Impressionists were more adventurous, but Seurat's work, at least, has suffered as a consequence of the darkening of the modern zinc yellows. Gauguin, who patronized

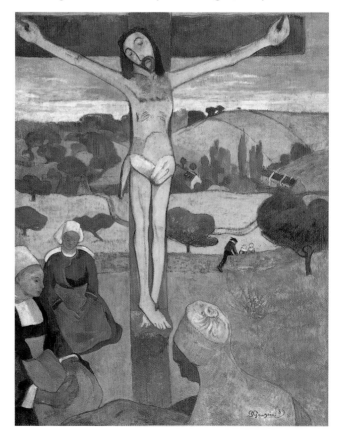

104. **Paul Gauguin**, *The Yellow Christ*, 1889. Gauguin shared his friend van Gogh's love of yellow, but used rather more reliable versions of it than did Vincent.

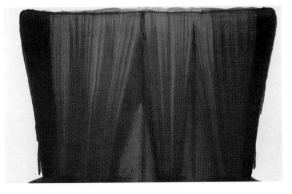

Lefranc, used the modern cadmiums as opposed to the older and
more unreliable chrome yellows [104]. When his friend van Gogh
asked his brother Theo in 1888 to procure for him in Paris a
number of the colours that the Neo-Impressionists 'have brought
into fashion', they were mainly bright but highly unstable, and van
Gogh knew it: 'Time', he said, 'will tone them down only too much.'

The thinness of Bocour's water-soluble Magna was crucial to
the veil technique of Morris Louis (1912–1962) [105]; and a revival
of highly transparent water-based paints had already been a major
element in the colour practice of early Modernists such as
Kandinsky and Klee. Watercolour had of course been in use for
many centuries and in many cultures, but in nineteenth-century
Europe it had moved from a marginal to a central position in the
repertory of techniques, notably in the work of Turner [106] and

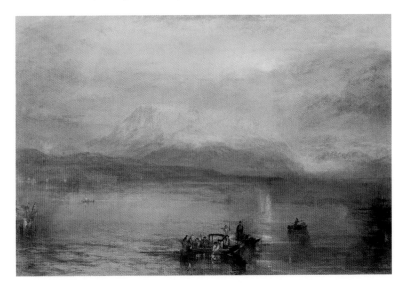

107. **Paul Cézanne**, *Peasant in a Straw Hat*, c. 1906. Like Turner, Cézanne came to work more and more in watercolour, a medium that gave him depth of transparency, as well as the freedom to work on many scales.

108. **Wassily Kandinsky**, *Composition*, 1911–12. The lack of body in watercolour allowed Kandinsky to focus on colour in his earliest non-representational works.

109. **Wassily Kandinsky**, *Riegsee-Dorfkirche (Riegsee Village Church)*, 1908. Working from nature, Kandinsky often echoed the substance of things in the substance of paint.

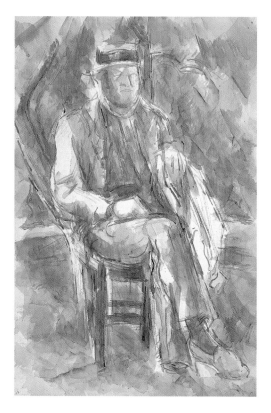

Cézanne [107]. Watercolour was vital to early abstraction. In the years around 1912, when Kandinsky was launching his new, non-representational style, he was using watercolour a great deal [108], in striking contrast to the impastose oil-painting style of his immediately preceding Murnau landscapes [109]. It is as if these thin patches of pigment which scarcely veil the white paper represent the disembodied, abstract character of colour itself. Nevertheless, in the 1914 Russian version of *On the Spiritual in Art*, Kandinsky was concerned to say that he was usually speaking of paint rather than colour: 'Apart from its abstract colour, the concept paint also embraces the material consistency with which the artist operates.'

For Kandinsky's later Bauhaus colleague Josef Albers, the variable consistency of his materials presented a particular challenge. 'Each color', he stated towards the end of his life, 'has different properties both as color and as buttery paste. Each has a different density. In spite of this, I want them all to *behave*; to do what *I* want and not what *they* want.' Albers tried, when he could,

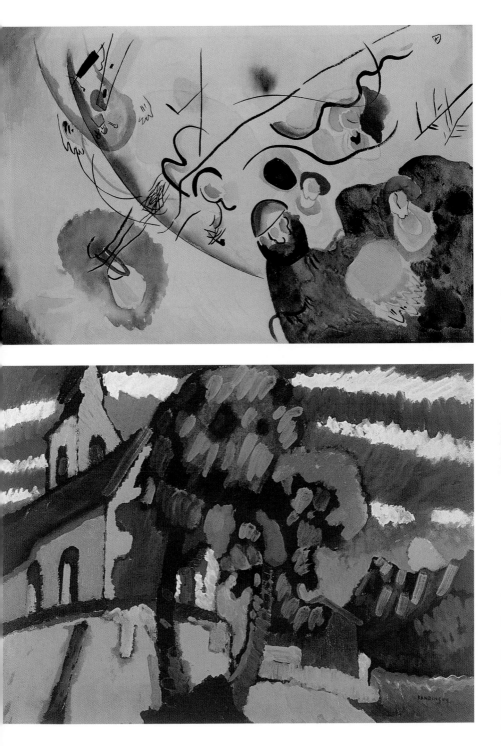

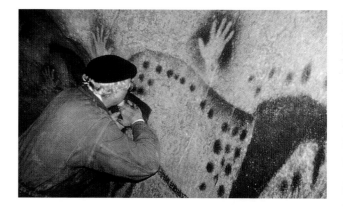

110. Michel Lorblanchet re-creating the spray-painted spotted horse panel at Peche-Merle cave in the Dordogne.

111. **Paul Klee**, *Emigrating Bird (No. 4176)*, 1926.

to buy his colours not simply from the same manufacturer, but from the same batch, time after time.

Kandinsky was also much involved in another colour innovation of the 1920s, the rather short-lived vogue for spray-painting at the Weimar Bauhaus (although Klee had experimented with it at early as 1907, and of course it is a technique as old as Palaeolithic art [110]). From around 1923 Paul Klee (1879–1940), Kandinsky and others made many works using this technique with stencils and water-based paints [111, 112]. In a letter of January 1924 Kandinsky wrote of applying paint 'more or less mechanically (all kinds of spraying processes)'. Like Klee, he was always open to new media and experimental techniques; but what is interesting here is his emphasis on the mechanical, although at Weimar it is

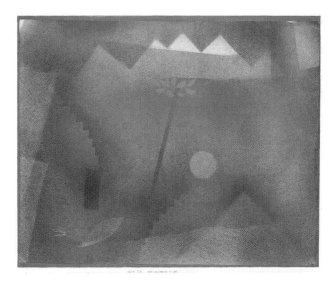

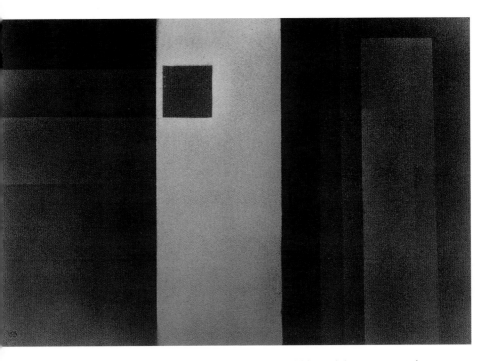

12. **Wassily Kandinsky**, *Rotes Quadrant [859]*, 1928.

13. Workshop for wall painting. Experimental for various spraygun techniques, Bauhaus, Dessau, c. 1927. Simple spray-painting techniques had been used by the cave painters of the Palaeolithic period, but the method had a particular vogue at the Bauhaus in Weimar and Dessau in the 1920s. Klee had already had some experience of it as a young artist, but he took it up again with great enthusiasm about 1924, and was followed by Kandinsky and other Bauhaus artists. In the more technologically oriented Dessau Bauhaus, large surfaces were painted with sprayguns powered by compressors.

unlikely that machines were available, and these spray-works are small. At the Dessau Bauhaus, however, after 1925, powerful compressors, developed in the automobile industry, operated sprayguns to test a variety of surfaces in the Wall-Painting Workshop [113]. Spray-painting gave an impersonal surface, but also the capacity for subtle layering and delicate nuances, for which quality the work of the head of the Dessau Wall-Painting Workshop, Hinnerk Scheper, was especially admired.

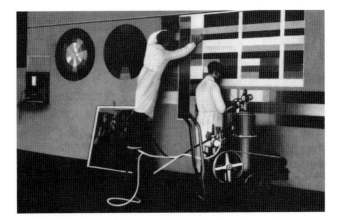

But by this time the emphasis had shifted from new colours and colour techniques to new media, and this was very much in tune with the new aesthetic valuation of surface texture as a means of expression, stimulated in particular by the late work of van Gogh and Monet. As the Russian theorist Nikolai Tarabukin wrote about 1920: 'We have seen in respect of colour that the modern painter is distinguished by the very special reverence he has for his materials, to the point that even when he is working with colours he gives through them the feeling of material as such, parallel to the effect produced by coloured sensations.' Tarabukin argued further that 'the same art-object affects us differently according to whether it is painted in oil, watercolour or distemper'.

Early Modernism is particularly remarkable for the widespread experimentation with media. Picasso was probably the first fine artist use house paint – Ripolin – around 1912, and he called it 'the health of colours' because of its directness and durability. Ripolin became one of the standard materials of Modernist painting; and at least one painter, the British artist Gillian Ayres, adopted it in the 1950s precisely because it had been sanctified by Picasso. By then it had become a 'fine-art' medium, but it was because house paints and industrial enamels were *not* associated with the fine-art tradition, and because they were cheaper to use on the now-standard wall-size canvases, that many British and American painters of the 1940s, 1950s and 1960s turned to using them.

The use of ordinary domestic paints in the New York of the 1940s was, indeed, partly for economic reasons. During and immediately after the Second World War there was a slump in the market for avant-garde art, and with no sales, artists could not afford traditional materials. But necessity soon became a virtue, and the unconventionality of the new materials was a major part of their attraction. Already in the 1930s the New York-based Mexican muralist David Sequeiros was using industrial paints and claiming that 'to a new society must correspond new material solutions'. Now, after the war, manufacturers of artists' materials were themselves beginning to use new synthetic resins, and Bocour, whose Magna was developed with Sam Golden in the late 1940s, was able to market it as 'the first new painting medium in 500 years'.

European artists in the 1950s and 1960s went to New York, as Italian Renaissance artists had gone to Venice, not simply because

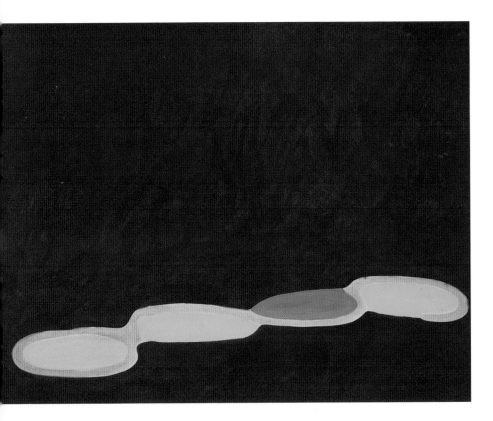

New York had, in a famous phrase, 'stolen the idea of modern art', but also because the city supplied the best materials for making it. The British abstract painter John Hoyland (b. 1934), for example, who had tried the new media in the United States, took to using the first acrylic available in England in 1963 [114], abandoning what he called the 'voluptuary [*sic*] of paint and surface that was generally considered to be fairly old hat at that time', because he believed 'historically, art always changed when techniques changed, from gesso to oil ... and this had the faint hum of new technology about it, that was behind the new philosophy'.

The materials of colour thus became part of the iconography of post-war painting. The precocious English artist Richard Hamilton (b. 1922) spray-painted his 1958 work *Hers Is a Lush Situation* [115] with nitro-cellulose, on the grounds that 'It's meant to be a car, so I thought it was appropriate to use car-colour'; and in *$he* of 1958–61, he used metallic paint to represent a toaster. Metallic paints were also much used in the 1950s in New York by Jackson Pollock (1912–56), and by Frank Stella (b. 1936) around

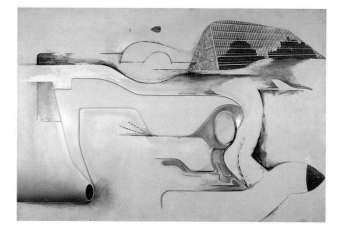

115. **Richard Hamilton**, *Hers Is a Lush Situation*, 1958. Hamilton felt car enamel was appropriate to rendering this motoring subject.

116. **Frank Stella**, *Itafa II*, 1964.

1960, to expand the range of abstract surface effects [116]. This was probably the first time since the Middle Ages that metallic materials had been used in flat paintings on a substantial scale. Hamilton argued in a quasi-medieval way that the function of the new paints and techniques was symbolic rather than representational: 'I tried to represent the images in a way that was related to the source ... I could use cellulose and spray because it symbolised the object.'

Yet this was not the first time that specific colouring materials had been fraught with ideology. The English Romantic colour-maker George Field had been anxious to develop pure pigments in the three primary colours since he believed that their chemical bases – silica for ultramarine, alumina for madder (the vegetable red that was precipitated onto aluminium hydrate to form a lake pigment), and lime for lemon yellow – were evidence of the triadic structure of nature, which in turn was an image of the Holy

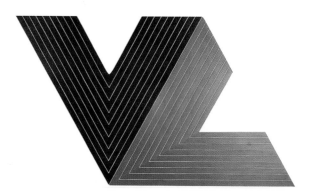

Trinity. Field was close to many artists throughout a long career, but he does not seem to have impressed them as much with his ideas as he did with his outstanding products [102], although some of his theories had a brief vogue in art education, especially in the United States and Japan.

That Field gave a religious inflection to colour ideas is in no way surprising in the context of Romanticism, which saw the early seeds of that characteristic nineteenth-century wish to revive the styles of pre-Renaissance art. He showed a strong interest in illuminated manuscripts, and was close to a major London collector of Early German and Italian painting, whose collection was also important for William Blake (1757–1827), a painter who was a reader of Cennini and who believed he understood the technique of Italian fresco [117]. The traditional mineral pigments

117. **William Blake**, *Ghost of a Flea, c.* 1819. Blake made his own colours and, characteristically, this technique of glue-tempera was revealed to him in a vision. He believed it was the same as early Italian fresco (hence the inscription), and was an eager reader of Cennini's *Book of Art* when it was first published – in Italian – in 1821.

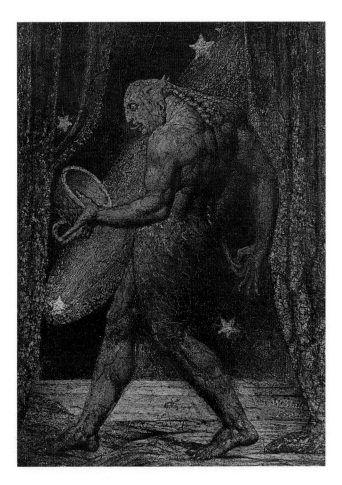

118. *The Colours of Urine*, from *The Physician's Calendar*, London, 15th century. Colour was vital in medical diagnosis, and the painter's most valuable colours often doubled as medicines, which in many cases worked by sympathetic magic, matching the colour, or hoped-for colour, of the sick organ.

had also been related in medieval thought to gemstones, and thus to moral and therapeutic powers. The thirteenth-century lapidary of Thomas of Cantimpré, for example, identified the Indian sapphire with lapis lazuli (which is not, in fact, translucent), and attributed a long list of virtues to it, including the relief of pains in the eyes and the forehead, and of ulcers on the tongue. It was also said to encourage chastity and offer protection against fraud, envy and terrors. In the Byzantine tradition this 'sapphire' was used as a purge. Similarly, the semi-precious stone haematite, often used as a red pigment and which was imported into Europe from Arabia or Ethiopia, by sympathetic magic could cure disorders of the blood and menstruation; and if powdered and mixed with wine could cure ulcers and protect against poisonous bites. And so on. Medical recipes were sometimes interspersed among pigment recipes in handbooks for artists, and until the rise of specialist colour-merchants, the raw materials of painting were to be had from apothecaries, who, in medieval Florence, included painters in their guild [118].

One context in which pigments, geography and religious values are closely intertwined is Australian Aboriginal painting,

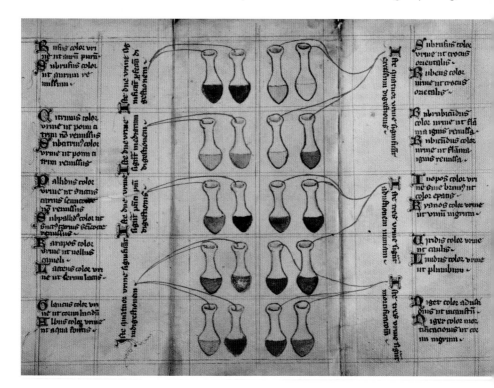

128

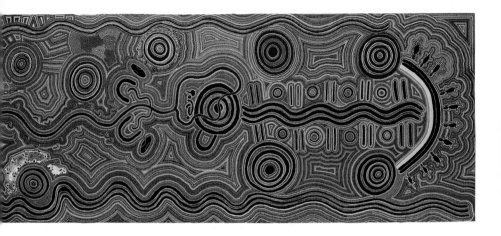

119. **Warlukurlangu Artists,** *arrku*, 1996. This vast canvas, y thirty-six artists from the ountry around Yuendumu in Central Australia, represents ritual tes near a famous sacred ochre ine, Karrku, in the Campbell anges. Natural ochres are elieved to have been created y Ancestors in the mythic Dreamtime.

which has undergone a remarkable transformation since the 1970s, and is now exhibited and collected throughout the world. Just as the work of a fourteenth-century French lapidary in the British Library (Sloane 1784) argued that the Ethiopian balas ruby (*Jagonice grena*), which protected against poisons, derived its red colour from the earth from which God created Adam, or, according to another authority, from the blood of the Second Adam, Christ, so the white, red and yellow ochres used in traditional Aboriginal rock and bark painting were the products of mines created by Ancestor figures in the mythology of the Dreamtime. The reds were the Ancestors' blood, the yellows their fat and the whites their faeces. Aboriginal art is primarily about land, country and their origins; and the identity of these colours found in that land is of the first importance. It is notable that recent bark painting from north-eastern Australia shows a great variety of formal invention by different artists who prize their individuality, yet in this region the traditional palette of four natural pigments – black, usually charcoal, but sometimes a mineral, white, red and yellow ochres – has been almost universally maintained.

It is thus somewhat paradoxical that the most valued of these ochres, such as the red of Karrku, a sacred mine in the Campbell Ranges, west of Yuendumu in the Central Desert [119], which were mined seasonally with great ceremony by tribes sometimes travelling several hundred kilometres to do so, should have been widely traded. The best known of the Central Desert painters, the late Clifford Possum Tjapaltjarri (c. 1932–2002) [129], explained how the use of particular ochres, such as Karrku, was

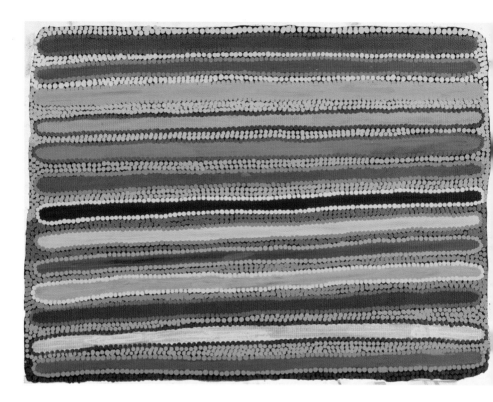

120. **Mitjili Napurrula**, *Spears at Ualki*, 1994. Napurrula, a female artist from Haast's Bluff in the Central Australian Desert, represents her father's Spear Dreaming in a style reminiscent of sand-painting, but with the brilliant palette of the new painting movement.

more or less strictly restricted to those who had traditional rights to the mine. He, for example, as a member of the Tjapaltjarri clan, was not able to use Karrku, which was only available to the Tjipurula, Tjakamarra, Tjangala and Tjamijinpa clans, who shared the Rain Dreaming site on which Karrku is situated. The Tjapaltjarris and the Tjungurayis from the same area used red ochre from another mine, called Yalkuti. Possum also described Karrku as characteristically pink, although in the Yuendumu painting [119] there are many saturated reds. Possum himself, as well as the large group who collaborated on *Karrku*, used modern acrylics.

The economy of ochres suggests an unexpected looseness in the connotations of Aboriginal colours; and even in pre-colonial times there is some evidence that more exotic colours, such as blue, were used in western Australia. When European settlement brought new products, such as washing-blue and carbon black from aircraft batteries, Aboriginal painters were happy to use them, even in the more conservative north. It was the introduction of modern synthetic paints in the late 1960s and

1970s that helped to create the astonishing rise of the painting movements in central and western Australia that has made Aboriginal art so widely admired and collected [120, 121]. At the same time, the new synthetics are often used to simulate the traditional four-colour palette, and this is a rare instance of pigments being used to *represent* other colours, not simply to *imitate* their precious materials in order to deceive, which was common enough in earlier periods in Europe. Perhaps there is no more telling indication than this of the great significance of the origin and physical character of pigments, beyond their simple capacity to colour.

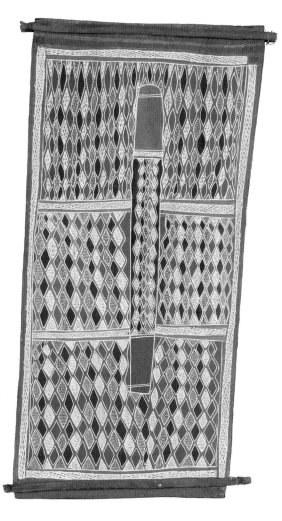

121. **Wakuthi Marawili**, *Fire Dreaming*, 1976. Marawili's dark-palette of four colours is characteristic of painting in Arnhem Land, in north-east Australia. The image is of a flaming log, sacred to the artist's Madarrpa people; the background is of clan designs used in ceremonial body-painting.

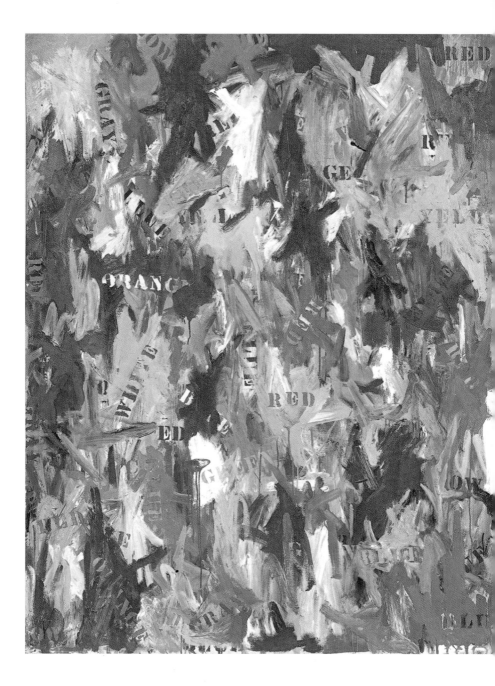

Chapter 5   Languages of Colour

In a remarkable study of 1989, the New York painter and teacher Patricia Sloane argued, in Modernist vein, that colour names, unless they are hallowed by centuries of use, are redundant and are, indeed, an obstacle to visual experience. That she devoted a book of more than three hundred pages to *The Visual Nature of Color* suggests that verbal colour language certainly throws up many problems, and Sloane, among many other topics, provided detailed critiques of the highly variable pigment terms used by manufacturers of artists' colours. Among the 125 English and French trade names for the same mid-blue, as identified by the US National Bureau of Standards, were Dresden Blue, Antwerp Blue, Peking Blue and Bleu de Lyon. Other names identified this same blue by reference to the artists Luca della Robbia, Raphael and Murillo.

Sloane was also highly critical of the modern colour systems of the American colour theorist Albert Munsell (1858–1918) [123]

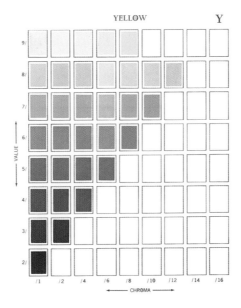

and the German Wilhelm Ostwald (1853–1932) [77], much used in the teaching of art and design, which in fact work largely with letter and figure notations. This allows them to cover a far wider range of nuances in colour-space than is recognized in ordinary languages, which, in industrial societies, tend to rest content with around a dozen very general terms. We saw in Chapter 1 how even this number of so-called 'basic' terms was further reduced by artists, in the light of the concept of 'primary' and 'secondary' colours. The distrust of verbal terms for colours was not felt by all painters – witness van Gogh's letters – but when, in the late nineteenth century, the colour range of their palettes began to be vastly expanded with synthetics, and exotic commercial colour names started to proliferate (causing artists to satirize them: *cuisse de nymphe émue* [thigh of excited nymph] and *caca-Dauphin* [dauphin's poo] are two examples), there were attempts to establish colour as a language itself. Already in 1850 George Field had subtitled a small student handbook 'A Grammar of Colouring', and in France the printmaker-friend of the Impressionists Félix Bracquemond was among a number of artists who looked forward to a grammar of colour, which seemed within sight because of the nineteenth-century development of colour systems based on the hue circle and the grey scale. The impact of Symbolism twenty or thirty years later shifted the emphasis from 'grammatical' structure to the more subjective, associative elements of colour, which were linked to phonetics: Arthur Rimbaud's poem *Voyelles* (*Vowels*), in which each vowel sound corresponds with a colour, stimulated a wave of scientific as well as aesthetic investigation into synaesthesia (see Chapter 7). Kandinsky, much attracted to Symbolism and the late-nineteenth-century psychology which was bound up with it, proposed to give *On the Spiritual in Art* the subtitle '*Farbensprache*' ('The Language of Colours'), although in its published form the book simply included a chapter entitled 'The Language of Forms and Colours'. This laid the basis for Kandinsky's association of yellow with the triangle, red with the square and blue with the circle, and it is striking that as late as this rejected design for the cover [124], of around 1910, these correspondences had not yet been clearly formulated – the triangle here is basically blue and the yellow in a rather rectangular form. Kandinsky's free use of the trio of geometrical forms in his Bauhaus years [80] shows that they were far from being dictionary definitions, but were analogous to the verbal richness and ambiguity of Symbolist or Expressionist poetry, of which he himself was a notable exponent.

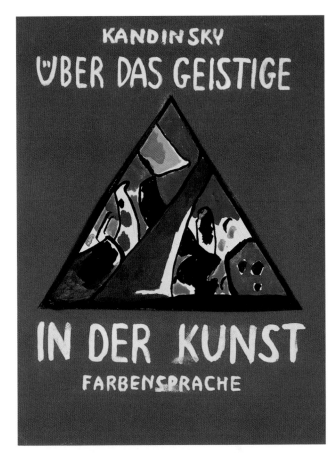

It is clear from his other early major publication, *The Blue Rider Almanac*, which he edited in 1912 with the Munich Expressionist Franz Marc and which included the scenario for one of his stage pieces, *The Yellow Sound*, that Kandinsky, who had begun professional life as an ethnographer, was very much concerned to promote a universal language of art. The *Almanac* included illustrations from Africa and Asia, Polynesia and the Americas, as well as folk art and the drawings of children, German medieval art and Romantic illustrations of medieval fantasies. It also illustrated and discussed the most up-to-date French and German art. This was probably the first time – outside the great international exhibitions of the nineteenth and early twentieth centuries – that such a range of artefacts had ever been shown together; and in contrast to the Eurocentric triumphalism of those other manifestations, this was in the interest of a universal

125. **Kazimir Malevich**, designs for backcloths of *Victory over the Sun*, 1913. The design on the right is generally regarded as the origin of Malevich's abstract style, Suprematism.

brotherhood of art. But universalism was also a major theme in linguistics at this time: the artificial languages Volapuek and Esperanto were launched in the 1880s, and Interlingua and Ido (supported by the colour theorist Ostwald) in the first decade of the twentieth century, all hoping to provide the world with a *lingua franca.* The Moscow Linguistic Circle was especially active in the 1910s, and it was investigating the phonetic basis of all languages in vowel and consonant sounds. Kandinsky, who paid regular visits to Moscow in the years before the publication of *On the Spiritual in Art*, was aware of these developments, and in *The Yellow Sound* he introduced an aria that recalls the nonsense sound-poems in a language called *Zaum* (transrational) by Alexei Kruschenykh: 'Suddenly a shrill, terrified tenor voice can be heard from behind the stage, rapidly shrieking completely unintelligible words (*a* can be heard frequently, for example, *kalasimunafakola*!).' This aria is also suggestive of those of Kruschenykh's friend, the poet and theorist Velimir Khlebnikov, who, in his collaboration in 1913 with Malevich on the anti-naturalist opera *Victory over the Sun*, introduced an aria entirely in consonants and another entirely in vowels.

This was a period in which the investigation of the phonetic fundamentals of language went hand in hand with the Modernist search for the fundamentals of form and colour. It was Malevich's designs for *Victory over the Sun* [125] that seem to have stimulated him to develop the most austere style of early geometrical abstraction, Suprematism. A few years after the opera, the Italian Futurist Fortunato Depero also wrote a short abstract stage piece, *Colours*, in which four coloured shapes in a bare blue room held a conversation in an abstract language. The dark-grey ovoid spoke interminably in an 'animal-like' voice, with many *i*s and *u*s, including frequent *blùs* and *bulùs*. The dynamic red triangular polyhedron spoke in a 'roaring, crashing' voice, with many sharp

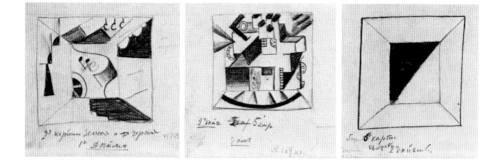

consonants, in words such as 'TORIAAAAKRAKTO'. The long, sharp, white shape spoke with a 'sharp, thin, brittle voice' with many *is* and *zs*, and the black multiglobe uttered deep, sonorous *ms* and *os* in a 'very profound, guttural voice'. *Colours* does not seem to have been performed, but it was published in an anthology of short Futurist scripts in 1916.

Colour came to have a role in this linguistic research through the phenomenon of synaesthesia. As Khlebnikov wrote in a manifesto of 1919: 'The task of the colour-painter is to give geometrical signs to the basic units of understanding.... It would be possible to have recourse to colour and express M with dark blue, W with green, B with red [other researchers identified A with red], E with grey, L with white...' So concepts of colour and language have long been intimately related, and in the last century this has offered a particular stimulus to artists. A psychological test of attentiveness, known as the 'Stroop Test' after the American psychologist who devised it, has even tended to suggest that the human mind – or at least that of randomly chosen test subjects – gives priority to names over perceptions. Jasper Johns (b. 1930) made a group of paintings around 1960 which play on this disjunction between seeing and reading, in which colour words are painted in other, contrasting colours [122]; and a video work, *Pli* (2003), by the Portuguese artist Cecilia Costa simply presents a variety of subjects attempting to rapidly identify the colours of a list of colour words in which only 'black' is in black letters. Most subjects opt for the colour word rather than the colour of the letters. Johns's series is perhaps no more than another example of his habitual playfulness, but it is also an instance of the way in which the verbal has precedence over the visual even in the realm of colour.

If language depends on a collective recognition of signs, one of the major obstacles to creating a colour language is the irreducible subjectivity of colour ideas. Although Kandinsky proposed that the German word *rot*, 'red', as opposed to red colouring materials, evokes 'of itself no particularly pronounced tendency towards warm or cold' (elsewhere he described it nevertheless as a 'characteristically warm colour'), his former colleague Josef Albers stated that in a group of fifty people, the word would suggest fifty different reds. For Kandinsky it was only when materialized in a concrete form that the 'rich and various' versions of red come into play. Ethnolinguists speak of a 'focal red', for example, about which there will be some general agreement. But in Chapter 6 I shall look at the 'redness' of 'purple' in the European cultures of antiquity and the Middle Ages, and in many non-European languages red, orange and yellow are covered by the same term.

Colour language offers even more paradoxical anomalies in non-industrial societies of the past and present. We have learned to classify colours by hue but, as we have seen, colours have other characteristics, such as purity (saturation), lightness or darkness, mattness or shininess, warmth or coldness, all of which are of great significance to artists. One of the puzzles of the pre-modern illuminated manuscript workshops is the interpretation of the many colour notes for illuminators that survive in the margins of some manuscript pages, and which represent a code of communication from the workshop master to the individual painter. Some French manuscripts, for example, have the letter 'v' close to areas of red, and this has quite reasonably been seen to stand for *vermeille* (vermilion). But how did the illuminator know that it did not stand for *vert* (green)? Was there a standard workshop code? Was the figure in question, for iconographic reasons, always dressed in red? The puzzle is complicated by the fact that in medieval France a single term could, in various contexts, signify red *or* green: *sinople,* a poetic word for red (from *sinopis*) in Old French, but green in the specialized language of heraldry. Old French is not the only language to include a red–green term; two modern Asian examples are cited by Heinrich Zollinger, and among a number of African tribes green is held to derive from red, as female from male.

In medieval Europe this paradox may have something to do with the technology of stained glass, where a single copper oxide was used to colour the liquid glass red and green, by varying the heating [13]. In the Chinese and Japanese examples cited by Zollinger, the green may have the primary meaning of 'fresh' (as in ancient Greek *chloron*), and a 'fresh red' is perfectly understandable. Technology may also be behind other anomalous medieval colour terms, *bloi* and *caeruleus,* which could refer to blue or yellow, just as processing the vegetable dyestuff woad transformed the yellow leaves into a deep-blue dye. Zollinger points to other examples of this particular union of opposites from central Europe, Asia, Africa and the United States. These anomalies make the understanding of some early colour texts particularly problematic, but they also suggest that artists in these periods were little concerned with a global theory of colour, but worked within the conventions of local usage, or even that of a particular workshop.

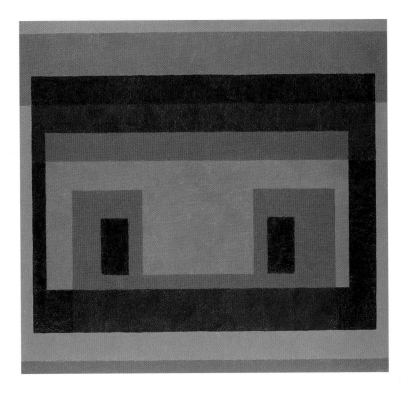

126. **Josef Albers**, *Variant:
4 Greens, 2 Grays*, 1948–55.

The study of colour vocabularies, which seemed to some early ethnographers to offer a key to the workings of 'the savage mind', in the French anthropologist Claude Lévi-Strauss's phrase, has flourished over the last half-century, but few ethnolinguists have included artists in their samples of respondents, not least because the category 'artist' was not recognized in many of the cultures they studied. One exception to this is a remarkable study of the 1970s that tested the response time for naming colour samples among art and science students in Israel and Switzerland. It found that science students responded far more rapidly than art students, and this was interpreted as showing that art students were more cautious in naming phenomena in which they had such a heavy investment as visually sensitive persons. If we look at the colour language of painters, when talking among themselves, it usually includes the names of pigments, often with specific brand names. Josef Albers, an unusually scrupulous technician, took in his later years to listing on the back of each painting precisely the colours employed. Thus, for example, on *Variant: 4 Greens, 2 Grays* [126]: 'Paints used (from center upward): Cobalt Green (Winsor & Newton); Cadmium Green (Winsor &

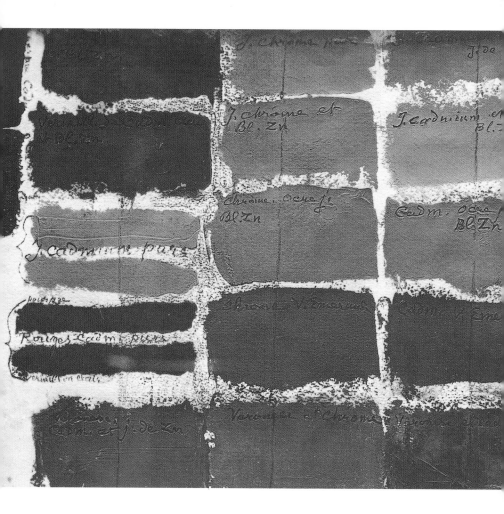

127. **Paul Gauguin**, oil paint samples and mixtures with autograph notes, on paper; thought to be the verso of *The Breton Calvary*, 1894. Unlike Albers, an exceptionally scrupulous technician, who listed paints from four suppliers, Gauguin simply itemized a range of red and purple mixtures made by himself. He, too, was a careful craftsman, although his list of samples includes mixtures with the rather unreliable chrome and zinc yellows. Many of these mixtures include zinc white, also a relatively new pigment, but safer than other whites, as here, with vermilion.

Newton); Perm. Green Lt (Pretested); Viridian Green (Winsor & Newton); Reilly's Neutral Gray No. 5 (Grumbacher); Chapin Neutral Gray (Shiva).' But here the context was, of course, future conservation of the work.

Yet when addressing the general public artists are equally content to use very general terms such as 'red', 'yellow' and 'blue'. Characteristically, it is the secondaries and especially the tertiaries that are given unusual, non-standard names. Already in the twelfth century the south Italian doctor Urso of Salerno confessed that he did not know the names of 'the many median colours mixed from the colours of the elements', which a 'good painter' could demonstrate rather than name (although we know of none who did). In modern times Van Gogh and Seurat occasionally spoke of 'unnameable' or 'indefinable' colours, which suggests how much the spread of colour-order systems in the late nineteenth century had led to the expectation that colours could indeed be defined, but not the subtle nuances of grey and violet which they created, largely by optical mixture. The indefinable colours were of special interest to Gauguin, who was careful to avoid the strong contrasts of his friend van Gogh, and who specifically exploited secondary and tertiary hues in the interest of what he called 'enigma' [127]. His surviving last palette also shows how thoroughly he would manipulate his colours into indefinable mixtures [128].

For all his aspirations to identify with non-European cultures, Gauguin remained very much involved in late-nineteenth-century French aesthetics, and in particular with the aesthetics of Symbolist literature. But how did colour language function in cultures without a literature; dependent, like the medieval workshops, largely on oral traditions? Again, the recent developments in Australian Aboriginal painting offer many important insights into the relationship of colour vocabulary to

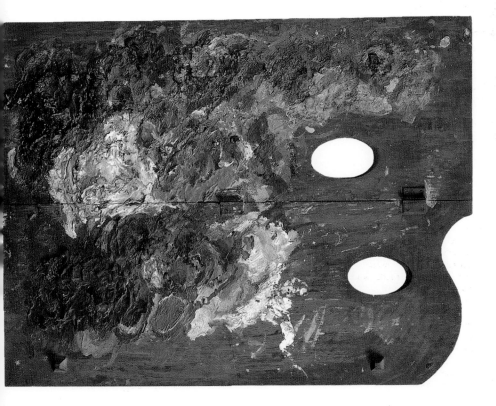

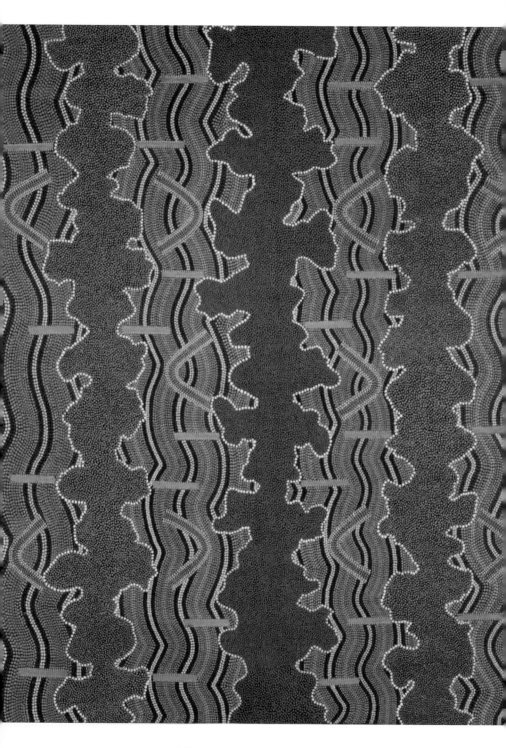

colour practice. As early as the European invasion of Australia in the late eighteenth century, it was noticed by the British that the Aborigines in what is now New South Wales had a very restricted colour vocabulary compared with their own. This is probably the earliest observation of these discrepancies in modern times; with colonial expansion and the simultaneous development of field ethnology, from the mid-nineteenth century they became the basis of a great deal of ethnolinguistic research, although little was done in Australia until the twentieth century. When, from the 1970s onwards, indigenous painters, especially in central and western Australia, began to use their brilliant palette of synthetic (usually acrylic) paints, including blues and greens, this was interpreted by many of the non-indigenous collectors for whom this work was made as being, for better or worse, a radical departure from the traditional palette. The artists themselves, on the other hand, have invariably insisted that their work communicates and promotes their traditional culture, and that this is, indeed, its primary function.

In an interview in the 1980s, Clifford Possum Tjapaltjarri, who knew six indigenous languages from three distinct language groups, spoke of his work in English [129]: 'put circle, circle n'dreamin. Body paint or might be ground paint [i.e., for dancing] – and after that one you put – im diffen diffen [very different] colour – Not them white men colour no – them native colour – them red one them white one, black one.' Yet Possum was one of the earliest Western Desert artists to use a wide range of acrylics, including blue and green.

The problem has been, essentially, a clash of languages. The viewers of these paintings see them through the veil of English – or French, or German, Italian, etc. – but the producers think of them in terms of their own indigenous languages, which divide up colour space in different, and usually more restricted, ways. This has been the case, as we saw, with many languages, ancient and modern, and it was so with ancient Egyptian, which subsumed 'blue' under a term for 'green', even though, as we saw in Chapter 4, this highly developed culture was famous for its production of the synthetic Egyptian Blue.

A recently deceased artist from Lajamanu in western Australia, for example, claimed that he spoke nine indigenous languages, plus English, but only one of them had a term for 'blue'. This multilingual painter, Jimmy Robertson, like the ancient Egyptians, made a very extensive use of blue, which his indigenous languages generally subsumed under a term for 'black'; blue could

130. **Ginger Riley Munduwalawala**, *Limmen Bight River Country*, 1992. Ginger Riley took to painting after seeing the work of Namatjira, the first Aboriginal artist to achieve fame in Australia [132]. Riley recognized that his palette was far wider than that of the traditional painters in his native Northern Territory [122], but he argued that the four-colour palette was strictly for ceremonial use.

well be seen as a variety of black, and hence a 'traditional' colour: 'Not them', in Possum's words, 'white men colour.' This linguistic displacement is particularly clear in the case of Kriol, an English-based creole very widely spoken in northern Australia, including Ngurr, the home of another painter using a brilliantly polychrome palette, Ginger Riley (c. 1937–2002) [130]. Kriol includes the term *blu*, but this term is seen as cognate with *blek*, and *blek* is often used to describe blue objects. Riley is an interesting artist in the present context because he rejected the traditional limited palette – black, white, red and yellow – on the grounds that it was only appropriate for ceremonial painting, or objects used in

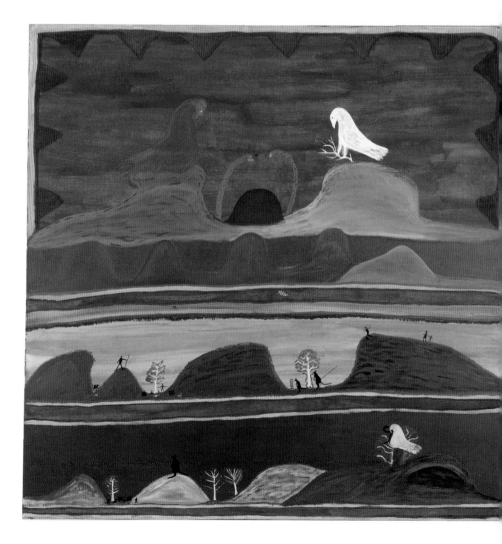

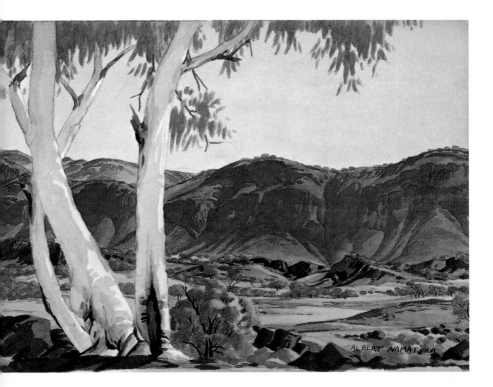

ceremony. He also adopted a figurative style and landscape imagery, stimulated by his earliest mentor, the first well-known Aboriginal painter, Albert Namatjira (1902–1959) [131]. Riley, like Possum, is well aware of the distinction between an indigenous and a non-indigenous palette, but language helped both of them to slip easily from one to the other without the conceptual obstacles faced by the non-indigenous viewer. The Australian experience suggests that we can only begin to think of a 'language' of colour if we have become familiar with the verbal language used to describe and even to think of it.

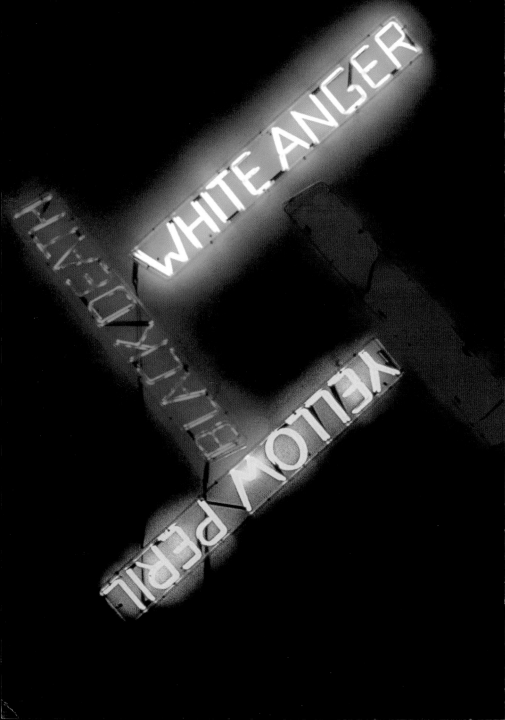

Chapter 6   Can Colours Signify?

Discussions of colour language outside the academic field of ethnolinguistics often involve the notion of colour as metaphor, and hence lending itself readily to symbolizing. The sculptor Anish Kapoor has spoken eloquently of the capacity of colours to transform things in the most immediate, formal way: 'It has a metaphoric value which is vast, and this is immensely interesting to me.' Thus colour symbolism is usually thought to be literary; even Kapoor's transfigurations must be verbalized if they are to be recognized; and here all the problems in the language of colour that I outlined in the last chapter begin to loom.

Although in the early twentieth century, at the high point of aspirations towards a universal verbal language, universal archetypal symbols were mooted by psychologists such as Carl Jung, colour symbolism has always remained inescapably local and contextual. A glance at the vast lists of colour meanings in the second edition of Alexander Theroux's *The Primary Colors* (1995) is enough to demonstrate that. It is true that some mileage has been had from the view that, for example, red connotes blood, and green, fresh vegetation or growth itself, yet it is invariably the objects symbolized rather than the colours that carry the meaning, for the colours of the same natural objects may well be highly variable. In his 1985 light piece *White Anger, Red Danger, Yellow Peril, Black Death* [132], Bruce Nauman (b. 1941) for technical reasons used blue to represent black, but this scarcely affects the meaning of the work, even though Nauman does not belong to a non-industrial society whose language routinely covers black and blue with a single term. Indeed, in the modern world 'black' is perhaps the most heavily freighted colour term of all, and in Nauman's United States the most political of all colours. With its rather swastika-like form, as well as its colours, Nauman's is indeed a highly political work.

Two contexts in which state ideology has impressed symbolic values on colours among members of the community have been Roman imperial attitudes to purple, and green in the national flags of the Islamic world. Shellfish purple was the most highly valued dyestuff in the ancient world because of its exceptionally laborious and hence costly processing, and its unrivalled light-fastness and durability. These characteristics made purple – at least in theory – for many centuries the legally enforced prerogative of the imperial household and government; and throughout the Middle Ages, and even in modern times, it has continued to be an emblem of royalty. But the colour purple remains a mystery, because the early literature suggests not only that it was classed as a type of red, but also that the best purple-red cloth looked dark by reflected light, but a fiery-red by transmitted light, and also had a much-admired surface sheen, which must originally have been well conveyed in the fresh mosaics of the emperor Justinian's court in S. Vitale at Ravenna [133]. The erosion of the surface and modern lighting make this original sheen very hard to appreciate now. The sumptuous so-called 'purple' codices of the Carolingian period also have pages that were often stained a bright red [134]; and in the Renaissance Aristotle's word for 'purple' (*halourgon*) was sometimes translated by the Latin word for the then most expensive *red* dye (*coccineus*). Goethe in his 1810 *Theory of Colours* gave his most valuable and prestigious red the name 'Purpur', in honour of Tyrian Purple, although he knew it had far less blue in it

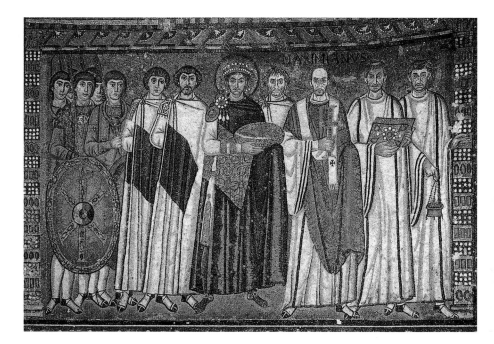

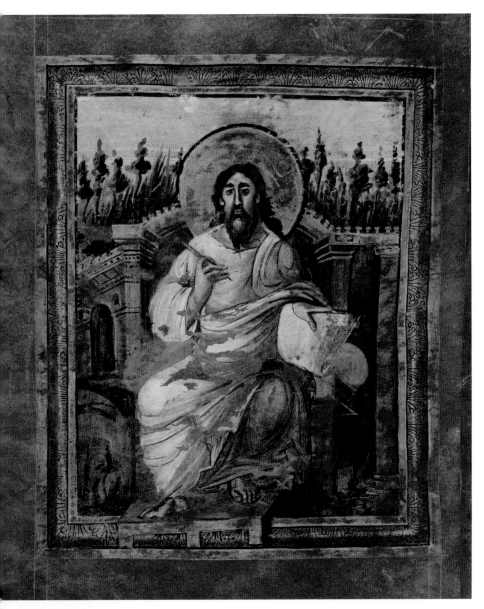

134. Gospel of St John, Coronation Gospels, 8th century AD. The sumptuous royal 'purple codices' were the manuscript equivalent of antiquity's purple cloth, but, as this example shows, 'purple' was often interpreted as bright red.

than the ancient variety; and yet, when he came to describe the photochemical changes in the shellfish dye during its processing, he characterized the final product as 'a pure bright red' (*eine reine hohe rote Farbe*). The question is further complicated by the fact that the chemistry of shellfish purple is very close to the chemistry of the blue vegetable dye indigo; and the Roman architectural theorist Vitruvius (first century BC) declared that the snails in colder, northern waters yielded a bluer purple than those in southern waters, which looked more red. In Hebrew, too, there are two terms for purple dyeing, *argaman* for a reddish colour and *tekhelet* for a bluish variety. So it was the preciousness of purple, rather than its specific colour, that was most impressive to early European and Middle Eastern cultures.

The context of green is rather different. Many modern flags that include green are those of Muslim countries [135], since the cloak and banner of Mohammed were said to be green, and in the Qur'an (XVIII, 31; LXXVI, 21) the Blessed in Paradise were to wear green silk robes. A fourteenth-century Persian theologian, Alaoddwa Semanani, held that Mohammed himself was a shining green in his role as the Divine Centre, since this was the colour most appropriate to 'the mystery of mysteries'. The Green Man, Khidr, of Muslim legend is green because of his role as mediator, and in the Western medieval tradition green was also regarded as the median colour between light and dark. But, outside the Islamic world, green in national flags has been given very different meanings. The green of the original Mexican state tricolour was glossed as symbolizing independence from Spain, although the present view is that, like the green of the Portuguese flag, it expresses hope, a concept taken over from the colour of hope

135. National flag of Saudi Arabia. Green often appears in the flags of Islamic countries because of the strong association of the Prophet Mohammed with this colour. The inscription reads: 'There is no God, but Allah, and Muhammed is his Prophet.'

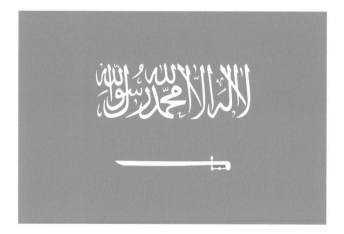

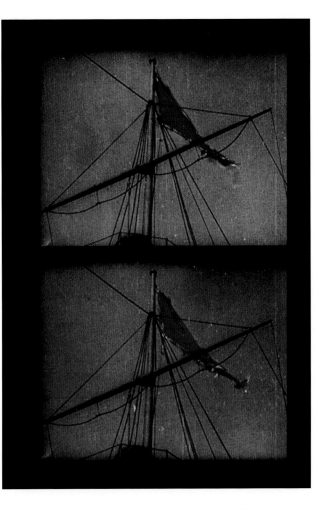

among the traditional Christian theological virtues. For many other states green in flags represents simply the verdant land.

Artists have not been slow to exploit the resonances of their flags. The Russian film director Sergei Eisenstein (1898–1948) introduced a red flag, painted on black-and-white filmstock, in his most famous film, *Battleship Potemkin* [136]. It was his first attempt at using colour in a film, and he emphasized that it gained its force, 'like a fanfare', not from the colour itself, but from its revolutionary meaning. It is rumoured that the Neoclassical painter Jacques-Louis David himself designed that most severely classical of flags, the French tricolour, at least the 1794 version, which had the revolutionary red flying free of the mast. The French tricolour has been perhaps the most influential flag design

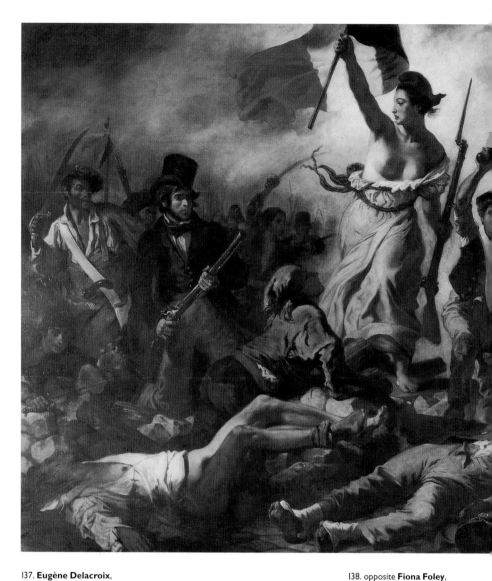

137. **Eugène Delacroix,**
Liberty Leading the People, 1830.
Delacroix's allegorical celebration
of the 1830 July Revolution gives a
prominent role to the new French
tricouleur, created as an emblem
of unity in the earlier Revolution
of 1789. In the distance to the
right, one of the towers of Notre
Dame bears a tiny image of this
same flag, whose raising there
rallied the people of Paris at the
beginning of July.

138. opposite **Fiona Foley,**
Untitled (Aboriginal Flag), 1991. The
Aboriginal flag, introduced in 1971,
four years after Aborigines gained
Australian citizenship, has become
a powerful political symbol in
much non-traditional Aboriginal
art. It introduces three of the four
'traditional' colours: red for the
earth, yellow for the sun and black
for the black skin. Only the fourth
colour, white, is, for obvious
reasons, excluded.

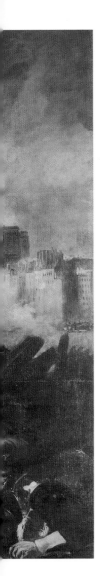

of all [137]; but, of course, it shares its combination of red, white and blue with many other flags, including that of its old friend, the United States, and that of its old enemy, Great Britain. The new Australian Aboriginal flag was designed by an artist, the Luritja Harold Turner, from South Australia, in 1971 [138]. Its colours are very close to those of the German tricolour, although the latter's yellow is called 'gold', and it represents, not the sun, but 'loyalty'. The Aboriginal sun is yellow, while in the Japanese flag it is rising in the east, and is therefore red. The black is the colour of the Aboriginal skin, whereas in the German flag it represents earth, iron and *Ernst* (seriousness). In Aboriginal Australia the earth is red, and so it is in the flag; but in the German flag red stands for blood and courage. Red is a common flag colour, but, according to the various official interpretations of the symbols of nationhood it can mean: war, blood, bravery, authority, fire, unity, revolution, soil, sacrifice, faith, sun, freedom, revolt, swordsmanship and horsemanship, independence, law and authority, brotherhood and equality, nation, charity, vitality and friendliness, warmth.

If flags represent most clearly the officially sponsored symbolism of colour in the modern world, they also inherit the very traditional ambiguities of colour meaning. But flag colours

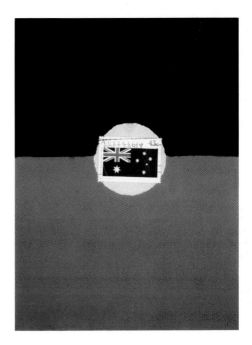

139. **Jasper Johns**, *White Flag*, 1955. Johns's draining of the red and the blue from the American flag in a series of grey and white flags was a typically impudent gesture towards the most potent of national symbols.

(and it is, of course, the 'colours' that we 'show') are always highly charged national symbols: Jasper Johns's American white flag of the late 1950s [139], rather than being the traditional sign of surrender, is another, and particularly impudent, Johnsian paradox.

The colours of flags present colour symbolism at its most public. Yet even in the modern world there are marginal groups that have proclaimed what amounts to a vocabulary of colour meanings. One is the Theosophical Society, founded in New York in 1875, and which, in a number of publications around 1900, published a key to the interpretation of coloured auras [140]. As these manifestations of colour and form above and around human bodies were visible only to clairvoyants, their status as a language is problematic, but since there is good reason to believe that their publication made them available to the pioneers of abstract painting, several of whom had a particular interest in the life of the spirit, they deserve, and have received, some attention well beyond the community they served. C. W. Leadbeater's *Man Visible and Invisible* (1902) discussed a series of 'astral bodies' representing the progress of man towards spiritual enlightenment. His account of the astral body of the Developed Man [141] emphasized his rationality: '[he] has his desires thoroughly under the control of the mind, and is no longer liable to be swept away

140. *Key to the Meaning of the Colours*, from C.W. Leadbeater, *Man Visible and Invisible*, 1902.

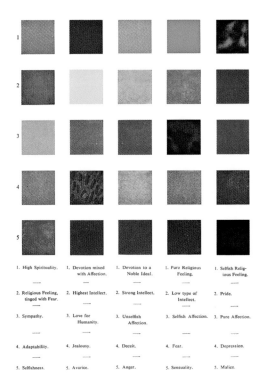

1. High Spirituality.	1. Devotion mixed with Affection.	1. Devotion to a Noble Ideal.	1. Pure Religious Feeling.	1. Selfish Religious Feeling.
2. Religious Feeling, tinged with Fear.	2. Highest Intellect.	2. Strong Intellect.	2. Low type of Intellect.	2. Pride.
3. Sympathy.	3. Love for Humanity.	3. Unselfish Affection.	3. Selfish Affection.	3. Pure Affection.
4. Adaptability.	4. Jealousy.	4. Deceit.	4. Fear.	4. Depression.
5. Selfishness.	5. Avarice.	5. Anger.	5. Sensuality.	5. Malice.

141. *Astral Body of the Developed Man*, from C. W. Leadbeater, *Man Visible and Invisible*, 1902. The Theosophist Leadbeater reveals the clairvoyant's view of the human (male) auras, and the interpretation of their colours.

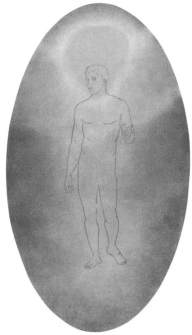

from the firm base of reason by wild surges of emotion'. This was particularly evident in the presence and position of strong yellow, the sign of intellect:

> When this colour is present in the oval, it invariably shows itself in the upper part of it, in the neighbourhood of the head; consequently it is the origin of the idea of the nimbus or glory round the head of a saint, since this is much the most conspicuous of the colours of the astral body, and the one most easily perceived by anyone who is approaching the verge of clairvoyance.... No doubt it was either from occasional glimpses of this phenomenon or from traditions derived from those who could see, that our mediaeval painters derived the idea of the glory round the head of the saint.

This coloured image bears a striking resemblance to William Blake's c. 1796 watercolour *Albion Rose* [142], and it may well be the work of the grandson of Blake's friend, the watercolourist and occultist John Varley, who was a specialist in Egyptian views and who is known to have been one of the illustrators of another influential Theosophical book, *Thought Forms* (1905), on which Leadbeater collaborated with Annie Besant. In the 1880s the younger John Varley (1850–1933) had been a member of the Theosophical circle of Helena Blavatsky, the co-founder of the Society; and he would also have had ready access to the Blake watercolour, which had been in the British Museum since 1856.

Varley's Developed Man is posed like a classical orator, and Leadbeater's view that he was an image of rationality is (probably coincidentally) entirely in tune with Blake's conception in *Albion Rose*, where Albion takes the pose of Vitruvian Man, the measure of all things, a supreme expression of proportion, and hence of reason. But, unlike Leadbeater, Blake did not see this in a positive light. His watercolour forms part of a polemical commentary on the world-picture of Newton, and the spectrum-like fan of colours round Albion is an image of divided light, of materialism, of the fallen world. In a later reworking of the design as an engraving around 1805, an inscription proclaims that Albion is dancing 'the dance of eternal death'.

An artist contemporary with Leadbeater, and who showed a significant interest in Theosophy, although he was never, it seems, a member of the Society, was similarly at odds with the Theosophical interpretation of the colours, and particularly of yellow. Kandinsky's approach to colour was rooted in the idea

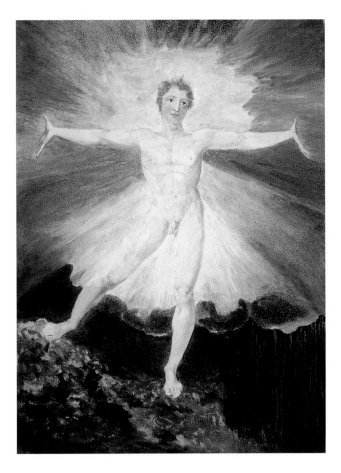

42. **William Blake**, *Albion Rose*, 1796. This may be a source of the images in *Man Visible and Invisible* [141], since the illustrations in that book were by the Theosophist grandson of Blake's close friend John Varley, who is known to have illustrated another book by Leadbeater. Albion's rainbow aura, like that of Leadbeater's Developed Man, implied reason, but for Blake, unlike Leadbeater, this was a negative attribute.

of polarity, which he developed largely on the basis of Goethe's *Theory*. Blue and yellow were for Kandinsky, as for Goethe, the fundamental chromatic opposition, and blue was for Kandinsky, as it was for the Theosophists, the highest spiritual colour. But yellow in Kandinsky, as the opposite to blue, was very far from being Leadbeater's rational hue. 'Yellow is the typically earthly colour', he wrote in *On the Spiritual in Art*. So far, so good, since for Leadbeater it was also characteristic of mind rather than soul. But Kandinsky continued:

> If one compares it to human states of mind, it could have the effect
> of representing madness – not melancholy or hypochondria, but
> rather mania, blind madness or frenzy – like the lunatic who
> attacks people, destroying everything, dissipating his physical
> strength in every direction, expending it without plan and without

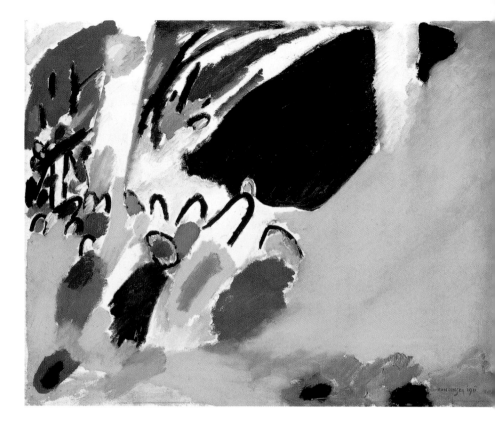

143. **Wassily Kandinsky**, *Impression III (Concert)*, 1911. The concert in question was a performance of Schoenberg's *Three Pieces for Piano*, and the yellow–black contrast seemed to Kandinsky to have an effect analogous to some of the composer's musical techniques.

limit until utterly exhausted. It is also like the reckless pouring out of the last forces of summer in the brilliant foliage of autumn, which is deprived of peaceful blue, rising to heaven. There arise colours full of a wild power which, however, lack any gift for depth.

Kandinsky noted in passing an intrinsic link between the canary's yellow and its high trill, so it is perhaps surprising that in the stage piece *The Yellow Sound*, published in *The Blue Rider Almanac* at the same time as *On the Spiritual in Art*, the singing of the five bright yellow giants in Scene 1 was 'very low'; and in Scene 3 the musical score (by Thomas von Hartmann) grew 'deeper and darker' as the yellow light bathing the totally empty stage rose from a dull to a bright lemon yellow. In the accompanying essay on stage composition Kandinsky articulated his wish to create striking contrasts and disjunctions; and these contradictions in the interpretation of yellow exemplify the 'Rule of Opposition' proposed by the major Romantic theorist of colour symbolism, Baron Frédéric Portal, by which, for example, red could signify both love and hate. This is very much in tune with medieval approaches to symbolizing as essentially a rhetorical device akin to metaphor (although Portal discussed examples from antiquity through to modern times – in his case 1837), but it sorted ill with the psychology-backed dogmatic streak in the Theosophists, and even in Kandinsky.

In 1911 Kandinsky made the acquaintance of the composer Arnold Schoenberg, with whom he corresponded over several years. Schoenberg's explorations of dissonance gave a powerful stimulus to Kandinsky's notion of the new harmony of 'opposites and contradictions', and it was probably with Schoenberg's compositions in mind that he painted his most yellow picture, *Impression III (Concert)* [143], after hearing a performance of *Three Pieces for Piano* (Op. II, 1909). Here the dominant oppositions are of yellow and black, and, as his Table I in *On the Spiritual in Art* shows [144], contrasts of yellow and blue were very close to the maximal contrasts of white and black, where yellow and white were the highly active elements and blue and black the completely withdrawn, or passive, elements. In the same manifesto, Kandinsky pointed to Schoenberg's isolation of individual musical elements in his quartets as a useful lesson for stage works, such as his own *Yellow Sound*, and in *Impression III (Concert)* he achieved the

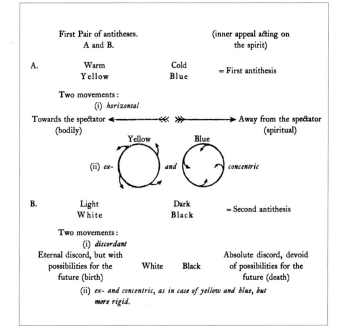

144. Wassily Kandinsky, Table I from *On the Spiritual in Art*, 1914.

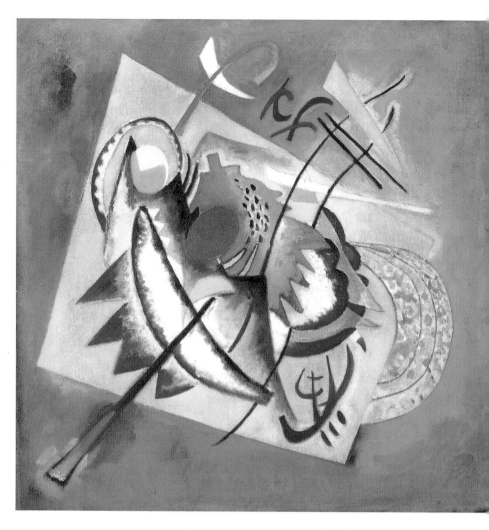

145. **Wassily Kandinsky**, *Red Oval*, 1920. This work was painted in Russia, and its forms, simpler and more geometrical than in Kandinsky's earlier work, are closely related to the new style of the Russian Constructivists. But the red oval is also highly charged with symbolic associations.

same independence for yellow and black. As a number of preparatory drawings show, the black shape is an abstraction from the grand piano used in the performance.

Although Kandinsky's repertory of forms was in a perpetual state of transformation during the second half of his life, his approach to colour remained remarkably constant. It is difficult to see, for example, that the claim he made in 1921 that after the October Revolution of 1917 his colours had become 'brighter and more attractive' was more than a sop to his Bolshevik masters, with whom he was often at odds. It is more remarkable that in the Neo-Constructivist atmosphere of the Dessau Bauhaus he was still sending his readers – in his Bauhaus book *Point and Line to*

Plane of 1926 – to his 1911 manifesto for ideas about colour. In the early 1930s Kandinsky was still expounding the notions of the Theosophist Rudolf Steiner, whose light dramas of the first decade of the century had been one of the primary inspirations for Kandinsky's own stage pieces, and whose articles on meditation, including an account of the meanings of colours, he had studied carefully about 1908. As late as 1938 he was restating colour principles from *On the Spiritual in Art*, for example that 'RED (Vermilion) can give the impression of loud beats of the drum'.

This percussive quality of red is especially striking in a painting from the Russian revolutionary years, *Red Oval* [145], a work that is witness both to the painter's extraordinary richness of formal ideas and to the difficulty we have in interpreting colours in terms of a single scheme of references. The relative simplicity of the formal structure and the new appearance of flat, hard-edged shapes has led some commentators to link the work with Russian Suprematism, and the frequent introduction of the trapezium in Malevich, Popova and others. The oval itself had been a common motif in Ivan Kliun's (1873–1943) formal experiments of around 1917 [147]; and there is a particularly closely related composition by Kliun of 1918, shown at the 'Jack of Diamonds' exhibition in Moscow that year, where a dull red oval is set within a trapezoidal

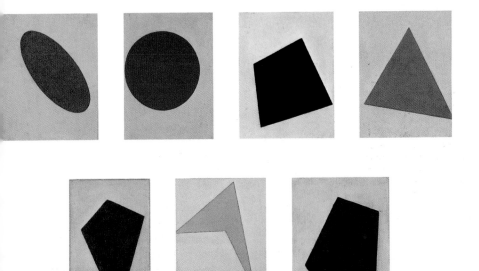

structure [147]. And there were other, and even more dynamic, red ovoids in circulation in Kandinsky's environment: for example, the 'thought form', *Definite Affection,* in Besant and Leadbeater's book, of which the artist owned a copy of the Leipzig edition of 1908 [148]. Yet, as we saw in Chapter 3, strong primary colours were usually linked in Suprematism with 'primary' forms, such as red with the circle (Popova), as they were in Kandinsky's own theory. In any case, Kandinsky soon expressed his distaste for what he saw as the too 'experimental' approach of Suprematist artists.

In her study of the continuing impact of Kandinsky's early ethnographic work, Peg Weiss has approached *Red Oval* in a more biographical vein. Kandinsky's son Volodia died in infancy in June 1920, and in Old Russia red eggs were taken after Easter to

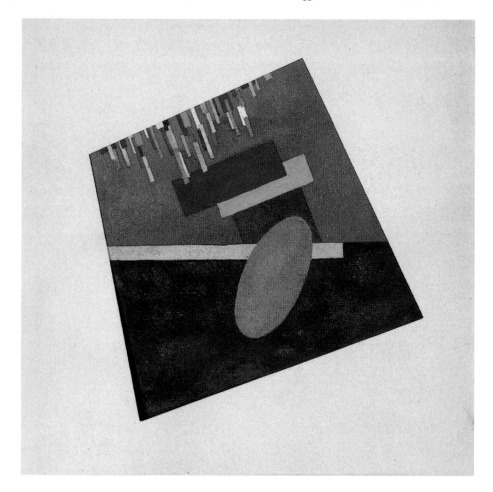

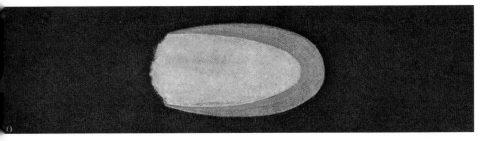

cemeteries to honour the dead. In parts of Russia, indeed, red eggs were thrown into streams at Easter to commemorate infants who died before they could be baptized. So this painting may be a memorial to the artist's dead son. The notion of a stream dividing the living from the dead is enhanced by the abstracted boat image, which Weiss links to an Old Russian belief that the soul after death would ride in a boat to the other world.

Red eggs, Red Revolution, Red Square – and Kandinsky's red square – as well as 'red' (*Krasnii*) in Russian, meaning 'beauty'. All these ideas may have coexisted in the painter's mind in Moscow in 1920. But perhaps the most important element for Kandinsky was the dynamic power of a rather warm red, in a dynamic shape and set obliquely, first against a strong green, and then against the trapezoidal yellow ground, which, itself set obliquely and butted with sharp blue shapes, is equally dynamic. Kandinsky was the most articulate expounder of the meaning of colour among early twentieth-century artists, yet even he was not able to confine colour to a single coherent meaning in his paintings.

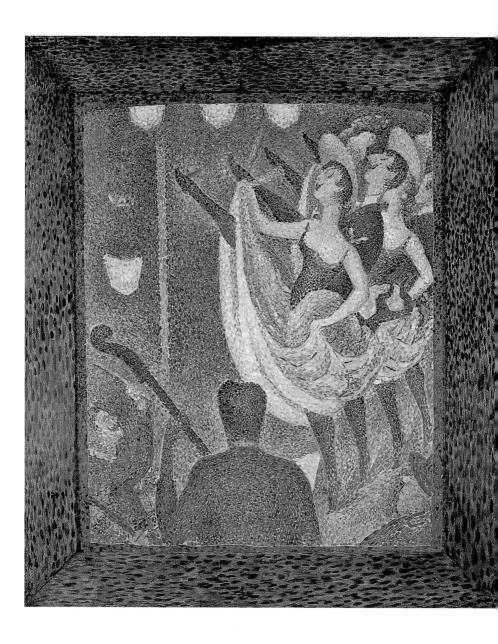

Chapter 7　The Union of the Senses

149. **Georges Seurat**, Final study for *Le Chahut*, 1889. Seurat's late work was very much under the influence of his friend, the mathematician Charles Henry, who proposed that rising lines and warm colours create a feeling of exhilaration, and falling lines and cool colours the opposite [61] Here the abstract idea is severely qualified by the dynamic subject and the Neo-Impressionist technique.

One of the arguments in favour of colour as a major element in visual representation was that it brought art closer to nature. We saw that this has been a far from universal view, and in many ways it seems implausible; yet from antiquity to the nineteenth century, and as long as the representation of nature was seen to be the primary function of painting, it was a dominant idea. In one of the earliest Italian Renaissance discussions of the relationships between the various arts, painting, sculpture and poetry (the Paragone), published in Baldassare Castiglione's *Book of the Courtier* (1528), which professes to record discussions at the court of Urbino in the early years of the century, one of the participants, Count Ludovico of Canossa, delivers a eulogy of painting (although even he prefaces it by asserting that everything in painting must depend on light and shade):

> *Do you think the imitation of natural colours in representing flesh and drapery is of little importance? This the marble-sculptor cannot achieve, nor even express the gracious glance of black and azure eyes, shining with their rays of love. He cannot show the colour of blonde hair, nor the glint of armour, nor a dark night, nor a storm at sea with bolts of lightning, nor a town on fire, nor the rosy colour of early dawn, with its rays of gold and purple; in short, [the sculptor] cannot represent sky, sea, earth, mountains, woods, meadows, gardens, rivers, towns or houses, all of which the painter is able to do.*

Here Canossa virtually lays out an agenda for the future of Western painting and, more important in the context of the present chapter, for the type of theatrical entertainment that became so popular in Europe and America in the eighteenth and nineteenth centuries. It is striking that his emphasis is on landscape (not a genre much cultivated in the early sixteenth century), for it was in landscape, from Rubens to Constable, the Pre-Raphaelites and Monet, that fidelity to the colours of the outdoor scene became a central aesthetic objective, although it is clear from even these few examples that what constituted 'fidelity' differed from one practitioner to the next.

It was in landscape, too, that the dependence of colour on lighting and context became most obvious, but whereas for the naturalistic painter this fact had to be taken as given, and used or neglected according to the particular needs of the moment, in the theatre it could, and did, become the basis of a powerful new medium. The history of art has rarely taken the history of theatrical design on board, even though it stimulated and engaged the talents of major artists such as Leonardo da Vinci, Edvard Munch, Kazimir Malevich, Wassily Kandinsky and Jasper Johns. But in the history of colour the theatre has had a substantial role to play, for it provided the first context for the integration of colour with light, and the need to make an impression over long distances led to the development of techniques of broken brushwork and sharp combinations of colours that anticipated by many decades their use by easel or mural painters.

We know little of the multi-media elements in the ancient performance arts, seen in the open air; but it is clear that the indoor religious rituals of the Middle Ages, with their moving processions, singing, incense and lamps and splendid vestments, engaged all the senses simultaneously. Religious drama furnished many of the ingredients of modern theatre, notably colour and lighting; and in a remarkable set of stage-directions for the Passion Play in the north Italian town of Revello in the fifteenth century we read that an improvised spotlight – a polished reflector – was to focus on Christ at the moment in the Transfiguration when he shed his crimson robe and appeared transformed in white. At Mons, in northern Europe, too, around 1500, Christ's face and hands in this scene were painted gold, his robe was of the whitest possible white, and the stage directions stipulate that a 'big sun' be placed behind him.

Artists were often called on to devise stage settings for their court patrons: at Milan in 1490 Leonardo da Vinci provided a set for a 'Paradiso' in a spectacle in honour of Duke Lodovico Sforza's wife, Isabella. It was shaped like half an egg, gilded on the inside and with many candles 'twinkling like stars'. Representations of the seven planets moved in the upper part and the signs of the zodiac were lit behind glass filters. This was the setting for a musical entertainment with Apollo, nymphs and other classical figures. Artists themselves staged elaborate banquets, especially in Italy, where their patrons were often invited as guests. The painter and art historian Giorgio Vasari described one such junket arranged by an unusually convivial artist, the sculptor Gian Francesco Rustici, who sponsored many thematic feasts and on this occasion had formed what sounds like an entirely impromptu 'Company of the Cauldron'. Instead of a table, guests sat in a large wine vat, formed into a cauldron and decorated with paintings. Guests and food 'appeared to be floating in the water', and the meal was lit by a bright light in the handle. The first course was brought from below on a 'tree with numerous branches', and when that was finished, the tree descended to where musicians were playing. This was repeated for the second course, and so on. The other artists brought fantastic offerings of food: Andrea del Sarto, for example, provided a model of the multi-coloured Florentine Baptistry made of jelly, sausages, Parmesan cheese, sugar icing and marzipan. Thus, at least four of the five senses – sight, hearing, taste and smell – were abundantly addressed.

The visual impact of these performances naturally depended heavily on lighting. An Annunciation play staged in the church of the Santissima Annunziata in Florence in 1439 re-created Heaven by means of some five hundred lamps continually revolving and rising and falling, and the performance included fire sent down

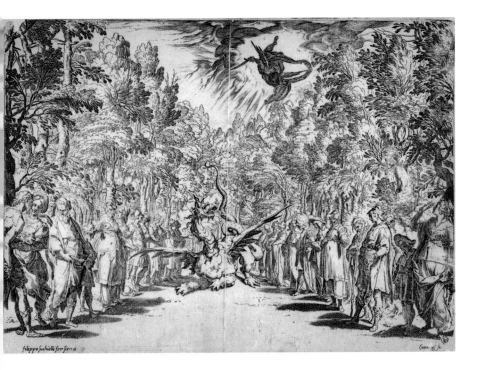

filippo suchielli for firma   (Caron) fe.

from this Heaven to the sound of thunder, and which 'poured forth and spread with increasing intensity and noise ... lighting the lamps in the church, but without burning the clothes of the spectators or causing any harm'. Modern tourists get a small echo of these effects at Easter in the Cathedral Square in Florence, when the Dove of the Holy Spirit flies out from the church and explodes fireworks on an ornate cart.

Sixteenth-century Italian staging used glass jars filled with distilled water to act as lenses and increase the light, as well as coloured liquids in crystal balls lit from behind. The architectural theorist Serlio described the precise chemical additives needed to create a blue sky in this way. The Florentine architect Bernardo Buontalenti (1531–1608) was apparently the first to use footlights in his intermezzo based on the multi-media cosmic tableau from Plato's *Republic*, staged in the Uffizi Gallery in 1589 [150]. This spectacle included a storm with lightning, a theatrical effect that became commonplace in later centuries.

Lighting and Colour in the Theatre

These vastly extravagant spectacles could be afforded only infrequently, but during the eighteenth century, especially in France, a new type of regular theatrical spectacle developed in which highly controlled lighting was crucial to the effect. A new means was provided by the improved oil lamp designed by the Swiss Aimé Argand, which shed up to twelve times more light than a good wax candle, and was patented in London in 1784. But this new technology nourished a popular taste already well established in France and England by the architect-designer Giovanni Niccolò Servandoni (1695–1766), who from 1728 was the chief scene designer at the Paris Opéra. In the 1720s Servandoni, working with transparencies, introduced spectacular stage effects, such as the silver gauze waterfall in Lully's *Prosperine* (1727); but it was with his *spectacle d'optique* at the Salle des Machines in the Tuileries, from 1738, that he created a new genre of light/sound shows with mechanical and live actors [151].

Servandoni's most brilliant follower was the landscape painter P. J. de Loutherbourg (1740–1812), an Alsatian, who emigrated to London from Paris in the 1770s to work for the actor, dramatist and theatre manager David Garrick at his Drury Lane theatre. Loutherbourg made an instant name for himself with effects like the fog scene – done with gauzes – in Garrick's *Christmas Tale* in 1773. He brought a far greater naturalism to the Servandonian repertory of phenomena, which had included in *Pandora* (1739)

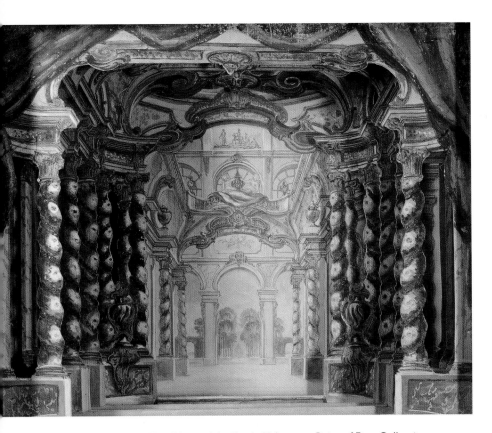

151. **Giovanni Niccolò Servandoni** (attributed), set design model, n.d. Servandoni began as a mainstream theatre designer, but it was his Paris *spectacle d'optique* (from 1738), an entirely mechanical theatre, that started a new trend, and anticipated the *Eidophusikon* of his pupil, Loutherbourg.

'Tremblings of the Earth, Volcanoes, Rains of Fire, Collapsing Cliffs, Thunder, Lightning, and all that might serve to represent a universal disorder'. But Loutherbourg's greatest claim on our attention in the context of colour is his permanent show *Eidophusikon (The Picture of Nature)*, which ran in London for a number of years from 1781, and subsequently toured the English provinces, under another manager, until it was destroyed by fire in 1800. *Eidophusikon* presented astonishingly realistic representations of natural events, such as changing effects of weather, or some recent and well-known shipwreck. At the opening performance in 1781 the first scene showed a dawn over London from down the Thames at Greenwich:

> This scene was enveloped in that mysterious light which is the precursor of day-break, so true to nature that the imagination of the spectator sniffed the sweet breath of morn. A faint light appeared along the horizon, the scene assumed a vapourish tint of grey; presently a gleam of saffron, changing to the pure varieties

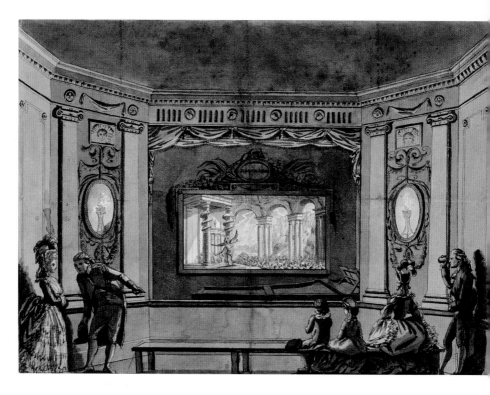

152. **Edward Burney,**
De Loutherbourg's Eidophusikon,
c. 1782. This restrained image
belies the excitement aroused by
this multi-media entertainment.
On the miniature stage is the scene
of Pandemonium from Milton's
Paradise Lost, which was often the
grand climax to Loutherbourg's
performances.

that tinge the fleecy clouds that pass away in morning mist; the
picture brightened by degrees, the sun appeared, gilding the tops of
the trees and the projections of the lofty buildings and burnishing
the vanes of the cupolas.

This contemporary account went on to record that the tableau
took the audience through the whole day, concluding with
moonlight and a storm, effects that in due course became
Romantic clichés, but at this time had the virtue of novelty in
England. Loutherbourg's second programme, the following year,
closed with a moving illustration of Milton's Hell from *Paradise
Lost,* showing the rise of the Palace of Pandemonium, and this,
too, was accompanied by dramatic changes of colour: a
newspaper report spoke of 'the intense red [which] changes to a
transparent white, exposing thereby the effect of fire upon metal'.
These vivid accounts make Edward Burney's (1760–1848) genteel
and unmoving watercolour of this finale [152] something of an
anticlimax. Musical accompaniment (note the harpsichord in
Burney's view) was sometimes provided by the composer and
keyboard virtuoso Michael Arne, who had also worked for

Garrick, but may have been a particularly congenial collaborator for Loutherbourg because of their common interest in alchemy. Another accompanist was the composer and celebrated historian of music Dr Charles Burney, and other music was provided by the vocalist Mrs Sophia Baddeley.

As in the case of Renaissance artists, Loutherbourg's services were also enlisted by private patrons. In the year that *Eidophusikon* was launched, the millionaire novelist and collector William Beckford engaged the painter to devise a décor to entertain his Christmas guests at his country seat, Fonthill Splendens in Wiltshire. In a later memoir Beckford recalled the:

> strange necromantic light which Loutherbourg had thrown over what absolutely appeared a realm of Fairy, or rather, perhaps, a demon Temple deep beneath the earth, set apart for tremendous mysteries ... the very air of summer seemed playing around us – the choir of low-toned melodious voices continued to soothe our ear, and that every sense in turn might receive blandishment, tables covered with delicious viands and fragrant flowers glided forth, by the aid of mechanism at stated intervals, from the richly draped and amply curtained recesses of the enchanted precincts.

In some respects this resembled the lavish private feasts of the Renaissance, but Loutherbourg's more popular mechanical theatre was more durable, and was often imitated: his successor, one Chapman, opened a *New Eidophusikon* in London in 1799, and the name was still being used for this type of London entertainment as late as 1837, just into Queen Victoria's reign, by the close of which the cinema was already firmly established. Loutherbourg's was the first of many rival moving spectacles whose aim was to convey a sense of absolute fidelity to a place or a building. It was this illusionism aided by these extraordinary effects of colour which earned them the contempt of imaginative artists such as Constable.

In the 1820s the French master of the medium, Louis Daguerre (better known for his later photographic innovations), joined with the painter Charles Bouton to develop the diorama, which, like the older but related entertainment the panorama, relied for its popularity on topical disasters: one [153] in Bouton and Daguerre's London repertory was *The Great Fire in Edinburgh, November 1824*. This same taste for sensation was exploited, in a very different style, by Turner in the following decade [63]. Daguerre enlarged the scale of his show to that of the panorama,

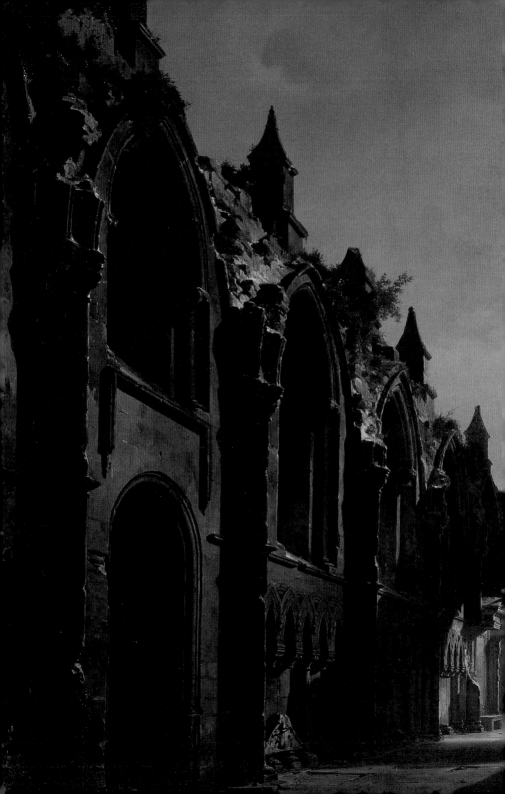

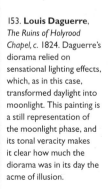

153. **Louis Daguerre**, *The Ruins of Holyrood Chapel, c.* 1824. Daguerre's diorama relied on sensational lighting effects, which, as in this case, transformed daylight into moonlight. This painting is a still representation of the moonlight phase, and its tonal veracity makes it clear how much the diorama was in its day the acme of illusion.

heightened the realism and extended the appeal to other senses, by, for example, introducing a goat as well as a three-dimensional chalet and alp-horns into a Swiss diorama shown in Paris. Bouton's Paris programme in 1836 included a scene of the interior of Santa Croce in Florence at sunset, where in the gathering darkness the lamps were lit, an organ played the Kyrie from Haydn's *Mass No. 1* and there was the tinkling of a liturgical bell and the smell of incense. All this, except for its attempt at absolute illusion, anticipated the multi-media theatrical performances of the French Symbolists at the close of the century. The diorama was so successful that it ran in Paris from 1822 to 1839 (when it was also destroyed by fire), and in its London version from 1823 to 1851.

In the nineteenth century Argand's principles were extended to gas lighting, which, like the later introduction of electricity, first used in the form of arc lamps at the Paris Opéra in 1849, made stronger and, most importantly, controllable lighting effects more and more feasible, although colour still played a comparatively minor role in these performances. The inventor of the first (mechanical) computer, Charles Babbage, did, however, propose in the 1840s to mount a rainbow ballet, using four limelights with coloured filters, which would project overlapping beams on the white-clad dancers, to mix the other hues. But it was prevented from being performed by the constant risk of fire.

What gave a new and decisive impetus to the development of multi-sensory performances was the idea of reviving the ancient Greek drama (about whose staging almost nothing was known), launched most vigorously by the highly innovative opera composer Richard Wagner (1813–83). The novelty of Wagner's theatrical reforms has sometimes been exaggerated: darkening the auditorium in order to concentrate the light on the stage, for example, had been introduced as early as 1683 at the Teatro San Giovanni Crisostomo in Venice, and it was a widespread practice in Italy in the early nineteenth century. One theatre where it was standard was La Scala in Milan, where a rather primitive anticipation of Wagner's *Gesamtkunstwerk* (total art work) was staged in 1813, a version of Beethoven's ballet *Prometheus* (1801), with additional music from Haydn's *Creation* (1801). The spectacle was devised by the dancer and choreographer Salvatore Viganò, with sets by Alessandro Sanquirico (1777/80–1849) [154]. But, in spite of the high reputation of these two artists, the spectacle was not universally approved. One spectator recorded:

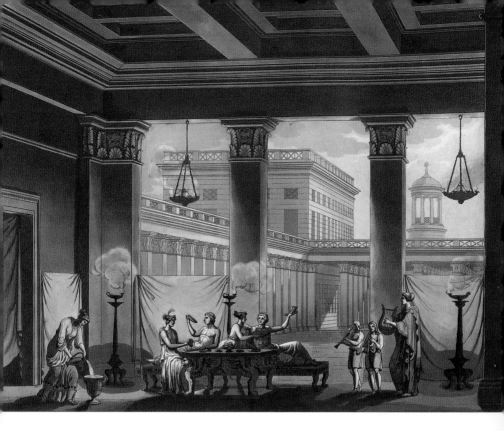

The firmament heavy with clouds appears at night with stars and a moon which is about to set and grow pale, thus the sky at the back of the stage whitens, the stars fade, it gets light, turns pink etc. as the appearance of the canvas slowly changes … then begins the celestial procession, brought on by machinery, poetically and picturesquely. Here, too, we may see what mechanics may do for the drama, which is not autonomous, as poetry itself is. This act, which will have been the ballet's success for the vulgar, was, for the discerning, its chief fault; for they knew Viganò to be above all the superlative poet of sentiment and painter of action. But the vulgar, who are not able to judge these things in the same way, at once proclaimed that this was the ballet of cosmoramic spectacle. If lavishness were enough, it was certainly not spared in Prometheus, *but for all its effort and expense, mechanics cannot imitate the constellations or the suns. Tithon appeared, beating back the darkness, and Lucifer on his fiery charger; Aurora scattering flowers; the dance of the Hours, the Months, and the blonde charioteer Apollo with his dazzling disc. But there was nothing but scraps of cloud to disguise the wires they hung from, which took them from one part of the stage to another;*

175

and these wires carried timid boys, quite unsuited to the actions they were required to perform, with flat, painted horses whose legs were fixed, although they were constantly moving through the air at a gallop. And then the sun appeared to be a glass globe filled with water, through which a light flickered violently. It could never have produced that flood of light which ought to have lit up the whole scene, and given an idea of the effect of this great planet in the world. Only the backcloth was beautiful, as it glowed orange at the arrival of the sun, illuminated brilliantly by light through the back. Magic, too, was Haydn's music, from that part of The Creation *which expresses the creation of light.*

The heterogeneous conventions and variable conditions of the stage spectacle demanded radical innovations if it was to hold its own with the orchestra and the dancers; and another Italian designer of this period, Pietro Gonzaga (1794–1877), put his faith in his new colouristic principles of stage painting [155]. A contemporary critic observed:

Until he achieved his fortunate revolution, scenery appeared very dull because the painters did not use pure black and white, but persisted in giving relief to each colour by darkening it far too much with black or by other means, in the background, thereby deadening the colouring. But Gonzaga, realising that the lighting illuminated not only the set, but also the clouds of dust continually thrown up by the dancers and the scene-changers, looked for ways of avoiding this. Seeing that these colours needed a natural

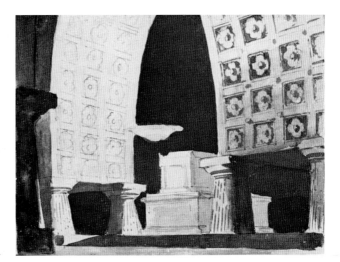

155. **Pietro Gonzaga**, stage scenery, n.d. Throughout the 18th and early 19th centuries Italian stage design dominated the field, and it was artists such as Gonzaga (who worked mainly in Russia) who found new colouristic techniques to give force to their décors.

*highlight and a very pronounced shadow, he started to paint with
pure white, and marked the shadows with the deepest available
black i.e. lamp-black, which his predecessors had believed was far
too strong, and had not liked to use pure except in small touches
… Furthermore, he continued to do without half-tones, or at least
to use them as little as possible, because when they were obscured
by flying dust they helped to confuse the general masses of
colouring, without contributing at all to that gradation demanded
in the painting of distance.*

Thus for purely pragmatic reasons at least one Italian scene
painter around 1800 had decided to use colour in a way that
we recognize more readily in the work of Thomas Couture
(1815–1879) and his pupil Édouard Manet [54], whose styles were
based on the simplification of tonal contrasts and much use of
unmodulated black.

But there is no doubt of the extraordinary impact of Wagner's
theory of the total work of art. His seminal essay 'Outlines of the
Art Work of the Future' (1849) juxtaposed the 'many-coloured
harmony' of the orchestration – in which Wagner was a great
innovator – with the 'finest blend of colours' of the landscape
painter responsible for the operatic décor. But here, as earlier at
La Scala, Wagner's ideas, and their realization, were not up to the
standard of the music. His tastes in visual art were thoroughly
conventional, and for the most part he employed undistinguished
naturalistic designers to create rather busy, humdrum sets that
added nothing to the imaginative power of the score. Small
wonder that he asked one of his guests at his great, purpose-built
Festival Theatre at Bayreuth to close her eyes during the
performance. And apparently the completely darkened
auditorium at the inauguration of his theatre was due to
the technical failure of the gas lighting. In the first Bayreuth
production of *Die Walküre* in 1876 the Ride of the Valkyries
was represented by projections lit by electricity.

It was, nevertheless, with Wagner – or rather with the
Wagnerian project – in mind that theatre reformers of around
1900 sought to pare down the décor and rely more on (electric)
lighting to match the mood of the music with light and colour.
For example, the Swiss designer Adolphe Appia (1862–1928)
[156] devised a radically minimalist staging for Wagner's *Parsifal*,
although it was never produced. Wagner was an iconic hero to
the French Symbolists, whose major literary vehicle in the 1880s
was *La Revue wagnérienne*; and the Theosophist Édouard Schuré

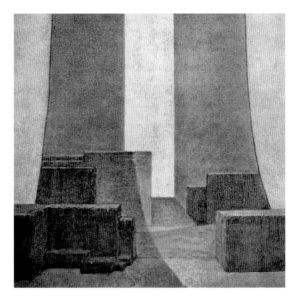

included him with Pythagoras, Christ and the Buddha as the last in his book of *The Great Initiates* (1889). In the Theosophical context, the overture to Wagner's *Meistersingers* also formed the monumental climax to Besant and Leadbeater's *Thought Forms* (1905), where a church performance of the piece generated a vast mountain of sounds and colours [157], each peak of which:

> has its own brilliant hue – a splendid splash of vivid colour, glowing with the glory of its own living light, spreading its resplendent radiance over all the country round. Yet in each of these masses of colour other colours are constantly flickering, as they do over the surface of molten metal, so that the coruscations and scintillations of these wondrous astral edifices are far beyond the power of any physical [sic] words to describe.

It was in French Symbolism that the ideal of the total art work came (briefly) to a head. The 1891 production of *The Song of Songs* at the Théâtre des Arts in Paris used colour, music and perfume in an entirely coordinated way, for the first – and perhaps last – time. The opening scene, presenting the meeting of King Solomon and the Queen of Sheba, was decorated in purple, the score was of C-major chords and the perfume was incense. Later scenes matched yellow with the scent of hyacinths, green with lily, and so on. The poet Paul Fort remembered that 'the projections changed colour with each change of scene and followed the various degrees of emotion rhythmically, while all the sweet scents flowed out'. They flowed a little too abundantly for some of the audience, who found them nauseous, and the work had a very short run.

Wagner also came to be a formative influence on the aesthetics of early abstraction. Kandinsky, who experimented with stage pieces using a light score around 1909 (see Chapters 5, 6), had been profoundly affected by a performance of *Lohengrin* in Moscow during his youth that gave him a new experience of colour. As he recalled: 'The violins, the deep tones of the basses, and especially the wind instruments at that time embodied for me all the power of that pre-nocturnal hour. I saw all my colours in my mind, they stood before my eyes.' Similarly, the Italian abstract filmmakers Arnaldo Ginna and Bruno Corra,

57. *Overture to Wagner's Meistersingers*, from A. Besant and C. W. Leadbeater, *Thought Forms*, 1905. This vast mountain of sounds, lights and colours is the most spectacular of the musical thought forms in the book. Characteristically, it is emitted from a church organ, and is visible to clairvoyants in tune with the Theosophical project.

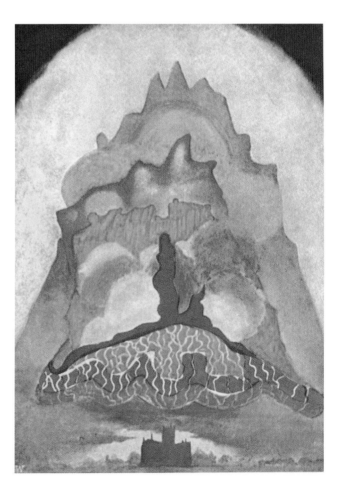

158. **Edward Gordon Craig**,
illustration for the stage set of
Henrik Ibsen's *The Pretenders*, Act
3, Scene 1, 'The Bishop's Death'.
Appia and Craig were in the avant-
garde of Wagnerian staging in the
early years of the 20th century,
when naturalistic décor was
replaced by the play of coloured
lights over simple three-
dimensional shapes.

159. **Richard Smith**, *Edward
Gordon Craig*, 1968. One of Britain's
leading Pop artists in the 1960s,
Smith produced an entire series of
lithographs dedicated to Edward
Gordon Craig and displaying simple
coloured forms such as those used
in Craig's designs. They reveal the
painter's and the theatre designer's
shared interest in the ability of
colour to define physical space.

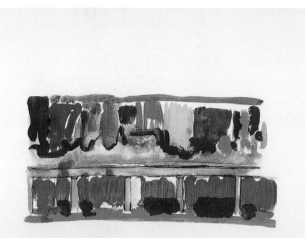

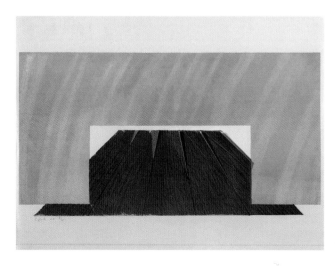

who were familiar both with Schuré and with *Thought Forms,* naturally cited Wagner's example in their manifesto of 1910, *The Art of the Future.*

But by this date radical theatre had moved, at least in theory, to a far more utopian position than had been envisaged in Wagner's total art work. One of the most original designers of the period, Edward Gordon Craig (1872–1966), wrote in 1891 to the director of the Théâtre des Arts that, unlike traditional painted scenery, which was simply a backdrop to the action: 'It is desirable that the décor, mobile as the sound, elucidates the phases of the drama in the same way as the music accompanies and underlines all movements, just as it develops in pace with the drama.' This was to be achieved largely by lighting, about which Craig [158] had learned a great deal from his stepfather, the actor-director Henry Irving. Already in the 1870s Irving, at the Lyceum Theatre in London, was using combinations of coloured lights, 'as a painter uses his palette': 'He had transparent lacquers applied to the glasses of the limelights,' wrote a contemporary, 'and when electric light came in [in 1891], to the bulbs of the electric lights, and thus produced effects of colour, both of intensity and delicacy up to then unknown.'

The Russian director Fyodor Komissarzhevsky similarly asserted in his autobiography: 'The rhythm of the music must be in harmony with the rhythm of the words, with the rhythm of the movements of the actors, of the colours and lines of the decors and costumes, and of the changing lights.' This complete interweaving of all the elements of a stage performance was to remain little more than a dream, but it was a dream fired by the rapid developments in, and expansion of, late-nineteenth-century psychology and technology. We saw how experimental psychologists, notably Charles Feré and Seurat's friend Charles Henry in the 1880s, had been exploring the relationship of colours and movements, and these lines of enquiry were soon taken up in performance. Komissarzhevsky may have been thinking of Kandinsky, who in his Russian years around the time of the First World War, for example, had collaborated with the dancer Alexander Sacharoff to translate some of his watercolours into dance. These experiments remained rather private, and little is known about them; but Ginna and Corra drew attention to the seminal influence of the most famous of all contemporary French cabaret dancers, the American-born Loïe Fuller, who in an early autobiography (1908) had also spoken of how the changes in lighting had induced her to make involuntary changes in her

160. **Henri de Toulouse-Lautrec**, *Study for Loïe Fuller*, 1893. Toulouse-Lautrec was one of the many artists who were attracted to the American dancer, who was the sensation of the Paris cabaret in the years around 1900. In this image, which he reproduced in many variants, Lautrec has conveyed the feeling of weightlessness and light that was the leading feature of Fuller's act.

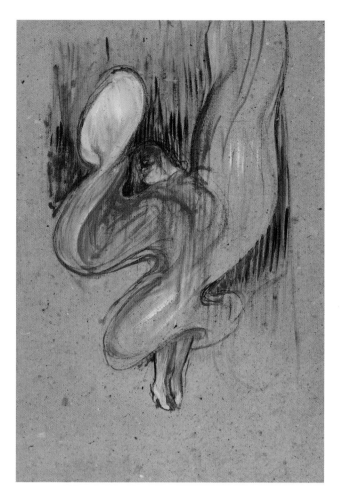

movements. Fuller's acts fascinated a whole generation of the French literary public, and she was portrayed by some seventy artists, including Auguste Rodin (1840–1917) and Henri de Toulouse-Lautrec (1864–1901) [160]. In 1893 the critic Roger Marx gave one of the many vivid descriptions of her performances, which began on a darkened stage:

> *From this night the apparition escapes, takes form, comes to life under the caress of the electric beams. She detaches herself from the gloomy background, takes on the dazzling whiteness of a diamond, then is covered with all the colours of a jewel-box full of precious gems…. The material [of her costume], dizzily swirling, is tinged successively with all the hues of the rainbow; and the vision*

is never so splendid, so magical, so enrapturing as at the moment
when she is about to disappear, to be plunged into nothingness,
to be lost in the darkness again.

As Toulouse-Lautrec's image and innumerable Art Nouveau
bronzes show us, it was Fuller's extravagant draperies that
marked her individuality – in one famous routine, *The Lily of the
Nile,* she wore around five hundred square metres of thin silk,
which, in the course of the dance, extended more than three
metres from her body – but it was also, as Marx's description
makes clear, her lighting that transformed a performance into
magic. Electric light was given enormous flexibility with the
development of the incandescent bulb by Thomas Alva Edison
around 1880. Fuller designed her own lighting rig, which included
ten to twenty lamps, depending on the dance, a light-box with
rotating coloured filters, and a double lantern for mixing coloured
beams. She also used glass floors lit from below. The Symbolist
writer J. K. Huysmans was one of the few spectators to remain
unimpressed; the glory, he said, 'goes to the electrician. It's
American.' But for us, Loïe Fuller is the direct ancestor of modern
high-tech performance artists such as Atsuko Tanaka [192].

Synaesthesia
Loïe Fuller's brilliant career was made possible only by new
technology but, as her remarks about light and movement
suggest, she had the good fortune to coincide with the earliest
phase of experimental psychology, which, as we have seen,
brought colour preferences and perceptions into the centre
of visual aesthetics. For probably the first time in history, poets
and artists became interesting as subjects of scientific enquiry;
and in one very active area of the new psychology, the study of
synaesthesia – the simultaneous response of two or more senses
to the same stimulus – they were among the most articulate
witnesses to the phenomenon. The most common and most
investigated type of synaesthesia was 'coloured hearing' (*audition
colorée*), and as the French psychologist Alfred Binet noted in
1892: 'While medical doctors have preferred to see in *audition
coloreé* nothing but a disturbance in sensory perception, literary
people believe that they have found in it a new form of art.'
Again it was Kandinsky – who is sometimes regarded as a
pseudo-synaesthete because it cannot now be ascertained
whether or not his multiple responses to the same stimulus were
involuntary – who gave the most comprehensive and eloquent

account of synaesthetic experiences. In his 1911 manifesto Kandinsky himself entered the debate on whether colours worked on the senses directly or by association: 'One might assume that, e.g., bright yellow produces a sour effect by analogy with lemons,' he wrote:

> It is, however, hardly possible to maintain this kind of explanation. As far as tasting colours is concerned, many examples are known where this explanation does not apply. A Dresden doctor tells how one of his patients, whom he describes as 'spiritually, unusually highly developed', invariably found that a certain sauce had a 'blue' taste, i.e. affected him like the colour blue … in the case of such highly developed people the paths leading to the soul are so direct, and the impressions it receives are so quickly produced, that an effect immediately communicated to the soul via the medium of taste sets up vibrations along the corresponding paths leading away from the soul to the other sensory organs (in this case, the eye). This effect would seem to be a sort of echo or resonance, as in the case of musical instruments, which, without themselves being touched, vibrate in sympathy with another instrument being played.… If one accepts this explanation, then admittedly sight must be related not only to taste, but also to all the other senses. Which is indeed the case. Many colours have an uneven, prickly appearance, while others feel smooth, like velvet, so that one wants to stroke them (dark ultramarine, chrome oxide green, madder). Even the distinction between cold and warm tones depends upon this sensation. There are also colours that appear soft (madder), others that always strike one as hard (cobalt green, green-blue oxide), so that one might mistake them for already dry when freshly squeezed from the tube.
>
> The expression 'the scent of colours' is common usage.
>
> Finally, our hearing of colours is so precise that it would perhaps be impossible to find anyone who would try to represent his impression of bright yellow by means of the bottom register of the piano, or describe dark madder as being like a soprano voice.

Here all the senses but smell are in play, yet for Kandinsky the musical analogy is central, and in his book he refers to the most recent attempt to bring colour and music together in a single, indivisible work of art. Due to repeated technical hitches in the early Russian performances, Alexander Scriabin's *Opus 60: Prometheus: A Poem of Fire* (1910–11) was first played in its complete form in New York in 1915. In one of his early sketches, subsequently abandoned, Scriabin had envisaged his audience, like Charles Feré's

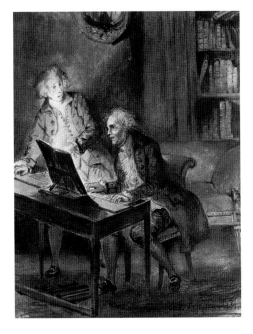

neurotic patients, bathed in coloured light; and in another, anticipating Kandinsky, that a dancer should mime the colour changes. In the event, only a colour keyboard was incorporated, played like a piano but producing coloured projections on a multiple screen. In a later, unexecuted work, *Mysterium,* Scriabin planned to add smell to the range of senses engaged in the performance. Typically for Russian Symbolism, the traditional ritual of the Orthodox Church, as well as the more recent practices of Theosophy, also played a shaping role. For Scriabin, as for the ancient and medieval theorists of music, it necessarily evoked moral feelings, and psychology had now made it possible to link colours precisely with these ideas. 'Creativity' he associated with blues and violets, and with E, Cb, Gb and Db; 'humanity' with Eb; 'passion' with Bb and, not surprisingly, with the pinks of the human skin.

Scriabin had (a not altogether encouraging) access to a colour organ, a type of instrument first mooted in eighteenth-century France, to exemplify these colour–note correspondences, and subtly illustrated by Delacroix [161], who loved the music of C. W. Gluck, in a pastel-drawing inspired by a story by the German composer and writer E. T. A. Hoffmann. In this short story, which was translated into French in 1829, at a time when Hoffmann's uncanny tales had begun to enjoy something of a vogue in France, his narrator encounters a strange old-fashioned gentleman at a concert of Gluck's music in Berlin in 1809. The gentleman shows a striking familiarity with Gluck's works, and is easily able to hum brilliant variations on them. He and the narrator strike up a friendship, and eventually the old man reveals his dreams, including one nightmare in which he is attacked by a monster who plunges him into the depths of the sea and then carries him up to the night sky. The darkness is illuminated with rays of light that are also clear musical notes: 'I awoke from my tortures and saw a great, bright eye which was looking at an organ and as it looked, notes came out shimmering and intertwining themselves in wonderful accords, such as I had never thought of.'

On a later occasion the narrator is taken to the old man's apartment, where, in a room furnished in an outdated style, there are shelves of Gluck's scores and a harpsichord. The old man takes down the score for one of his last operas, *Armida* (1779), and begins to play with great emotion, his face aglow, and again with many improvisations. Delacroix's drawing shows the moment when the narrator sees that the score-book is completely blank, but is the source of light illuminating the musician's excited face. He is, of course, Gluck himself, who had died twenty years earlier. This is perhaps the earliest illustration of a synaesthetic experience; and it is remarkable that, as early as 1831, Delacroix was imaginatively concerned with the relationship between the aural and the visual, something which was to intensify during his later friendship with Chopin. Delacroix loved Gluck's music and painted a number of subjects from his operas; and it was, coincidentally, Gluck's *Orpheus and Euridice* to which the Swedish director Per Lindberg gave a complex symbolic light score in a Gothenburg production of 1919. In the second act, for example, the presence of the Furies was signalled in red, and that of Orpheus in blue, so that there was 'a struggle between the blue and the red'. Delacroix's most influential critic, the poet Charles Baudelaire (1821–67), was the father-figure of French Symbolism, as E. T. A. Hoffmann was the grandfather-figure, and in his poem 'Correspondances' he set the agenda for late-nineteenth-century aesthetics by proposing synaesthetic links between perfumes, colours and sounds. In another poem, on the beacons of painting ('Les Phares'), Baudelaire characterized the work of Delacroix as 'a lake of blood, haunted by evil angels', and the composer to whom he compared this most Romantic of painters was another German: not the Neoclassical Gluck, but the Romantic Carl Maria von Weber (1786–1826).

The late nineteenth and early twentieth centuries saw a plethora of colour pianos [162] and organs lit by electricity, but

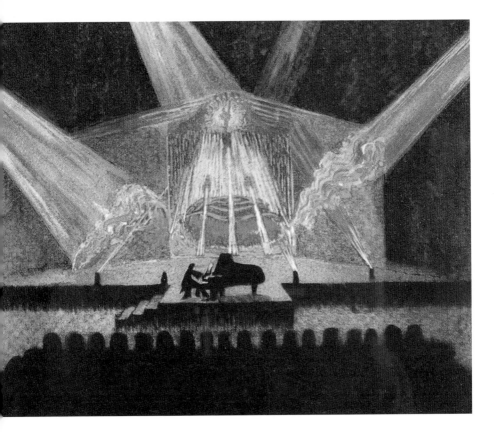

62. Alexander László, *Colour-Musical Performance* (after a watercolour by Matthias Holl), from A. László, *Colour-Light Music* (*Die Farblichtmusik*), 1925. László was probably the best known of the concert pianists touring Europe in the 1920s and 1930s who introduced a coloured light show into his performances. This was the heyday of colour music, which, after the Second World War, became almost the exclusive preserve of pop concerts. László used the system of Wilhelm Ostwald [78] – who was also much interested in colour music – to establish the correspondences between notes and colours, and he included Ostwald's eight-step grey scale. But his colour accompaniments were designed by the painter Matthias Holl.

technical problems and high cost meant that they never became popular as an art medium or developed a coherent aesthetic. After the Second World War the introduction of laser light, video and digital technology made these cumbersome early experiments quite obsolete. But, as the 1916 Italian *Futurist Cinema* manifesto, signed by Ginna and Corra as well as by the founding-father of Futurism, the writer Filippo Tommaso Marinetti, and the painter Giacomo Balla, proclaimed, 'the music of colours' would play a significant role in the development of film, which was destined to be the most important new medium of the modern era.

Colour in Film

As usual, it was the limitations of technology that inhibited the early introduction of colour into the cinema. Ginna and Corra hand-painted the filmstock for their first abstract productions, as had the very early feature-filmmaker Georges Meliès, whose fantasies such as *Voyage to the Moon* (1902) were to be much admired by the Surrealists. Arnold Schoenberg, too, hoped that a film of his opera *Die Glückliche Hand* (1910–13) would be hand-coloured by Kandinsky or, closer to home, by the Viennese stage designer Alfred Roller. This project was never realized. It was not until the 1930s that new methods of creating coloured filmstock – Dufaycolor and Gasparcolor in 1934; Kodachrome in 1935; Agfacolor in 1936 (although the Technicolor Motion Picture Corporation had been founded as early as 1915, and had already had some successes in the 1920s) – made moving pictures capable of being shot in colour, and in the early years the economics of filmmaking made colour the almost exclusive province of popular American musicals such as *The Wizard of Oz* (1939) or cartoons such as Walt Disney's *Fantasia* of the following year. *Fantasia* is remarkable for Disney's having engaged the Hungarian Constructivist and ex-Bauhaus teacher László Moholy-Nagy to design some abstract sequences, but these were cut from the released version.

In popular cinema, colour has never looked back, and in recent years even some old black-and-white films have been revamped with computer 'colorization' to give them a new lease of life. But ambitious art-film directors remained reluctant to abandon black and white. And if colour it must be, then not American colour. As Sergei Eisenstein, one of the few such directors to venture into colour at the end of his career after the Second World War, wrote in 1940 in *Notes of a Film Director*: 'The tasks of colour in the film are *not* what we see in the technically perfect American films.'

Eisenstein had a lifelong love of colour, and he wrote almost as much about it as his compatriot Kandinsky. He had been impressed with what he called the 'natural colouring' of some documentaries he had seen at Riga on the Baltic as early as 1910 or 1912. But his own use of colour film was beset with problems. A 1939 colour documentary on the building of a Soviet canal was mysteriously abandoned at the behest of the authorities on the first day of shooting. A film of the life of the poet Pushkin, which used colour in a much more thoroughgoing way, was never released because of its technical flaws. Eisenstein was not able to find an appropriate colour film before the Red Army brought back some looted Agfa filmstock from Germany in the Second World War. He used this new and chance resource in Part II of *Ivan the Terrible* (1946, released 1958), yet it was in one of his several commentaries on this film that he pinpointed the virtues of black and white: 'Traditional black, grey and white has the richest variety of textures, from the metallic gleam of the brocade, with its varying quality and style, through

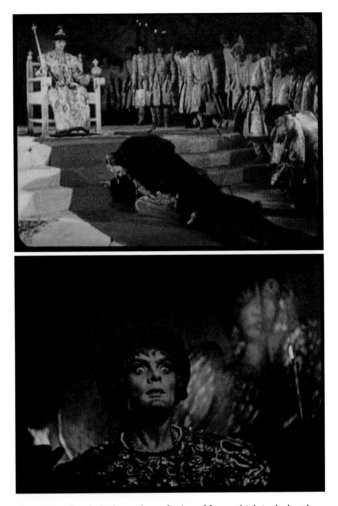

the material and cloth, to the soft play of furs, which includes the
whole range of shades, from sable and fox to wolf and bear; brown
when it is worn and white for carpets and bedcovers.' In Eisenstein's
experience of filmmaking, 'Colour was not an obedient servant ... it
was a terrible and savage tyrant who demanded so much light that
it damaged the actors' costumes and melted their make-up; it was
a scoundrel who wrung the heart of the colour idea dry; a
vulgarian who rode roughshod over perceptions of colour; an
idler who was unable to achieve even one per cent of the idea, the
fantasy, the flight of what had been imagined in colour.'

    In *Ivan the Terrible* colour was confined largely to red, black
and blue, and these were used in the interest of expression [163,
164]. During the dance scene:

At first all the colour themes are tied up in a knot. Then the red theme is gradually teased out, then the black, then the blue. What counts is that they are torn away from their original associations with an object. Suppose that the red theme begins with a red sleeve; it is repeated with the red background of candles; when Vladimir Andreyevich goes to his death, the theme is picked up by the red carpet.... You need to distance yourself from the various red objects, take their overall redness and combine the objects according to their common feature.... I wanted there to be red drops of blood in the black-and-white part, after the murder of Vladimir Andreyevich, but [the assistant director] would not have it, saying that it would be Formalism.

Formalism, which had been a major strand in the Russian aesthetics of literature since before the Revolution, had later been denounced as 'bourgeois' by the Soviet authorities. But it did play

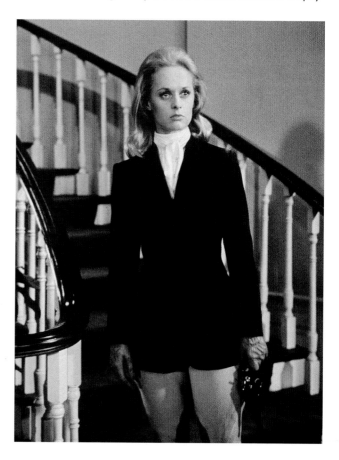

a role in some decisions taken during the filming of *Ivan the Terrible*. Eisenstein wanted to dress the tsar in black and gold, for example, a tradition that 'survived from black-and-white photography'. But the tonality was wrong, and he switched to red.

Even in Hollywood the famously imperious director Alfred Hitchcock (1899–1980) was unable to resist a star such as Grace Kelly's insistence that she wear a filmy nightgown – emblem of vulnerability – rather than red as she answers the fatal phone-call in *Dial M for Murder* (1954). Hitchcock, like Eisenstein, was certainly anxious to exploit the notional symbolic force of red: in *Marnie* (1964) red blood, red gladioli, hunting scarlet and red ink were the leitmotifs of the heroine's phobia; yet even here her hair, envisaged as red in one scene in the early treatment, became blonde in the final version [165]. Hitchcock, too, used washed-out colour for flashbacks, whereas black and white is often adopted by more recent directors – and the advertising industry.

Eisenstein felt that colour should perform a function very similar to the musical soundtrack – by Prokoviev in the case of *Ivan*: it was to be 'an exact replica' of the score, 'emotionally colouring the events'. He was aware of the theories of Wagner and the practice of Scriabin and had, in fact, directed a Bolshoi production of Wagner's *Die Walküre* in 1940 at exactly the same time as he was planning the detailed use of colour in film. In spite, again, of technical limitations, he felt that he had effectively combined the elements of Wagner's score with the changing play of coloured lights. In the finale of the Magic Fire, for example, he arranged that Wagner's leitmotif for the wizard Loge ran 'like a thread of blue through the purple of fire'.

For Eisenstein, for colour to become expressive, it had to become abstract, and this was far more problematic than in the case of music.

> The notion of 'orange colour' [must] be separated from the colouring of an orange, before colour becomes part of a system of consciously controlled means of expression and impression. Before we can learn to distinguish three oranges on a patch of grass both as three objects in the grass and as three orange patches against a green background, we dare not think of colour composition.
>
> Because unless we develop that ability, we cannot establish the colour-compositional connection between these oranges and two orange-coloured buoys floating on the surface of limpid greenish-blue water.

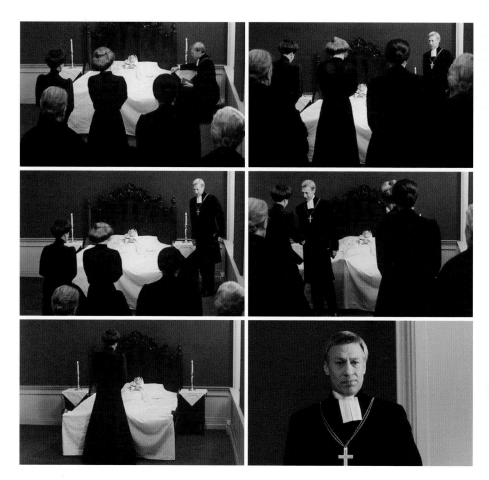

166. Ingmar Bergman, *The Mourners and Anders Ek at the Deathbed*, stills from *Cries and Whispers*, 1972.

Eisenstein's films were few, but he probably wrote more about them – and about colour – than any other director, and was one of the most influential film theorists of the first half of the twentieth century. Ingmar Bergman (b. 1918) is one later director whose approach to colour has a good deal in common with Eisenstein's, and he, too, had worked for many years in the theatre. Bergman's most significant production in colour was *Cries and Whispers* (1972), where, as he said, 'Everything is red', and in which every scene fades to red. 'All my films can be thought in black-and-white, except for *Cries and Whispers*', he wrote. 'In the screenplay I say that I have thought of the colour red as the interior of the soul. When I was a child I saw the soul as a shadowy dragon, blue as smoke, hovering like an enormous winged creature, half bird, half fish. But inside the dragon everything was red.'

Just as Eisenstein prepared every shot with many drawn
sketches, so Bergman and his cameraman Sven Nykvist tested
every aspect of the sets and costumes before shooting *Cries and*
Whispers, 'not only the make-up, the hair, the costumes, but every
object, wallcovering, the upholstery, every inch of carpeting.
Everything had been controlled down to the last detail.' And
where Eisenstein studied Russian icons and wall-paintings to
establish his colours, Bergman based his colour compositions in
Cries and Whispers on the deathbed scenes of Edvard Munch [166,
167]. Munch was himself designing for the theatre in the 1890s,
and in his half-dozen sickroom scenes of that period we sense
the dramatic tensions of a Strindberg or a Maeterlinck, where
characters often address the audience rather than each other.
We saw in Chapter 2 that Munch had no fixed view on colour
symbolism, and in these paintings the dominant colour may be
green as well as red; but in *Cries and Whispers* it is red that carries
most of the burden in establishing the intolerable claustrophobia
and bloody violence of the screenplay. Like Eisenstein, Bergman
treated red as the archetypal symbol of blood.

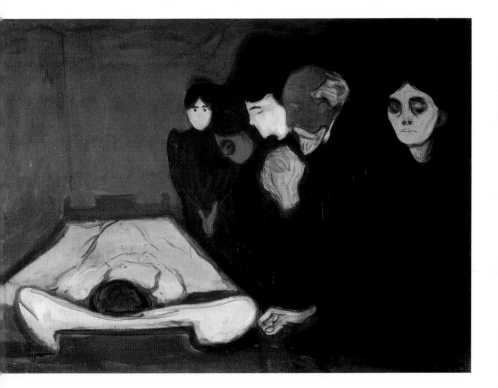

Not so Jean-Luc Godard (b. 1930), another highly innovative film colourist of the mid-century. In an interview about his film *Pierrot le fou* (1965), Godard contradicted an interviewer who had seen a good deal of blood in the film [168]. 'Not blood,' said Godard, 'red.' *Pierrot,* which, according to Godard had colour as one of its main attributes, and has something of the garishness of Pop Art, was his attempt to use colour, like Eisenstein, more abstractly. When Ferdinand (played by Jean-Paul Belmondo) in the last scene of the film blows himself up with sticks of dynamite coloured red, yellow and blue, it is the universal status of these three primaries, the source of all colours, that creates the meaning. Negation is comprehensive. Godard's style of direction could not be less like Eisenstein's and Bergman's. Although, like them, he worked like a painter, it was like an improvising painter of the 1960s rather than a painter with a traditional academic

168. **Jean-Luc Godard**, still from *Pierrot le fou*, 1965. Godard disclaimed any symbolic concerns in this garishly coloured film, but the coloured sticks of dynamite used in its violent ending suggest the annihilation also of the whole world of colour.

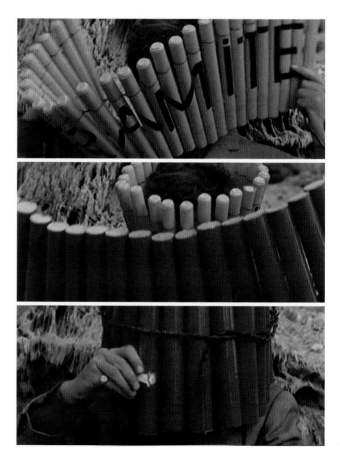

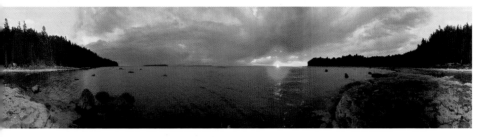

69. **Dan Sandin**, landscape environment from *CAVE*, 1991. The use of colour in the new developments of Virtual Reality is often highly abstract.

training: 'Most of it came out of my head just before it was shot. I worked without notes, like a painter. With Antonioni, the colour seems to be inside the camera. With me, it's simply what is in front of the camera.' But what is in front of the camera must be put there, and Godard's abstraction was far less casual than he suggests. Of the sequence in *Pierrot le fou* in a car, with reflections of lights in the windscreen flashing by – one of the most painterly scenes in the film – Godard said: 'When you drive in Paris at night, what do you see? Red, green, yellow lights. I wanted to show these elements but without necessarily placing them as they are in reality. Rather as they remain in the memory – splashes of red and green, flashes of yellow passing by. I wanted to recreate a sensation through the elements which constitute it.' The sensation was of pure colour.

Colour in film has continued to be used in varied and sensitive ways, but, like the musical score, in most cases it has hardly been noticed. Cinema-goers generally have other priorities. Outside the cinema, too, the colour element in multi-media works, with rare exceptions such as Terry Flaxton's *Colour Myths* (1991, distributed by London Video Arts), has hardly been primary. On the television screen, the modification of colour is at the finger-tips of the viewer, which makes the medium, I suppose, a part of community art. Freedom devalues. The intense and bizarre colours created by thermal-imaging cameras have brought abstraction and reality closer together, and the idea of the real has returned in Virtual Reality programmes that, as in Dan Sandin's *CAVE* [169], use colour in a neo-Expressionist way, but with the intention of giving the viewer a sense of 'being there'. Colour may be available, but it may not necessarily be taken up. Film theory was for many years fixated on black and white; and to help to understand why, I shall in my final chapter look at some ways in which, in many periods and many cultures, colour has been a troubling element of experience.

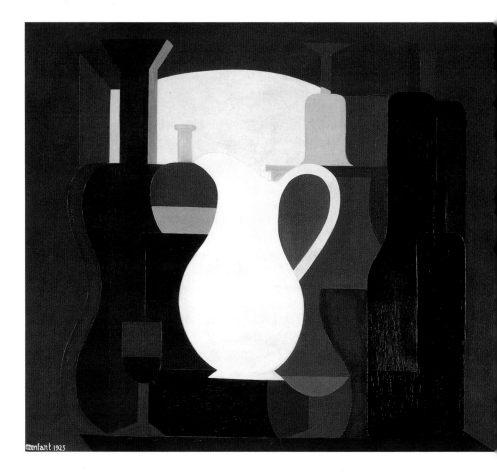

Chapter 8   Colour Trouble

The story told in this book so far has, for the most part, been
that of one of the most potent visual sources of delight, but I am
concluding it on a rather different, more sombre note. Just as the
artist and writer David Batchelor's essay *Chromophobia* (2000),
on the recurrent distrust of colour in European societies as purely
decorative, as oriental, as feminine, closed with a chapter on
'chromophilia', so this one must give some space to the disquiet
felt among many artists, Eastern and Western, that a love of
colour would take art into mere decoration, cosmetics and kitsch.
Batchelor's study began with the white cube of Modernist
architecture, and it was the propagandist of the white cube,
Le Corbusier, in his earlier incarnation as the painter Charles-
Édouard Jeanneret (1887–1965), who, together with his painter-
friend Amédeé Ozenfant (1886–1966) [170], framed in 1920 a
philosophy of Purist colour, which classified three scales.
The first was a major scale of black, white and the earth-yellows
and red, plus, rather surprisingly, ultramarine blue. This was
the constructive scale, which created volumes; and it had been
used, they maintained, by Michelangelo, Rembrandt, El Greco,
Delacroix and Renoir, who had all aimed at unified colour
compositions. The second scale was the dynamic scale: lemon
yellow, chrome and cadmium orange, vermilions, emerald green
and light cobalt blues, all used by 'local' colourists such as Raphael
and Ingres: 'They are the disturbing elements.' The last scale was
of the pure tinting colours: the madders and lakes, and Veronese
Green, none of which had any constructive function. Painting, said
Jeanneret and Ozenfant, echoing the Renaissance advocates of
disegno, could not do without colour, but 'Let us leave to the
clothes-dyers the sensory jubilations of the paint tube.' These
'sensory jubilations' were, as we have already seen, uppermost
in the mind of Arman in the 1960s, who made art works with
nothing more than tubes of coloured paint [98].

Yet, when Ozenfant turned to interior decoration in England
in the 1930s, he was happy to exploit the spatial effects of bright

171. **Amédée Ozenfant**, *Plan Diagram of Curtain Arrangements for Living Room/Colour Laboratory*, 1937, from *Architectural Review*, no. 81, January 1937. Ozenfant was, with C. E. Jeanneret (Le Corbusier), the founder of Purism, and his *Le Pot blanc* [170] exemplifies the simple flat planes and subdued desaturated colour of the Purist aesthetic. As an interior designer in England in the 1930s, this palette was abandoned in favour of the bright, clear colours of the decorative scale, disparaged earlier as without constructive power.

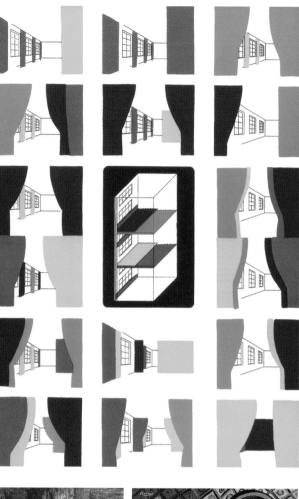

172. **Pablo Picasso**, *Ma Jolie*, 1911–12.

173. **Pablo Picasso**, *Girl before a Mirror (Marie-Thérèse)*, 1932. Picasso was one of many modern painters whose palette changed in phases, here from almost monochrome in the Analytical Cubist period to almost garish in the late 1920s and early 1930s.

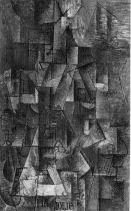

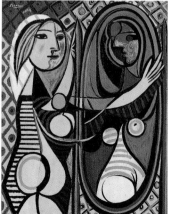

colours [171], basing his work on the chromatic system of Ostwald. He was one of many modern painters – Pablo Picasso (1881–1973) was another [172, 173] – who veered from a subdued chromatism to brilliantly varied palettes in the course of their careers. But the reverse movement, from bright colour to an ascetic achromatism, has been equally followed, and nowhere more so than in New York, where several of the colour painters of the 1950s turned in the following decades to black and white, grey and drab monochromes. Frank Stella made an ironic comment on Jasper Johns's working simultaneously with a chromatic and achromatic palette in his *Jasper's Dilemma* of 1962–63 [174, 175]; and one of the most poignant moments in the neurologist Oliver Sacks's story of the abstract painter Jonathan I., who continued to paint after an accident had destroyed his colour vision, was when his new black-and-white paintings, stimulated by his accident, proved highly successful in New York, where they were greeted simply as a new phase in his work.

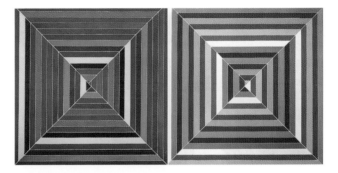

174. Frank Stella, *Jasper's Dilemma*, 1962–63.

175. Jasper Johns, *Gray Numbers*, 1958. Johns's series of inert grey paintings provoked Stella's gentle satire.

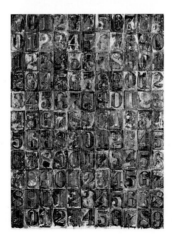

Jonathan I.'s transformed vision was at first a source of great anxiety to him, but it is well known that congenital colour blindness is so small a functional disability that it often goes unnoticed; and black-and-white prints and photographs have, of course, long been seen as adequate representations of the world, and even of paintings. This might be regarded simply as an example of the way in which cognition is more actively engaged by contour and contrasts of value than by colour, a view that, in the Renaissance, lay behind the appeal to *disegno,* in the interest of imitating both nature and the art of antiquity. In seventeenth-century Rome landscape painters were using the black mirror that came to be known as the Claude Glass (although it does not seem to have been used by Claude himself), which edited colours out of the scene reflected in it, and allowed painters – largely northern artists – to concentrate on relationships of tone. It was in the north of Europe, too, at this time, that etching developed, especially in the hands of Rembrandt, into a largely chiaroscuro technique, and the newly invented technique of mezzotint brought a new concept of monochromatic 'colour' into printmaking. But anti-colourism involved far more than that, and it was in ancient Rome that the moral idea of colouristic restraint was first clearly articulated. The elder Pliny complained in a familiar Roman vein that:

> *Four colours only [white, black, red, yellow] … were used by Apelles, Aetion, Melanthius and Nikomachus in their immortal works; illustrious artists, a single one of whose pictures the wealth of a city would hardly suffice to buy, while now that even purple clothes our walls, and India contributes the ooze of her rivers and the blood of dragons and elephants, no famous picture is painted. We must believe that when the painters' equipment was less complete, the results were in every respect better, for … we are alive only to the worth of the materials and not to the genius of the artist.*
> (*Natural History*, XXXII, 50)

Pliny apparently knew nothing of the Greek painting five centuries before his time (he was writing from Greek literary sources), and we know little more; but Greek classicism survived into the modern period in the form of marble sculptures, whose very colourlessness – for the paint had usually worn off – was taken as a guarantee of their ideal beauty. That white marble (and 'white' skin) was most beautiful because it reflected most light was one of the key aesthetic concepts of the eighteenth-century historian of Greek art J. J. Winckelmann, whose most famous phrase, 'noble simplicity and quiet grandeur', was quoted by the most

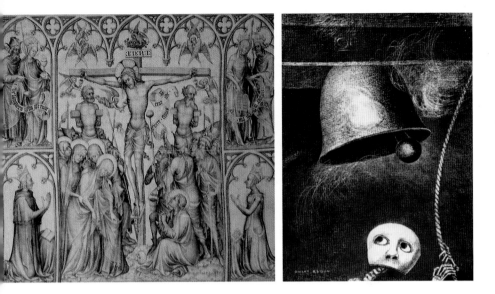

176. *The Parement de Narbonne* (detail), *c.* 1375. The greatest of the few surviving Lenten altar-covers, used to represent the sombre Passion story in terms of grey monochrome.

177. **Odilon Redon**, *A Mask Tolling the Hour of Death*, 1882.

radical of modern classicizing painters, Ad Reinhardt. But Reinhardt, as we shall see, also made a particular virtue of black.

Pliny's moral stance set the tone for many complaints about colour in the European art of the following millennia. In the late Middle Ages in northern Europe many coloured altarpieces were closed during Lent, to display their modestly monochromatic outer wings, often painted in imitation of unpainted sculpture, and altars were covered with *grisaille* paintings such as the *Parement de Narbonne* [176]. Similarly, the French Symbolist Odilon Redon (1840–1916) wrote during his period of mastery as a black-and-white artist, before his work burst into a blaze of colours: 'One must respect black. Nothing prostitutes it. It does not please the eye or awaken another sense. It is the agent of the mind even more than the beautiful colour of the palette or prism.' Here the illustrator of Edgar Allan Poe and the great exponent of visual mystery [177] was making a plea for rationalism against the unruly consequences of the then so fashionable synaesthesia. But it would not be long before the most intellectually engaged painters, such as Kupka or Delaunay, would be deploying the entire resources of the prismatic spectrum [30, 32, 34].

One of the many paradoxes in attitudes to colour among modern Western artists lies in their widespread enthusiasm for oriental thought. The rich and subtle colouring of Middle Eastern and Asian textiles has invariably been prized in the West, and they brought a new and vibrant colourism into the work of many

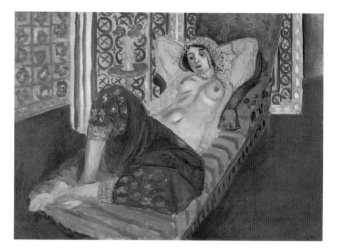

178. **Henri Matisse**, *Odalisque with Red Culottes*, 1921. Matisse often used his fascination with oriental fabrics and designs (he visited Morocco in 1912–13) as a vehicle for his lavish colour.

179. bottom left **Utagawa Hiroshige**, *The Plum Tree Teahouse at Kameido*, 1857.

180. bottom right **Vincent van Gogh**, *Japonaiserie: Plum Tree in Blossom (after Hiroshige)*, 1887. Van Gogh's 'copies' of Japanese woodblock prints, of which he had a significant collection, stopped short of imitating their subtle colouring.

nineteenth- and twentieth-century painters, such as Ingres, Delacroix and Matisse [178]. At the same time, Japanese coloured woodcuts by artists such as Hokusai (1760–1849) and Hiroshige (1797–1858) were much collected in Europe, and often imitated, although, at least in the case of van Gogh's 'copies', their delicate colouring was revised in the direction of more strident Western complementary contrasts [179, 180]. Yet it was for his greys that the hedonist James Abbott McNeill Whistler (1834–1903) [181] attracted the notice of the great nineteenth-century oriental scholar Ernest Fenellosa:

He, the first of occidentals, has explored the infinite range of tones that lie wrapped around the central core of grays. His grays themselves pulsate with imprisoned colors. Years ago I said of the

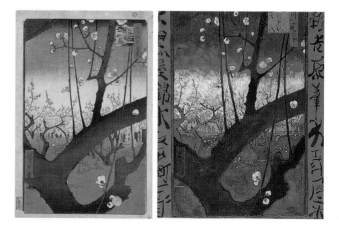

old Chinese school of colouring, that it conceived of color as a flower growing out of a soil of grays. But in European art I have seen this thought exemplified only in the work of Whistler.

Particularly among American painters since the 1940s, oriental thought has connoted asceticism, renunciation, emptiness, in colour as well as form. Such asceticism has indeed formed a major strand in oriental aesthetics: the Taoist Lao Tzu warned in the *Tao Teh Ching* (c. 300 BC): 'The five colours blind the eye. The five tones deafen the ear. The five flavours cloy the palate. Racing and hunting madden the mind. Rare goods tempt men to do wrong.' The five traditional colours in China were the scale of black, white, yellow, red and green, of which yellow – the most important, central, royal colour, representing the element of earth – could harmonize all the others. But in the modern, post-imperial Chinese world, yellow has lost its aura: it is now usually the colour – for safety reasons – of industrial machinery, and its traditional name, *huang*, has fallen out of use.

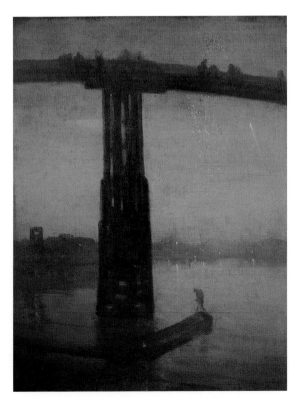

181. **James Abbott McNeill Whistler**, Nocturne: Blue and Gold - Old Battersea Bridge, c. 1872–75. Whistler was one of the earliest painters to be famous for his handling of grey.

182. **Ad Reinhardt**, *Abstract Painting No. 5, 1962*, 1962. Reinhardt's black paintings, with their barely perceptible transitions from area to area, owe much to his reading of ancient Chinese philosophy.

Negative Colour

American Modernist artists, from the black-and-white photographer Alfred Stieglitz in 1929 to the immigrant Josef Albers in 1950 and Ad Reinhardt in the 1960s, similarly arrived at aesthetic statements through negation. As Reinhardt (1913–1967), the most vocal and most radical of them, wrote in 1962: 'The only and one way to say what abstract art or art-as-art is, is to say what it is not.' He often quoted Lao Tzu on colour, and in his best-known manifesto, *Twelve Rules for a New Academy* (1957), Rule 6 was: 'No colors. "Color blinds." "Colors are an aspect of appearance, so only of the surface." Colors are barbaric, unstable, suggest life, "cannot be completely controlled" and "should be concealed." Colors are a "distracting embellishment."'

Reinhardt had been a brilliant colourist in the 1930s and 1940s. He had also painted a number of white monochromes, but white, too, was now to be outlawed as 'a color and all colors', 'antiseptic and not artistic, appropriate and pleasing for kitchen fixtures, and hardly the medium for expressing truth and beauty'. From this date until the end of his life Reinhardt made exclusively black paintings. He had long been interested in close tones, but here the tones are so close as to be barely distinguishable. As Lao Tzu had written: 'Even if we try to see the Way, it cannot be seen. In this respect it may be described as "dim and figureless" …

utterly vague, utterly indistinct, and yet there is something there.' Although they are of a subtlety that is impossible to reproduce, I illustrate here an *Abstract Painting* [182] that can be seen in a public collection. Reinhardt pointed to the morality of his decision to confine himself to blacks in a panel discussion of 1960: 'Someone once asked me about color and I used the occasion to mention a number of times and places in art where color was excluded – Chinese monochrome painting, analytic cubism, Picasso's *Guernica*, etc. There is something wrong, irresponsible and mindless about color, something impossible to control. Control and rationality are part of my morality.'

Even Reinhardt's *Black Paintings* are not strictly monochromatic since, like Malevich's *White on White* series [183], they deploy hard-edged areas of slightly modulated colour which our linguistic habits would have to class as 'off-black', or even 'grey'. But the interior rectangles have to be searched out, and it is this protracted, meditative searching that gives meaning to the works.

Gerhard Richter, that protean figure, who followed Jasper Johns's grey paintings of the 1950s with his own grey series some twenty years later [185], has given a more secular version of the attractions of emptiness. '[Grey] makes no statement whatever', he wrote in 1975, 'it evokes neither feelings nor associations; it is really neither visible nor invisible. Its inconspicuousness gives it

184. **Kazimir Malevich**, paintings
displayed at the 'Last Futurist
Exhibition, 0.10 (Zero Ten)',
Petrograd, December 1915.
Malevich placed his *Black Square*
high across the corner of the
room, a position traditionally
reserved for the most important
icon in the house. The black
square thus became again the
spiritual symbol of the infinite it
had been for the 17th-century
alchemist Fludd.

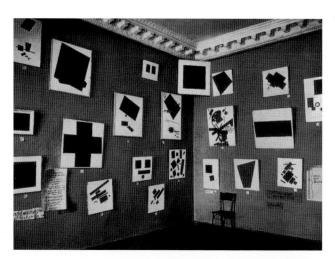

185. **Gerhard Richter**, *Cell*
(*Zelle*), 1988. Richter chose grey
as a colour of total indifference.

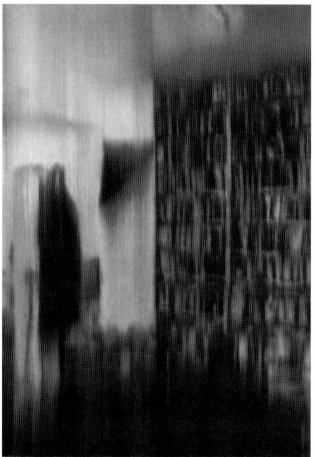

86. **Robert Fludd**, *Et sic in
finitum,* from *Utriusque cosmi
maioris I: de macrocosmi historia,*
617.

87. **Antoni Tàpies**, *Flud*, 1988.

the capacity to mediate, to make visible in a positively illusionistic way, like a photograph. To me, grey is the welcome and only possible equivalent for indifference, non-commitment, absence of opinion, absence of shape.'

There has been a strong tradition of monochromatic painting in the twentieth century, from Malevich's *Black Square* [184], Aleksandr Rodchenko's suite of three 'primary' rectangles (1921, Moscow, Rodchenko Archive) and Yves Klein's various monochromes, not confined to blue, to Ellsworth Kelly's spectral series [1] and the single canvases of Robert Ryman, Gerhard Merz and Joseph Marioni [189]. The ancestry of these monochromatic rectangles would include the alchemist Robert Fludd's image of infinity in his treatise *Utriusque cosmi maioris* of 1617 [186], an image that has been quoted directly, and on a vast scale, by the Spanish painter Antoni Tàpies (b. 1923) [187].

But in its most radical form, the blank canvas, the monochrome also has its roots in oriental aesthetics. A master of the Japanese tea-ceremony in the sixteenth-century Tokugawa Period, Yoken Fujimura, is credited with introducing the 'white paper inscription' (*haku-shi-san*), in which a text at the top interprets a picture of which there is no sign on the blank sheet. This is clearly the source of a work by the American artist John Baldassari, a blank canvas exhibited in 1966 with its text: 'Everything is purged from this painting but art.' As another Japanese painter, Ike-no Taija, put it in the eighteenth century: 'Drawing a white space where absolutely nothing is drawn – that is the most difficult thing to accomplish in painting.'

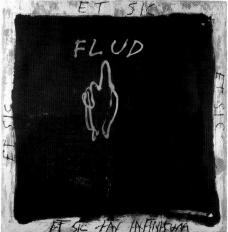

207

It might well be thought that monochromes are the final homage to individual, irreducible, independent colour, but they depend more than any other colour-paintings on the environment and the ambient lighting. Robert Ryman has stated that he takes account of the walls on which his white paintings hang; and the French painter Claude Rutault takes this notion to its logical conclusion, and paints the wall itself, according to the character of his monochrome. Joseph Marioni (b. 1943) [188] has observed: 'As the light source changes the color shifts. The perceptual context of a painting is the atmosphere of the environment in which it hangs ... the painting is not just an expression of color alone but rather the painted quality of color within its gestalt as an object.'

These considerations tend to qualify the independence of the monochrome as a painting, and to bring it closer to installation works, such as James Turrell's large monochromatic light pieces of the 1970s and 1980s [52], which require a radical adaptation of the eye on the part of the spectator, and hence must be shown in total darkness.

The aesthetic impact of a dim yet colour-filled environment was also a feature of the Japanese tea-house, perhaps the paradigm of the wilfully restrained environment. The Japanese writer Junichiro Tawizaki recalled in the 1950s 'an unforgettable vision of darkness' he had experienced in an old Kyoto tea-house:

It was a wide room ... and the darkness, broken only by a few candles, was of a richness quite different from the darkness of a small room.... On the far side of the screen [behind the candle], at

188. **Joseph Marioni**, *Red Painting No. 5*, 1996.

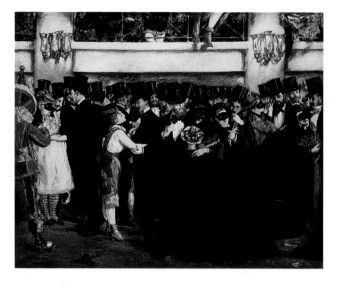

39. **Édouard Manet**, *Masked Ball at the Opera*, 1873–74. Baudelaire's comment in the 1840s that the French male was in a perpetual state of mourning had, by the 1860s, been transformed into a celebration. Manet shows vividly how the universal black evening dress could counterpoint the bright costumes of the dancers.

the edge of the little circle of light, the darkness seemed to fall from the ceiling, lofty, intense, of a color, the fragile light of the candle unable to pierce its thickness, turned back as from a black wall.... It was a repletion, a fullness of tiny particles like fine ashes, each particle luminous as a rainbow.

Here in the darkness was the voluptuousness of an all-but-colourless world.

For all Ad Reinhardt's active engagement in left-wing politics in the 1930s and 1940s, he was an elitist, campaigning long against popular art and the notion that it was open to anyone to be an artist. He was always anxious to detach art from life. The radical colouristic restraint that characterizes his work had always had connotations of exclusivity, and nowhere more so than in the matter of dress. In Renaissance Europe restraint in dress, and the widespread sumptuary laws that sought to enforce it, was largely an index of nobility, for it was directed against the lavish display thought to be the mark of the *nouveaux-riches* and crippling to the public economy in the days before rampant consumerism. We are at the beginning of the gentlemanly fashion for black and grey, so brilliantly represented by Velázquez and Frans Hals, by Whistler and Manet [189]: what Baudelaire celebrated as early as 1846 as a symbol of 'the heroism of modern life', 'the necessary garb of our suffering age, which uses the symbol of a perpetual mourning even upon its thin black shoulders ... Great colourists know how to create colour with a black coat, a white cravat and a grey

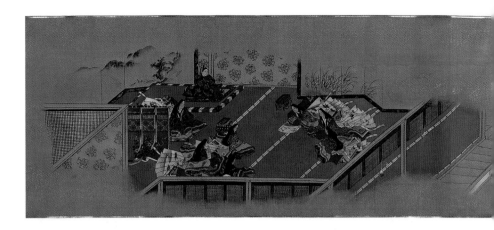

190. **Kano Ryusetsu Hidenoku**, *Tale of Genji*, chapter 35, 17th–18th century. Lady Murasaki's celebrated *Tale of Genji* continued to be illustrated in Japan for many centuries. This image of the imperial court at Kyoto gives a sense of how court dress was a type of uniform, highly regulated as to form and colour.

191. **Mary Cassatt**, *Young Girl at a Window*, 1883. The white summer dresses fashionable in France in the 1870s and 1880s proved an ideal vehicle for the display of coloured shadows and reflections in Impressionist painting.

background'. But social hierarchies of colour were by no means confined to Europe. In the Heian period in Japan (eighth–twelfth centuries AD), where the most subtly coloured silks were prized at the imperial court in Kyoto, the courtier and diarist Lady Murasaki (the Japanese word for 'purple'), author of the classic *Tale of Genji* [190], kept a watchful eye on who was wearing which colour at what time; and in several passages of her diary she alludes to the colours forbidden to the lower ranks of the court ladies – yellows, greens, reds and purple – and notes that these ladies:

> dressed simply in beautiful robes of three or four layers, mantles of figured silk and plain jackets; some had robes decorated with damask and gauze ... Their trains and jackets had, of course, been embroidered. The jackets had decorated cuffs; the silver thread stitched down the seams of the trains had been made to look like braid; and silver foil had been inlaid into the figured patterns on the fans. You felt as if you were gazing at mountains deep in snow in clear moonlight. It was so bright, indeed, that you could hardly distinguish anything, as if the room had been hung with mirrors.

We are reminded vividly of the female equivalents of the nineteenth-century men in black – the dazzling women in white of Impressionist France, of a Renoir, a Berthe Morisot or a Mary Cassatt [191].

The traditional layering of subtly coloured fabrics has survived in the more strident culture of modern Japan in the form of art. In the 1950s the clothes-artist Atsuko Tanaka (b. 1932) devised a performance entitled *Stage Clothes*, in which she removed layers of brightly coloured dresses, each layer contrasting with the

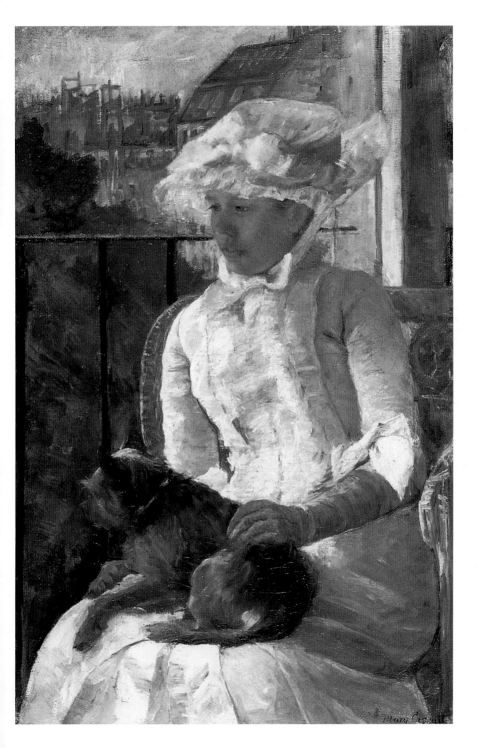

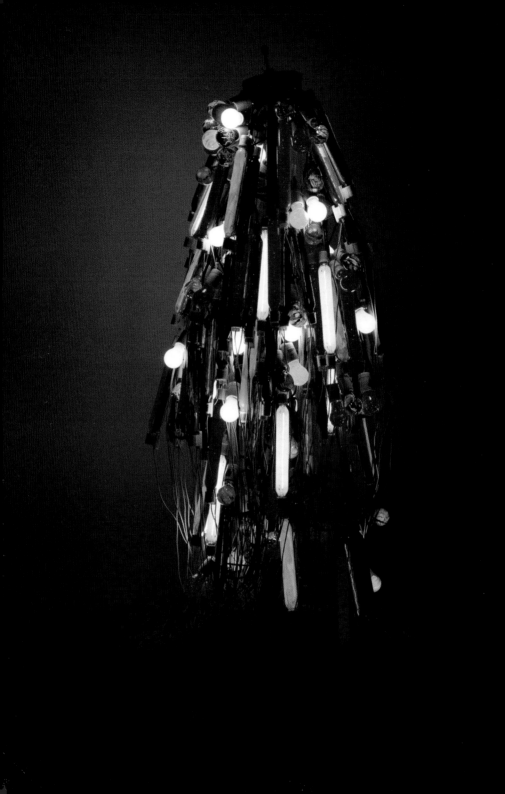

192. **Atsuko Tanaka**, *Electric Dress*, 1956 (reconstructed 1986). Tanaka brought modern techniques to bear on the traditional Japanese fashion for translucent layered dresses, creating many indefinable and changing effects of colour.

previous one, until she finally appeared in a black leotard. Tanaka at this time also created an 'Electric Dress', constructed out of layers of white and multi-coloured electric bulbs [192]. An interesting sidelight on these recent changes in Japanese colour sensibilities is thrown by the modern Japanese colour vocabulary, where loan words derived from English sit side by side with older Japanese terms, and in some cases are more frequently used than their native equivalents. But the imported terms are generally thought to indicate brighter versions of the same hues than the native terms: the focus of 'purple', for example, the traditional term for which, as we saw, is *murasaki*, is located several steps lower on the scale of lightness, and covers a wider range of nuances, than *paapuru*, the Japanese version of the English word. Here is another indication of the crucial interaction of language and perception, and variations in loan words offer a rich field for the investigation of colour sensibilities that, as yet, has hardly been exploited.

Social Contexts for Aboriginal Colour

Dress codes, like most hierarchical codes, have now largely lost their force throughout most of Western society, except among teenagers and in some nostalgic environments such as clubs and smart restaurants.

Although the almost complete absence of a clear colour iconography meant that drapery was one of the most freely improvised and abstract elements in European figurative art before the twentieth century, it is clear from the sumptuary laws and dress codes that colour could indeed be subject to severe social pressures. Nowhere are these pressures clearer in contemporary art than in Aboriginal Australia, where, as we saw, the rise of the painting movements in the late twentieth century has led to a radical revaluation of the role of colour. Until the attempts of the European invaders in the nineteenth century to assimilate indigenous Australians into Christianity and white cultural practices, the very active visual culture of the Aborigines largely took the form of rock-painting in sacred sites, body-painting, ground-painting and sculpture in connection with ceremonial dancing and, in the rainy tropical north, the painting of bark shelters and hollow log coffins. The colours generally available were natural ochres, pipeclay and charcoal; and since every element of the natural world played a part in the many creation myths peculiar to each tribal grouping, these colouring materials had, as we saw, a far from purely visual significance. This has led students of Aboriginal art and ceremonial to believe that the 'authentic' Aboriginal palette must be confined to the four 'natural' colours, black, white, red and yellow; and this palette and these pigments have been for the most part retained by the bark-painters of the north, who now, however, work almost exclusively for a non-Aboriginal public [121]. The situation is strikingly similar to that in ancient Rome, as described by Pliny in his account of Apelles and his contemporaries. Even in central Australia, where the painting movement that began at Papunya in the 1960s introduced the European media of composition board, canvas and multi-coloured synthetic paints, there have been attempts by white art advisors, whose presence has been crucial to the economics of Aboriginal art, to restrict the available colours to the traditional four. The most striking instance of this restriction is the 1988 *Barunga Statement* [193], where the unity of northern and central tribes in the Northern Territory is expressed in the *lingua franca* of these four colours, even though the several designs are peculiar to each region.

Yet there is good reason to believe that indigenous artists were and are eager to use any colours available to them, including blues and greens. Even in Arnhem Land in the north-east, where ceremonial accessories had always included plumage of many colours, artists in the 1940s showed a great flair for deploying all the many coloured crayons supplied to them by ethnographers gathering visual information about Dreaming stories [194]. There is no need to emphasize the fact that the acrylic painters of central and western Australia have, from the 1960s until the present, been quite without inhibitions in their use of a brilliant

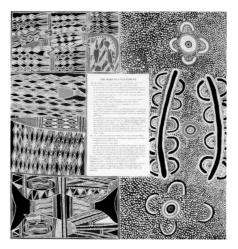

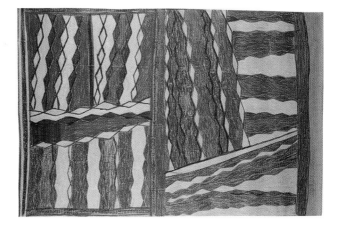

94. Munggaraui, *Flame Dreaming,* 1947. In the 1930s Munggaraui, head of the Gumatj clan in north-east Arnhem Land, was one of the first commercial bark painters, using traditional ochres [121]; but when the anthropologists Ronald and Catherine Berndt collected clan designs a decade later, on the basis of coloured crayon drawings, he was happy to use a full range of colours.

and wide-ranging palette [119, 120]. The Aboriginal art of central Australia found a ready market in the West because the ground had been prepared by Abstract Expressionism in the 1960s. Yet there are few links with American-influenced art in the paintings produced in remote outback communities, and even the wide range of bright colours is habitually designated 'traditional' by the artists themselves. This is crucial to the function of works which, from the point of view of the painters, are not simply their access to the money economy, but are designed to introduce Aboriginal culture to a wider world. With their emphasis on land both in iconography and in tonality, they are the keystones of indigenous politics. We saw in Chapter 5 that this apparent paradox may be resolved by considering Aboriginal colour vocabularies, which, as in many other languages in the world, including early European languages, invariably subsume blues under 'black' and greens under 'yellow', or, rather, use the same term to cover both.

The reasons for avoiding colour have thus been as various, and as inflected by social and political ideologies, as the reasons for using it abundantly. As I have attempted to demonstrate in this book, colour in art is no less a cultural phenomenon than in any other branch of human activity. Even in physics and chemistry, where the causes and materials of colour were always available, it has a history, because what we understand as 'colour' is essentially psychological, and human consciousness is a historical development. All colour practices have their specific contexts and their specific rationale, so that colour must be at last not simply a branch – and a minor one – of formal analysis, but must be fully integrated into the history of art.

Glossary

ADDITIVE MIXTURE
Adding one coloured light to another until white light is achieved. The 'primary colours' in additive mixture are red, blue and green, but since yellow is, additively, a mixture of red and green, blue and yellow lights will also suffice to mix white.

COMPLEMENTARITY
Two colours are regarded as complementary when their mixture adds up to white or near-white. They are the colours usually placed opposite each other on the colour circle.

CONSTRUCTIVISM, NEO-CONSTRUCTIVISM
An art movement originating largely in post-Revolutionary Russia, which regarded the art work not as representing something else, but as existing in its own right and functioning according to its own laws, sometimes mathematical laws. Neo-Constructivism, which paid more attention to colour than the original movement, was particularly active in Poland and Switzerland.

DADA
One of the earliest anti-art movements, started in neutral Zurich during the First World War. Drawing some of its ideas from Italian FUTURISM, Dada (the French word for 'hobby-horse') fostered performance and interactive art, as well as giving art status to utilitarian objects such as a urinal and a shovel. Paradoxically, for an anti-art movement, Dada has been one of the most influential movements of twentieth-century art, stimulating aspects of Pop Art and its twenty-first-century offshoots, and even the Op Art of the 1960s.

DIORAMA
A popular visual entertainment developed in Paris in the 1820s. It presented exotic scenes and topical events (usually disasters) in a quasi-theatrical space, but by means of painted transparencies, which allowed the lighting of the same scene to change. The term is now often used for contextual displays in natural history museums.

EXPRESSIONISM
An anti-naturalistic art movement of the early twentieth century, based largely in Germany, but much influenced by van Gogh and Munch. Coarse forms and violent colour are two of the hallmarks of Expressionism, and the wide interests of Expressionists, in child art, in non-European art, in medieval art and in folk-art are well illustrated in *The Blue Rider Almanac* of 1912.

FAUVISM
An early twentieth-century French movement related stylistically to EXPRESSIONISM, particularly in its bright colour and broad brushwork. An exhibition of a group of artists' work, notably that of Matisse, in 1905 led critics to brand them as '*fauves*' (the French for 'wild beasts').

FORMALISM
Originally an early twentieth-century Russian literary theory stressing the self-referentiality and artificiality of language, and directing attention especially to phonetics rather than sense. Later it was taken over into visual aesthetics, and related to CONSTRUCTIVISM. Most abstraction rests on some variety of formalism, and in painting it had its final fling in the New York of the 1950s and 1960s.

FUTURISM
An Italian movement, but begun in Paris in 1909, and proclaiming through many published manifestos as well as lecture-performances throughout Europe, the virtues of modernity and the bankruptcy of traditional art-culture, especially in Italy. Members of the group particularly interested in colour were Giacomo Balla (1871–1958), who wrote the only manifesto on the subject, Gino Severini (1885–1966), and Fortunato Depero (1892–1960).

GESAMTKUNSTWERK
(total art work)
Multi-media art has always existed, but with the German opera-composer Richard Wagner (1813–1883) in the mid-nineteenth century, the idea that all these media – poetry, music, décor and costumes, movement (dance) and even (briefly) perfume – should be totally integrated, became a major and very influential aesthetic aspiration. However, it has remained largely at the level of theory.

HOLOGRAM
The possibility of generating light of a single wavelength (laser light) in the 1940s led to the realization that, if a beam of light reflected from a three-dimensional object (the object beam) hit another beam of the same frequency playing over a plate bearing light-sensitive emulsion (the reference beam), the slight differences in the time for the wave-fronts of light from each plane of the object to reach the reference beam, would create variable interferences there, which the emulsion would record. The emulsion, developed like a photograph, will re-create the original three-dimensional object if lit by light of the same frequency and at the same angle as the original registration. The flat plate will show deep space, sometimes with the image in front of the plate, but always in monochrome. In the 1960s a new type of hologram, coloured and viewable in ordinary white light, but with a much shallower space, was developed, and this is the type now familiar on credit cards and other security devices.

HUE
That aspect of colour which depends on wavelength, and distinguishes blue from green, yellow from orange, and so on.

LIGHTNESS (BRIGHTNESS)
The proportion of light reflected from any HUE. Some, notably yellow, are intrinsically higher up the scale of lightness; others, notably blue, are lower down. Any hue can be made lighter or darker by mixture, but this results in a loss of SATURATION.

OPTICAL MIXTURE
If the eye cannot resolve the identities of small patches of closely juxtaposed contrasting colours, scanned at a certain distance; or if sensations of different colours move rapidly across the field of vision, optical mixing is the result. Since optical mixtures are due to reflection from surface colours, they are not as luminous as the ADDITIVE MIXTURES of lights, but they are more so than palette mixtures where a large percentage of the incident light is absorbed. Optical mixtures were thus of particular interest to the early Neo-Impressionists, for whom the rendering of light was a high priority.

PANORAMA
A large, usually circular painting of a townscape or exotic scenery or, often, a battle, designed to give the spectator the illusion of being there. The panorama existed in the form of painted rooms in the earlier eighteenth century, but the first independent Panoramas were made in Edinburgh in the 1780s and soon spread to many other European and American centres, often housed in purpose-built round buildings. Panorama painting was seen as a branch of topography, and was thus disparaged by imaginative painters, for whom illusion was far below art.

POSITIVISM
The ideological position dominant in Europe in the nineteenth century, which held that only the empirically verifiable was 'real'. It was a position much influenced by science and technology.

PRIMARY COLOURS
The smallest number of colours considered necessary to mix the whole range of perceivable colours, or, in the case of coloured lights, to mix white light. In the SUBTRACTIVE MIXTURE of paints, the primary colours are considered to be red, yellow and blue; but in mixing lights, it

was found in the mid-nineteenth century that any two colours sufficiently far apart in the spectrum could mix to white. Nevertheless the ideal ADDITIVE primaries are found to be red, green and blue.

SATURATION
The maximum purity of a HUE, without any admixture of white or black.

SIMULTANEOUS CONTRAST
When two large juxtaposed patches of contrasting colours are looked at for some time, their contrasts seem to be heightened at their junction. This is particularly marked with black and white and with complementary colours, where the complementary after-image of each patch forms a sort of halo along the junction, intensifying each of the pair.

SUBTRACTIVE MIXTURE
The more colours are added to a pigment mixture the more wavelengths of light are absorbed in the mixture, and the fewer reflected to the eye. Hence pigment mixtures get darker, while ADDITIVE MIXTURES of lights get lighter.

SURREALISM
A French literary and art movement developing in the 1920s under the influence of Freudian psychoanalysis and highlighting the activity of the unconscious. In visual art Surrealism's two main strands were automatism and the development of random techniques, the ancestors of American Abstract Expressionism (many European Surrealists were in New York during the Second World War); and the highly detailed representation of dreams. The automatists showed little interest in colour, although they developed a number of original techniques; but the dream-painters suggested universally that we dream in colour.

SYMBOLISM
Symbolizing is a universal human phenomenon (although the connotations of particular symbols vary from culture to

culture and even from individual to individual), but it became a particular aesthetic creed in the late nineteenth century, particularly in France. Symbols always convey more than they show; and it is usually only those spectators who are in the know who are able to penetrate far below the surface.

THEOSOPHY
A spiritualist movement founded in New York in the 1870s, with its roots in the distant, usually non-European past, but also anxious to incorporate some aspects of modern science. The Theosophical Society is notable for using visual indications of spiritual states, and for making these available to a general public. These visual manifestations of spirituality, published in a number of well-illustrated books after 1900, were of great interest to early abstract artists in search of ways to give a profound content to abstract signs.

Bibliography

INTRODUCTION
Many of the themes in this book have received a more extended treatment in my earlier studies, *Colour and Culture: Practice and Meaning from Antiquity to Abstraction* (1993) and *Colour and Meaning: Art, Science and Symbolism* (1999). For a short, but wide-ranging and up-to-date overview by a chemist, H. Zollinger, *Color: A Multidisciplinary Approach*, 1999. The colour-interests of more recent artists have been reviewed in two exhibition catalogues: H. C. Cousseau (ed.), *Colour Since Matisse: French Painting in the 20th Century*, 1985 (with an important essay by Georges Roque); and J. Alison (ed.), *Colour after Klein: Re-Thinking Colour in Modern and Contemporary Art*, 2005. Blue has attracted a lot of attention in recent years, with mammoth exhibitions in Heidelberg: 'Blau: Farbe der Ferne' (1990), and Marseilles, 'Sublime Indigo' (1987) and a smaller one at the

New Art Gallery, Walsall: 'Blue, Borrowed and New' (2000). All have catalogues with important essays and are well illustrated. Blue has also been the subject of a monograph: M. Pastoureau, *Blue: The History of a Color*, 2000. Red was the subject of the exhibition, 'Seeing Red', New York, 2004 (catalogue ed. by M. Fehr) Collections of international conference-papers often include items in English: K. Blomstroem (ed.), *Fargen mellom Kunst og Vitenskap/ Colour between Art and Science*, 1998 (all papers in Norwegian and English); E. Alliez and E. von Samsonow (eds), *Chroma Drama: Widerstand der Farbe*, Vienna, 2001 (some articles in English).

CHAPTER 1
Ancient ideas on colour have been gathered in J. J. Pollitt, *The Ancient View of Greek Art* (1974), and Ancient practices have been studied by V. J. Bruno in *Form and Color in Greek Painting* (1977), as well as by myself in *Colour and Culture*, Chapters 1 and 2. The best edition of the Peripatetic *On Colours*, is now M. F. Ferrini (ed.), *I Colori*, 1999 (Greek text and Italian translation, with extensive commentary).

For medieval mosaic and stained glass, see *Colour and Culture*, chapters 3 and 4. I have also looked at medieval and Renaissance prismatic experiments in *Colour and Meaning*, chapter 8.

Barnett Newman's remarks on the primaries are in J. P. O'Neill (ed.), *Barnett Newman: Selected Writings and Interviews*, 1990. For Richter, see H.-U. Obrist (ed.), *Gerhard Richter: The Daily Practice of Painting: Writings and Interviews 1962–1993*, 1995; and for Kelly, see Y.-A. Bois, J. Cowart, A. Pacquement, *Ellsworth Kelly: The Years in France, 1948–1954*, 1992.

Kupka's colour has been studied by V. Spate, *Orphism: The Evolution of Non-Figurative Painting in Paris, 1910-1914*, 1979; see also M. Rowell in the Guggenheim Museum's *Frantisek Kupka: A Retrospective*, 1975.

Mondrian's comments on Vantongerloo are in H. Holtzman and M. James,

The New Art – The New Life: The Collected Writings of Piet Mondrian, 1987; and for Vantongerloo himself, C. Blotkamp et al, *De Stijl: The Formative Years, 1917–1922*, 1986. For Lohse, see B. Holeczek et al (eds), *Richard Paul Lohse, 1902–1988*, Ludwigshafen, Wilhelm-Hack Museum, 1992.

For holography, see the issue of *Leonardo* (vol. 22, nos. 3–4, 1989) devoted to this medium, which includes an essay by Sally Weber and Suzanne St Cyr. See also, on Weber's work, M. Fehr (ed.), *Im Licht/In Licht*, Hagen, Karl Ernst Osthaus-Museum, 1995 (in English and German).

Van Gogh's remarks on colour, cited here, are included in R. Pickvance, *Van Gogh in Arles*, 1984; see also *The Complete Letters of Vincent van Gogh*, 1958. Chevreul's impact on artists has now been extensively studied by G. Roque, *Art et Science de la Couleur: Chevreul et les Peintres de Delacroix à l'Abstraction*, 1997. See also my *Colour and Meaning*, chapter 15. I have examined Seurat's approach to colour in *Colour and Meaning*, chapters 16, 17. Many of the documents are translated in N. Broude (ed.), *Seurat in Perspective*, 1978. See also J. Leighton and R. Thompson, *Seurat and the Bathers*, 1997, and P. Smith, *Seurat and the Avant-Garde*, 1997.

For *Cyclorama 2000*, see S. Wurmfeld, *Cyclorama 2000*, Hagen, 2000 (in English and German).

CHAPTER 2
For colour-psychology in general, E. G. Boring, *Sensation and Perception in the History of Experimental Psychology*, 1942; and for von Allesch's sceptical view of colour-preferences, A. R. Chandler, *Beauty and Human Nature: Elements of Psychological Aesthetics*, 1934. I have discussed the role of the psychology of colour in modern art in *Colour and Meaning*, chapter 20.

I have looked in more detail at the role of darkness in picture-making in 'Under color of darkness', in M. Fehr (ed.), *Seeing Red*, 2004, and at 'black light' in *Colour and Meaning*, chapter 18. For fashion, see J. Harvey, *Men in Black*, 1995.

Colour in infancy has been studied by J. W. van der Zanden, *Human Development* (2nd ed., 1981), and Frank Lloyd Wright's observations are in *An Autobiography* (1932), 1977.

Malevich's essay, 'An attempt to determine the relation between colour and form in painting', is in T. Andersen (ed.), *K. Malevich, Essays on Art*, II, *1928–1933*, 1968. For Bauhaus furniture and toys, see M. Siebenbrodt (ed.), *Bauhaus Weimar: Designs for the Future*, 2000.

The Goethe quotations throughout this book are from, J. W. von Goethe, *Theory of Colours*, trans. C. L. Eastlake (1840), 1970.

The fullest examination of Seurat's aesthetic is now R. L. Herbert, *Seurat and the Making of 'La Grande Jatte'*, 2004.

Kandinsky's *On the Spiritual in Art*, is conveniently translated and extensively annotated in K. Lindsay and P. Vergo (eds.), *Wassily Kandinsky: Complete Writings on Art*, 1982, vol. I.

One of many modern accounts of the use of colour in healing is R. Amber, *Color Therapy*, 1983; for a sceptical assessment of the practice, P. Kaiser, 'Physiological responses to color: a critical review', *Color Research and Application*, IX, 1984, 29–36.

Zollinger's account of colour-temperature is in his *Color*, 1999, 139–40; I have looked at the history of the idea in a paper 'When warm was cool: on the history of colour-temperature' (2004; in the press). Wayne Roberts's mapping of the spectrum on to the grey scale is discussed in his book *Principles of Nature: Towards a New Visual Language*, 2003.

CHAPTER 3

For the essays by Malevich and Kandinsky see bibliography for Chapter 2. Léger's essay, 'Les réalisations picturales actuelles', 1914, is translated by E. F. Fry, *Cubism (World of Art)*, 1966. For the Bauhaus, E. Lupton and J. Abbott-Miller (eds), *The ABCs of Triangle, Square, Circle: The Bauhaus and Design Theory*,

(1991), 1993. Gerstner has discussed his series in H. Stierlin (ed.), *The Spirit of Colors: The Art of Karl Gerstner*, c. 1982; see also E. Gomringer (ed.), *Karl Gerstner: Review of Seven Chapters of Constructive Pictures, Etc.*, 2003.

Juan Gris, 'On the possibilities of painting' was published in English in *Transatlantic Review* in 1924, and in German in *Querschnitt*, 1925; it is reprinted in D. H. Kahnweiler, *Juan Gris: His Life and Work*, 1947.

For *disegno* and *colore*, see T. Puttfarken, 'The dispute about "Disegno" and "Colorito" in Venice: Paolo Pino, Lodovico Dolce and Titian', in P. F. Ganz et al (eds), *Kunst und Kunsttheorie, 1400–1900*, 1991. See also my *Colour and Culture*, chapter 7.

Bridget Riley's observations have come largely from Bridget Riley, *Dialogues on Art*, 1995; see also M. de Sausmarez, *Bridget Riley*, 1970, Anton Ehrenzweig, *The Hidden Order of Art*, (1967), 1971, and P. Moorhouse (ed.), *Bridget Riley*, Tate Gallery, 2003.

For Kelly, see T. Kamps, in San Diego Museum of Cotemporary Art, *Ellsworth Kelly: Red, Green, Blue: Paintings and Studies, 1958–1965*, 2003.

I looked at Rothko's approaches to colour in 'Rothko: Color as Subject', in J. Weiss (ed.), *Mark Rothko*, 1998.

Donald Judd's comments on colour come from *Complete Writings, 1959–1975*, 1975; and for colour in his practice, D. Elger (ed.), *Donald Judd, Colorist*, 2000. Judd's Albers exhibition was 'Josef Albers', The Chinati Foundation, Marfa, Texas, 1991. Albers's *Interaction of Color* was published in a monumental edition, with silk-screened plates in 1963, and a modest abbreviated paperback in 1971.

CHAPTER 4

The history of pigments and dyes has been given a general treatment by P. Ball, *Bright Earth: Art and the Invention of Color*, 2001. For indigo, J. Balfour-Paul, *Indigo*, 1998, and the exhibition, 'Sublime Indigo', Marseilles, 1987. English materials have been given an exemplary treatment by R. D. Harley,

Artists' Pigments, c. 1600–1835, 2nd ed., 1982.

Many medieval documents on the powers of coloured gemstones have been gathered by J. Evans in *Magical Jewels of the Middle Ages and the Renaissance* (1922), 1976. Cennino Cennini's *Libro dell'Arte*, has been translated by D. V. Thompson, Jr. as *The Craftsman's Handbook*, 1933 (now available as a Dover Paperback). For Renaissance patronage and pigments, see A. Thomas, *The Painter's Practice in Renaissance Tuscany*, 1995; and for the Venetian colour-trade, L. C. Matthew, 'Vendicolori a Venezia: the reconstruction of a profession', *Burlington Magazine*, CXLIV, 2002, 680–86. Seventeenth-century attitudes to Venetian techniques have been studied by P. Sohm, *Pittoresco: Marco Boschini, his Critics and their Critiques of Painterly Brushwork in Seventeenth- and Eighteenth-Century Italy*, 1991.

I have examined the career and influence of George Field in an exhibition, 'George Field and his Circle, from Romanticism to the Pre-Raphaelite Brotherhood', Fitzwilliam Museum, Cambridge, 1989, and 'A Romantic Colourman: George Field and British art', *Walpole Society*, LXIII, 2001. For late-nineteenth-century pigments and media, A. Callen, *The Art of Impressionism: Painting Techniques and the Making of Modernity*, 2000.

For the modern industrial paints used by artists, J. Crook and T. Learner, *The Impact of Modern Paints*, 2000.

For watercolour, see J. Gage, 'Turner: a watershed in watercolour' in M. Lloyd (ed.), *Turner*, Canberra, National Gallery of Australia, 1996; M. Schapiro, 'Cézanne as a watercolorist', in *Modern Art: Nineteenth and Twentieth Centuries*, 1978. Kandinsky's use of watercolour and experimental media has been discussed by R. H. Wackernagel, '"Watercolour with 'oil'…, oil with 'watercolor' and so on"': on Kandinsky's studio and his painting techniques', in

V. E. Barnett, *Vasily Kandinsky: A Colorful Life: The Collection of the Lenbachhaus, Munich*, 1995.

On Aboriginal ochres, H. Morphy and M. Smith Bole (eds), *Art from the Land: Dialog with the Kluge-Ruhe Collection c Australian Aboriginal Art*, 1999; J. Gage, *Restricting the Palette: Colour and Land*, Canberra School of Art Gallery, Austra National University, 2000; J. Ryan, *Colour Power: Aborigina Art Post-1984 in the Collection of the National Gallery of Victori* 2004.

GHAPTER 5

For a general discussion of the problems of colour-vocabularies, J. A. Lucy, 'The linguistics of color', in C. L. Hardin and L. Maffi (eds), *Color Categories in Thought and Language*, 1997. The Swiss comparative study (by A. von Wattenwyl and H. Zollinger), has now been summarized in an updated, in chapter 6 of his *Color*, 1999, which also include much more linguistic material gathered by Zollinger.

For the Stroop Test, D. R. Davies, D. M. Jones, A. Taylor, 'Selective and sustained attention tasks: individual and group differences', in R. Parasuraman and D. R. Dav (eds), *Varieties of Attention*, 198 395–447.

Old French, *bloi* has been discussed by Pastoureau, *Blue: The History of a Color*, 2000. I have looked at colour in the manuscript workshops in *Colo and Meaning*, chapter 5.

Josef Albers's annotations are recorded in G. Nordland (ed.), *Josef Albers: The American Years*, 1965.

Depero's stage-piece *Color* has been translated in M. Kirb *Futurist Performance*, 1971, 278–79.

I have looked at Ancient Egyptian colour-terms in relation to Egyptian painting ir 'Did colours signify? Symbolisn in the red', *Cambridge Archaeological Journal*, vol. 9/1, 1999, 110–12. For indigenous Australian colour-vocabularies see S. Hargrave, 'A report on colour term research in five Aboriginal languages', *Work*

apers of the Summer Institute of
inguistics, Australian Aboriginal
ranch, Series B, vol. 8, 1982;
ee also my Restricting the
alette, 2000. A somewhat
dited version of Clifford
ossum's interview is published
n V. Johnson's well-illustrated
monograph The Art of Clifford
ossum Tjapaltjarri, 1994, 142.

CHAPTER 6
The most useful general
ictionary of symbolism is
Chevalier and A. Gheerbrant,
enguin Dictionary of Symbols,
969.

Anish Kapoor's interview
was with M. Allthorpe-Guyton,
nd was published in Anish
Kapoor, British Pavilion, XLIV
Venice Biennale, 1990.

For some of the problems
vith purple, see P. Ball, Bright
Earth, 2001; G. Henderson,
The colour purple: a Late
Antique phenomenon and
ts Anglo-Saxon reflexes',
n Vision and Image in Early
Christian England, 1999.

For flags, A. Znamierowski,
The World Encyclopedia of Flags,
999; S. R. Weitman, 'National
lags: a sociological overview',
Semiotica, VIII, 1973, 328–67;
or the French tricouleur,
Pastoureau, Blue, 2000, 145ff.;
or Eisenstein's red flag,
S. Eisenstein, Notes of a Film
Director (1940–48), 1970.

For Theosophical
Symbolism, M. Tuchman (ed.),
The Spiritual in Art, 1890–1985,
1986; C. W. Leadbeater, Man
Visible and Invisible (1902), 1971.
I have looked at Blake's Albion
Rose in Colour and Meaning,
chapter 10. Portal's study of
symbolism was translated into
English by W. S. Inman, and
published in 1845.

For Kandinsky and Steiner in
1930, see Marty Bax, Bauhaus
Lecture Notes, 1930–1933, 1991.
For the Red Oval, see C. Poling
n Kandinsky: Russian and Bauhaus
Years, 1983, 21–22; and for the
ethnographic interpretation,
P. Weiss, Kandinsky and Old
Russia: The Artist as Ethnographer
and Shaman, 1995.

CHAPTER 7
Several of the seminal texts on
multi-media are reprinted in
R. Packer and K. Jordan (eds),

Multi-Media: From Wagner to
Virtual Reality, 2001; see also
M. Rush, New Media in Art, 2nd
ed., 2005.

For medieval multi-media
and ritual, see L. James, 'Sense
and Sensibility in Byzantium',
Art History, 27, 2004, 522–37;
W. Tydeman (ed.), The Medieval
European Stage, 500–1500,
2001.

Vasari's Life of Giovanni
Francesco Rustici is in G. Vasari,
Lives of the Painters, Sculptors and
Architects, trans. A. B. Hind,
(1927), 1963, vol. IV.

Hoffmann's story, 'Ritter
Gluck' does not seem to have
been translated into English.
Delacroix probably knew it in
Oeuvres Complètes d'Hoffmann,
1830, vol. VIII. I have used the
Frankfurt Insel edition of E. T. A.
Hoffmann, Werke, I, 1967.

On Servandoni, D. J. Hough
and N. Wild , 'Giovanni Niccolò
Servandoni', New Grove
Dictionary of Music and Musicians,
2nd ed., 2001.

I have given a brief outline of
de Loutherbourg's work and
reputation in 'Loutherbourg:
Mystagogue of the Sublime',
History Today, 13, 1963; for the
context and history of the
Eidophusikon, see R. Altick,
The Shows of London, 1978.

The most comprehensive
study of stage-lighting in English
is G. Bergman, Lighting in the
Theatre, 1977.

For Loïe Fuller, R. N. and
M. E. Currunt, Loïe Fuller,
Goddess of Light, 1997.

For the history and
problematics of synaesthesia,
see my article on the topic in
M. Kelly (ed.) Encyclopedia of
Aesthetics, 1998, IV. See also
K. Brougher, J. Strick, A.
Wiseman, J. Zilczer, Visual Music:
Synaesthesia in Art and Music
Since 1900, 2005.

The Manifesto of Futurist
Cinema is translated in
U. Apollonio (ed.), Futurist
Manifestos, 1973, and M. Kirby,
Futurist Performance, 1971.

A useful chronology of
the development of the
colour-movie is in B. Coe,
'The development of colour
cinematography' in R. Manvell
(ed.), The International
Encyclopedia of Film, 1972,
29–48.

For Eisenstein, S. Eisenstein,
Selected Works (ed. R. Taylor), II,
IV, 1995–6; S. Eisenstein, Notes
of a Film Director (1948), 1970.

Bergman has written of his
interest in colour in Images: My
Life in Film (1990), 1994; see also
H. I. Cohen, Ingmar Bergman: The
Art of Confession, 1993. For the
influential images of Munch,
A. Eggum, 'The theme of death',
in R. Rosenblum (ed.), Edvard
Munch: Symbols and Images,
1978.

On Hitchcock's Dial M for
Murder, B. Krohn, Hitchcock at
Work, 2000. Hitchcock's 1961
treatment of Marnie is in
D. Aniler, Hitchcock's Secret
Notebooks, 1999, 220; and for a
synopsis of the film as released,
J. E. Sloan, Alfred Hitchcock: A
Filmography and Bibliography,
1995.

For Godard's Pierrot le Fou,
J. Narboni and T. Milne (eds),
Godard on Godard (1968), 1970;
J. Leyda (ed.), Film Makers Speak:
Voices of Film Experience, 1977.
A symbolic view of Godard's
work has been put forward by
A. Dalle Vacche, Cinema and
Painting: How Art is Used in Film,
1996.

On Flaxton, S. Cubitt,
Videography: Video Media as Art
and Culture, 1993

CHAPTER 8
For the Purist view of colour,
C-E. Jeanneret and A. Ozenfant,
'Purism', trans. R. L. Herbert,
Modern Artists on Art, 1964. For
Ozenfant's interior decorations,
W. W. Braham, Modern
Color/Modern Architecture:
Amédée Ozenfant and the
Genealogy of Color in Modern
Architecture, 2002

Fellenosa's comments on
Whistler are cited in C. A. Riley
II, Color Codes: Modern Theories of
Color in Philosophy, Painting and
Architecture, Literature, Music and
Psychology, 1995.

Redon's remarks on black
are in R. Arnheim, Art and Visual
Perception: The New Version, 1974.

For Winckelmann and white,
A. Potts, Flesh and the Ideal:
Winckelmann and the Origins of
Art History, 1994, 160–64.
For Jonathan I., O. Sacks,
'The case of the colour-blind
painter', in An Anthropologist on
Mars, 1995, esp. 36.

For the earliest use of the
'Claude Glass' (by Pieter van
Laer ('Bamboccio') and Gaspar
Dughet), M. Merrifield, Original
Treatises on the Arts of Painting,
(1849), 1967, I, cxxv.

Some of Ad Reinhardt's
extensive writings have been
gathered by B. Rose, Art-as-Art:
The Selected Writings of Ad
Reinhardt, 1975.

For a useful general survey
of oriental aesthetics, T. Munro,
Oriental Aesthetics, 1965. See also
T. Izutsu, 'The elimination of
colour in Far-Eastern art and
philosophy', in Color Symbolism:
Six Excerpts from the Eranos
Yearbook 1972, 1977. For
language, Lu Ching-Fu, 'Basic
Mandarin color-terms', Color
Research and Application, 22,
1997, 4–10; and for the modern
Japanese loan-words, J. Stanlaw,
'Two observations on culture
contact and the Japanese color
nomenclature system', in C. L.
Hardin and L. Maffi (eds), Color
Categories in Thought and
Language, 1997.

A well-illustrated survey
of monochrome painting is
B. Epperlein, Monochrome
Malerei, 1997; see also
T. de Duve, 'The monochrome
and the blank canvas', in
Reconstructing Modernism, 1990.
For Marioni, Joseph Marioni: Blue
Paintings, Boston, Howard
Yezerski Gallery, 2002.

For dress-codes,
A. Hollander, Seeing through
Clothes (1978), 1995; J. Harvey,
Men in Black, 1995.

The Diary of Lady Murasaki,
has been translated by R.
Bowring, 1996; see also Miyeko
Murase (intro.), The Tale of Genji:
Legends and Paintings, 2001.
Atsuko Tamaka's work has been
illustrated and discussed in
M. Kato and M. Tiampo,
Electrifying Art: Atsuko Tamaka,
1954–1968, 2004. Junichiro
Tawizaki's
description of the tea-house
was published in 'In praise of
shadows', Atlantic Monthly, 195,
January 1955, 141–44.

For the new Australian
Aboriginal art, E. Michaels,
Bad Aboriginal Art: Tradition, Media
and Technological Horizons, 1994;
F. R. Myers, Painting Culture: The
Making of an Aboriginal High Art,
2002.

Illustration list

Dimensions of works are given in centimetres then inches, height before width.

1 Ellsworth Kelly, *Spectrum I*, 1953. Oil on canvas, 152.4 x 152.4 (60 x 60). Collection San Francisco Museum of Modern Art (EK 59). © Ellsworth Kelly. **2** Josef Albers, Interaction of Colour, 1963. © The Josef and Anni Albers Foundation/VG Bild-Kunst, Bonn and DACS, London 2006. **3** Wilhelm von Bezold, *Colour Circle*, plate no. 2 from 'The theory of color in its relation to art and art-industry', translated from the German by S. R. Koehler, Boston, L. Prang and Company, 1876. V&A Images/Victoria and Albert Museum. **4** Advertisement. © 2002 Hewlett-Packard Company. **5** Henri Matisse, *Harmony in Red/La desserte*, 1908. Oil on canvas, 180 x 220 (70⅞ x 86⅝). The Hermitage Museum, St Petersburg. Formerly collection Sergei Shchukin. © Succession H. Matisse/DACS 2006. **6** Wassily Kandinsky, study for the cover of *The Blue Rider Almanac*, 1911. Watercolour and pencil on paper, 27.7 x 21.8 (10⅞ x 8⅝). Städtische Galerie im Lenbachhaus, Munich. © ADAGP, Paris and DACS, London 2006. **7** *Life of the Virgin* window, *The Visitation*, *c.* 1150. Stained glass. Chartres Cathedral. **8** *Iris and Turnus*, from *The Aeneid*, Book IX, fol. 74v, the Virgilius Romanus, 5th century AD. **9** Garden painting on north wall of diatea (garden room) of the House of the Wedding of Alexander, Pompeii, 1st century AD. **10** Penthesilea Painter, detail from a red-figure vase, *c.* 450 BC. Museum of Fine Arts, Boston. **11** Game of Knucklebones, Herculaneum, 1st century AD. Museo Nazionale, Naples. Photo Scala, Florence, courtesy the Ministero Beni e Att. Culturali. **12** Bust reliquary of S. Donato, 1346. Silver gilt, enamels and cabochon gemstones. Santa Maria della Pieve, Arezzo. **13** The prophet Isaiah, *c.* 1130. Stained glass. Augsburg Cathedral. © AKG-images/Erich Lessing. **14** French School, *The Crucifixion and the Ascension*, 13th century. Stained glass. Poitiers Cathedral, Poitiers. Paul Maeyaert/The Bridgeman Art Library. **15** Medieval people in silver stain, from the Lady Chapel, *c.* 1340–49. Stained glass, Ely Stained Glass Museum, Ely Cathedral, Cambridgeshire, UK/The Bridgeman Art Library. **16** Masaccio, *The Shadow Healing*, 1425. Fresco, 232 x 162 (91⅜ x 63¾). Brancacci Chapel, Santa Maria del Carmine, Florence. **17** White-ground kylix with Apollo wreathed with myrtle, 5th century BC. Delphi, Museum. Photo Scala, Florence. **18** Bernardo Strozzi, Adoration of the Shepherds, *c.* 1618. Oil on canvas, 97.8 x 139.4 (38½ x 54⅞). Walters Art Museum, Baltimore. **19** Cornelius van Eesteren with colour by Theo van Doesburg, *Axonometric from below, Winkelgalerij Shopping Mall, The Hague*, 1924. Tempera on photostat, 35 x 72.5 (13¾ x 28½). Collection van Eesteren-Fleck and van Lohuizen Archive. **20** Herbert Bayer, *Design for a newspaper kiosk*, 1924. Tempera, 64.5 x 34.5 (25⅜ x 13⅝). Bauhaus-Archiv/Museum für Gestaltung, Berlin. © DACS 2006. **21** Barnett Newman, *Who's Afraid of Red, Yellow and Blue I*, 1966. Oil on canvas, 190 x 122 (75 x 48). Private Collection, New York. © ARS, NY and DACS, London 2006. **22** Johannes Vermeer, *The Girl with a Pearl Earring*, *c.* 1665. Oil on canvas, 46.5 x 40 (18¼ x 15¾). Royal Cabinet of Paintings, Mauritshuis, The Hague. **23** Henri Matisse, *Zulma*, 1950. Gouache on paper, cut and pasted, and crayon, 238 x 133 (93¾ x 52⅜). Statens Museum for Kunst, Copenhagen, J. Rump Collection. © Succession H. Matisse/DACS 2006. **24** William Hogarth, diagram of palette, detail from engraving of *The Analysis of Beauty*, plate II, 1753. **25** William Hogarth, *Self-portrait painting the Comic Muse* (detail), *c.* 1757. Oil on canvas, 45.1 x 42.5 (17¾ x 16¾). National Portrait Gallery, London. **26** Philipp Otto Runge, Colour Harmonies, from *Farben-Kugel* by Philipp Otto Runge, Hamburg, 1810. **27** Benjamin West, *Moses shown the Promised Land*, 1801. Oil on wood, 50.2 x 73 (19¾ x 28¾). Metropolitan Museum of Art, New York. **28** Sir Isaac Newton, Colour Wheel from '*Newton Opticks*', Book I, part II, London, 1704. **29** Moses Harris, *Prismatic Circle*, *c.* 1776 from T. Phillips, 'Lectures on the History and Principles of Painting', London 1833. **30** Frantisek Kupka, *Study for Disks of Newton*, 1911–12. Gouache on paper, 32 x 25 (12⅝ x 9⅞). Centre Pompidou, MNAM, Paris. © ADAGP, Paris and DACS, London 2006. **31** Ogden Rood, *Diagram of Contrasts* from *Modern Chromatics*, London, 1879. **32** Frantisek Kupka, *Disks of Newton (Study for 'Fugue in Two Colours')*, 1911–12. Oil on canvas, 49.5 x 65 (19½ x 25⅝). Centre Pompidou, MNAM, Paris. © ADAGP, Paris and DACS, London 2006. **33** Sir Isaac Newton, *Colours of Thin Plates* from *Opticks*, Book II, part I, London, 1704. **34** Robert Delaunay, *Formes circulaires (Circular Forms)*, 1930. Oil on canvas, 128.9 x 195 (50¾ x 76¾). Solomon R. Guggenheim Museum, New York. Robert Delaunay © L&M Services B.V. Amsterdam. **35** Sonia Delaunay, *Finlandaise*, 1908. Oil on canvas, 42.5 x 46 (16¾ x 18⅛). © L&M Services B.V. Amsterdam. **36** Sonia Delaunay, *Composition*, 1938. Gouache on cardboard, 105 x 74 (41⅜ x 29⅛). © L&M Services B.V. Amsterdam. **37** Piet Mondrian, *Composition in Red, Blue and Yellow*, 1930. Oil on canvas, 46 x 46 (18⅛ x 18⅛). Kunsthaus, Zurich. © 2006 Mondrian/Holtzman Trust c/o HCR International, Warrenton, VA USA. **38** Georges Vantongerloo, *Study, Brussels*, 1918. Oil on canvas, 52 x 61.5 (20½ x 24¼). Private Collection. © DACS 2006. **39** Gerhard Richter, *256 Colours*, 1974 (repainted 1984). Enamel paint on canvas, 222 x 414 (87½ x 163). Städtisches Kunstmuseum, Bonn. © Gerhard Richter. **40** Ellsworth Kelly, *Spectrum Colours Arranged by Chance*, 1951–53. Oil on wood, 152.4 x 152.4 (60 x 60). San Francisco Museum of Modern Art (EK 63). © Ellswo[rth] Kelly. **41** Richard Paul Lohse, *Fifteen System Colour Series in a Circular Form*, 1952/83. Oil [on] canvas, 150 x 150 (59 x 59). Lohse Foundat[ion,] Zurich. **42** Sally Weber, *Alignment*, 1987. Holographic optical element and cast acryl[ic,] 213 x 92 x 50 (83⅞ x 36¼ x 19⅝). Karl Ernst Osthaus-Museum, Hagen. Photo Achim Kukulies, Düsseldorf. **43** Robert Waring Darwin, Ocular Spectra, from *Philosophical Transactions of the Royal Society*, LXXVI, 178[6]. **44** Dan Flavin, *Untitled (to Pat and Bob Rohm* [...] 1969. Red, green and yellow fluorescent lig[ht,] 244 (96). Private Collection. Photo Rury Fischelt. © ARS, NY and DACS, London 20[06]. **45** *The Trinity with Christ Crucified (Austrian)*, *c.* 1410. Egg tempera on silver fir, 118.1 x 11[4] (46½ x 45¼). © National Gallery, London. Bought with a contribution from the Natio[nal] Art Collections Fund, 1922. **46** Vincent van Gogh, *Bedroom at Arles*, 1888. Oil on canvas, 72 x 90 (28 9/16 x 35 7/16). Van Gogh Museum, Amsterdam. **47** Eugène Delacroix, *Dante et les esprits des grands hommes*, 1841–45. Oil [on] canvas, 680 (267 11/16) diameter, 2,040 (803½) circumference. Cupola of Senate, Palais du Luxembourg, Paris. **48** Georges Seurat, *A Sunday on La Grande Jatte* (detail), 1884–86. Oil on canvas, 207.5 x 308.1 (81¾ x 121¼). Helen Birch Bartlett Memorial Collection, A[rt] Institute of Chicago. **49** Georges Seurat, *Le Couple*, 1884–85. Conte crayon, 31.2 x 2[...] (12¼ x 9¼). The Trustees of the British Museum. **50** Sanford Wurmfeld, *Cyclorama*, 2000. Acrylic on cotton, 230 x 280 (90 9/16 x 110¼). Karl Ernst Osthaus-Museum, Hagen. Photo Achim Kukulies, Düsseldorf. **51** Sanf[ord] Wurmfeld, *Cyclorama*, 2000 (detail). Acrylic on cotton, 230 x 280 (90 9/16 x 110¼). Karl Ernst Osthaus-Museum, Hagen. Photo Ach[im] Kukulies, Düsseldorf. **52** James Turrell, *Nigh[t] Passage*, 1987. Rectangular cut in partition wall, fluorescent and tungsten lamps, and fixtures. Dimensions vary with installation; outer room and entry: 450 x 1260 x 1050; sensing space: 410 x 300 x 1050; cut in partition wall: 230 x 525 placed 100 from floor, as installed at the Guggenheim Museu[m] Bilbao, 2000–01, 365.8 x 1097.3 x 1828.8 (144 x 432 x 720). Solomon R. Guggenheim Museum, New York, Panza Collection, Gift, 1991, 91.4080. Photograph by Erika Barahor[a] Ede. **53** Pierre-Auguste Renoir, *La Loge*, 187[...] Oil on canvas, 80 x 63.5 (31½ x 25). The Samuel Courtauld Trust, Courtauld Institute of Art Gallery, London. **54** Édouard Manet, *Portrait of Zacharie Astruc*, 1866. Oil on canva[s,] 90 x 116 (35⅜ x 45⅝). Kunsthalle, Bremen. **55** Kazimir Malevich, *Sportsmen*, *c.* 1930–32 Oil on canvas, 142 x 164 (56 x 64½). Russian Museum, St Petersburg. **56** Kazimir Malevic[h,] *The Artist (Self-Portrait)*, 1933. Oil on canvas, 73 x 66 (28¾ x 26). Russian Museum, St Petersburg. **57** Gerrit Rietveld, *Red-Blue Ch[air]*, *c.* 1923 (reconstruction). Black-stained fram[e]

:quered seat and back, 88 x 65.5 x 83 4⅝ x 25¾ x 32⅝). Cassina SpA. © DACS 006. **58** Peter Keler, *Crib*, 1922. Painted ood. Photo Hochschule für Architektur d Bauwesen. **59** Eberhard Schrammen, ooden construction game, *c.* 1922. Wood, loured, 70 parts, height up to 18.2 (7⅛). unstsammlungen zu Weimar. **60** Friedrich verbeck, *Italia und Germania*, 1828. Oil on nvas, 94.4 x 104.7 (37⅛ x 41¼). Bayerische aatsgemäldesammlungen, Neue Pinakothek unich and Kunstdia-Archiv ARTOTHEK, D-/eilheim. **61** Georges Seurat, *The Side Show arade)*, 1888. Oil on canvas, 101 x 150.2 9¾ x 59⅛). Metropolitan Museum of Art, ew York. Bequest of Stephen C. Clark, 1960. **2** James Clerk Maxwell, *Maxwell's Discs*, *c.* 355. Cavendish Laboratory, Cambridge. **63** M. W. Turner, *The Burning of the House of rds and Commons, October 16th 1834*, 1834. il on canvas, 92.5 x 123 (36⅜ x 48⅜). leveland Museum of Art. **64** Frank Howard, *rner's Principle*, from *Colour as a Means of Art*, 338. **65** Wassily Kandinsky, *Farbstudien mit ngaben zur Maltechnik*, 1913. Watercolour, ouache and pencil on paper, 23.9 x 31.5 (9⅜ x 2⅜). Städtische Galerie im Lenbachhaus, unich. © ADAGP, Paris and DACS, London 006. **66** Wayne Roberts, *Low Tide, Cancale*, 995. Acrylic on schut paper, 39 x 49 (15⅜ x 9¼). Collection of the artist. **67** Wassily andinsky, *Black Lines*, 1913. Oil on canvas, 29.5 x 131.1 (51 x 51⅝). Solomon R. uggenheim Museum, New York. © ADAGP, aris and DACS, London 2006. **68** Wassily andinsky, *Colour System*, 1911. Figure III from Concerning the Spiritual in Art' first ublished in English translation under the title he Art of Spiritual Harmony', London, 1914. **9** Paul Gauguin, *Be Mysterious (Soyez ystérieuses)*, 1890. Painted linden wood, 73 x 5 x 5 (28¾ x 37⅜ x 2). Musée d'Orsay, Paris. cquired in 1978, RF 3405. Photo © RMN - an Schormans. **70** Edvard Munch, *The Lonely nes (Two Human Beings)*, 1899. Colour oodcut. Munch Museum, Oslo (MMG 601-2). **71** Edvard Munch, *The Lonely Ones (Two uman Beings)*, 1899. Colour woodcut. Munch useum, Oslo (MMG 601-42). **72** Anish apoor, *Mother as a Mountain*, 1985. Wood, esso and pigment, height 140 (55). Walker rt Center, Minneapolis. © the artist. **3** Wassily Kandinsky, jacket illustration from 1980 edition of *On the Spiritual in Art* (1914), ublished by Oriental Research Partners, lewtonville, Mass. © ADAGP, Paris and ACS, London 2006. **74** Ivan Kliun, *Forms and olours*, *c.* 1931. Colour lithograph, 22.5 x 17 3⅞ x 6⅝). Costakis Collection. **75** Eugen atz, *Colours and Forms*, 1929–30. Tempera on aper, 42.3 x 32.9 (16⅝ x 13). Bauhaus Archiv, erlin. © DACS 2006. **76** Karl Gerstner, The olor Form Model, Diversion Cycle, *c.* 1979.) Karl Gerstner. **77** Wilhelm Ostwald, olour-circle, from Wilhelm Ostwald, 'Die arbenfibel', 1916. **78** Karl Gerstner, Color orm Objects, Diversion cycle, 1970–75/82. Nitrocellulose on phenolic resin plates. © Karl Gerstner. **79** Oskar Schlemmer, *Point, Line, Plane (Kandinsky)*, 1928. India ink and gold bronze, collage with silver foil, tinted paper and photomontage, with three printed, cut out, and collaged words 'fläche punkt linie' on white card, 20.1 x 20.1 (8 x 8). Schlemmer Nachlass. **80** Wassily Kandinsky, *Tension in Red*, 1926. Oil on card, 66 x 53.7 (26 x 21⅛). Solomon R. Guggenheim Museum, New York. © ADAGP, Paris and DACS, London 2006. **81** Fernand Léger, *Contrast of Forms (Contraste de formes)*, 1913. Oil on burlap, 130.2 x 97.6 (51¼ x 38⁷⁄₁₆). Philadephia Museum of Art, The Louise and Walter Arensberg Collection. © ADAGP, Paris and DACS, London 2006. **82** Juan Gris, *Seated Harlequin*, 1923. Oil on canvas, 73 x 92 (28¾ x 36¼). The Carey Walker Foundation, New York. **83** Titian, *The Assumption*, 1516–18. Oil on panel, 690 x 360 (271⅝ x 141¾). Santa Maria Gloriosa dei Frari, Venice. Photo Archivio RCS Libri, Milan. **84** Titian, *Study for Christ in the Garden*, *c.* 1559–63. White chalk on blue paper, 23.2 x 19.9 (9⅛ x 7⅞). Uffizi, Florence. **85** Michelangelo Buonarotti, *Christ on the Cross between the Virgin and St John*, *c.* 1562. Black chalk and white lead, 38.2 x 21 (15 x 8¼). Royal Collection © 2006 Her Majesty Queen Elizabeth II. **86** Michelangelo Buonarotti, *Roboam-Abias lunette*, 1508/10. Fresco. Sistine Chapel, St Peter's, Rome. **87** El Greco, *The Opening of the Fifth Seal (The Vision of St John)*, 1608–14. Oil on canvas, 222.3 x 193 (87½ x 76). Metropolitan Museum of Art, New York. **88** Rosso Fiorentino, *Deposition from the Cross*, 1528. Oil on panel, 270 x 201 (106¼ x 79⅛). Sansepolcro, San Lorenzo. **89** David Lucas after John Constable, *Old Sarum*, 1830. Mezzotint, 14 x 21.5 (5½ x 8). Tate, London 2006. **90** Mark Rothko, *Orange and Yellow*, 1956. Oil on canvas, 232.4 x 181.3 (91½ x 71⅜). Albright-Knox Art Gallery, Buffalo, New York. Gift of Seymour H. Knox, 1956. © 1998 Kate Rothko Prizel & Christopher Rothko/DACS 2006. **91** Josef Albers, *Homage to the Square*, 1950. Oil on masonite panel, unframed 52.3 x 52 (20⅝ x 20½). Yale University Art Gallery, New Haven, Gift of Anni Albers and the Josef Albers Foundation, Inc. © The Josef and Anni Albers Foundation/VG Bild-Kunst, Bonn and DACS, London 2006. **92** Bridget Riley, *Song of Orpheus 5*, 1978. Acrylic on linen, 195.6 x 259.7 (77 x 102¼). Museum of Fine Arts, Boston. © 2006 Bridget Riley, 2006. All rights reserved. **93** Bridget Riley, *Winter Palace*, 1981. Oil on linen, 212.1 x 183.5 (83.5 x 72¼). Leeds City Art Gallery. © 2006 Bridget Riley, 2006. All rights reserved. **94** Donald Judd, *Untitled*, 1973. Stainless steel and red plexiglass. 10 units measuring 23 x 101.6 x 78.7 (9 x 40 x 31), with each interval. Centre Georges Pompidou, MNAM, Paris. Art © Judd Foundation. Licensed by VAGA, New York/DACS, London 2006. **95** Donald Judd, *Untitled*, 1984. Enameled aluminum, 30 x 180 x 30 (11¹³⁄₁₆ x 70⅞ x 11¹³⁄₁₆). Private Collection, Switzerland. Art © Judd Foundation. Licensed by VAGA, New York/DACS, London 2006. **96** Tony Cragg, *Hassocks*, 1986. Lapis lazuli and serpentine, *c.* 55 x 175 x 45 (21⅝ x 68⅞ x 17¾). Galerie Museum, Basel. Copyright the artist. **97** Fra Angelico, *Linaiuoli tabernacle*, 1433. Tempera on panel, 260 x 266 (102⅜ x 104¾) (open). Museo di San Marco, Florence. **98** Arman, *La Vie dans la ville pour l'oeil (Life in the Town for the Eye)*, 1965. Accumulation of paint tubes and caps with paints in polyester, 123 x 101 x 8 (48½ x 39¾ x 3⅛). Galerie Beaubourg, Paris. © ADAGP, Paris and DACS, London 2006. **99** Titian, *The Entombment of Christ*, 1559. Oil on canvas, 137 x 175 (53⅞ x 68⅞). Prado, Madrid. **100** Vincent van Gogh, *Portrait of Père Tanguy*, 1887–88. Oil on canvas, 65 x 51 (25½ x 20). Private Collection. **101** Advertisement for Thomas Miller's Van Eyck Glass Medium for oil painting, p. 194 from *The Art Union*, 1841. V&A Images/Victoria and Albert Museum. **102** John Everett Millais, *The Bridesmaid*, 1851. Oil on wood, 27.9 x 20.3 (11 x 8). Fitzwilliam Museum, Cambridge. **103** Yves Klein, *Monochrome Bleu*, 1960. Pure pigment and synthetic resin on canvas mounted on wood, 199 x 153 (78⅜ x 60¼). Centre Georges Pompidou, MNAM, Paris. © ADAGP, Paris and DACS, London 2006. **104** Paul Gauguin, *The Yellow Christ*, 1889. Oil on canvas, 92 x 73 (36¼ x 28⅞). Albright-Knox Art Gallery, Buffalo, New York. General Purchase Funds, 1946. **105** Morris Louis, *Golden Age*, 1958. Acrylic on canvas, 231.1 x 378.5 (91 x 149). Ulster Museum, Belfast. **106** J. M. W. Turner, *The Red Rigi*, 1842. Watercolour, 30.5 x 45.8 (12 x 18). Felton Bequest, 1947, National Gallery of Victoria, Melbourne. **107** Paul Cézanne, *Peasant in a Straw Hat*, *c.* 1906. Watercolour, 47.5 x 31.4 (18¾ x 12⅜). Art Institute of Chicago. **108** Wassily Kandinsky, *Komposition*, 1911–12. Watercolour, ink and pencil, 31.5 x 48 (12⅜ x 18⅞). Karl Ernst Osthaus-Museum, Hagen. Photo Friedrich Rosenstiel, Cologne. © ADAGP, Paris and DACS, London 2006. **109** Wassily Kandinsky, *Riegsee-Dorfkirche*, 1908. Oil on cardboard, 33 x 45 (13 x 17¾). Von der Heydt Museum, Wuppertal. © ADAGP, Paris and DACS, London 2006. **110** Michel Lorblanchet re-creating the spotted horse panel at Pech Merle. Courtesy Michel Lorblanchet. **111** Paul Klee, *Emigrating Bird (no. 4176)*, 1926. Gouache sprayed and hand-applied on wove paper bordered with gray gouache, mounted on cardboard, 37.5 x 47.3 (14¾ x 18⅝). Metropolitan Museum of Art, New York, Berggruen Klee Collection, 1984. © DACS 2006. **112** Wassily Kandinsky, *Rotes Quadrant [859]*, 1928. Watercolour on paper, 32.2 x 48.3 (12⅝ x 19). Long Beach Museum of Art, Long Beach, CA, The Milton Wichner Collection. © ADAGP, Paris and DACS, London 2006. **113** Workshop for wall painting. Experimental wall for various spray-gun techniques, Dessau Bauhaus, *c.* 1927. **114** John Hoyland, *17.5.64*. Acrylic on cotton duck, 213 x 274 (84 x 108). © Collection of the Artist/Bridgeman Art Library. **115** Richard Hamilton, *Hers is a Lush Situation*, 1958. Oil, cellulose, metal foil and collage on panel, 81 x 122 (32 x 48). Private Collection. © Richard Hamilton 2006. All Rights Reserved, DACS. **116** Frank Stella, *Ifafa II*, 1964. Metallic powder in polymer emulsion on canvas, 196.9 x 331.5 (77½ x 130½). Museum für Gegenwartskunst der Öffentliche Kunstsammlung, Basel. © ARS, NY and DACS, London 2006. **117** William Blake, *Ghost of a Flea*, c. 1819. Tempera and gold on panel, 21.4 x 16.2 (8⅜ x 6⅜). Tate, London 2006. **118** *The Colours of Urine*, from *The Physicians Calendar*, London, 15th century. Harley MS 5311. The British Library, London. **119** Warlukurlangu Artists, *Karrku*, 1996. Acrylic on canvas, 280 x 680 (110¼ x 267¾). University of Virginia, Kluge-Ruhe Collection. © DACS 2006. **120** Mitjili Napurrula, *Spears at Ualki*, 1994. Synthetic polymer paint on canvas, 56 x 76 (22 x 30). Purchased 1994. Art Gallery of New South Wales. © the artist. **121** Wakuthi Marawili, *Fire Dreaming*, 1976. Earth pigments on bark, 119.3 x 65.4 (47 x 25¾). Purchased through the Art Foundation of Victoria with the assistance of the Utah Foundation, Fellow, 1990. National Gallery of Victoria, Melbourne. Courtesy of Buku-Larrngay Mulka Centre, Yirrkala, NT. **122** Jasper Johns, *False Start*, 1959. Oil on canvas, 170.8 x 137.2 (67¼ x 54). Private Collection, New York. © Jasper Johns/VAGA, New York/DACS, London 2006. **123** Albert H. Munsell, yellow (constant hue) chart of the Munsell Colour Solid, first published in *Color Notation*, 1905. **124** Wassily Kandinsky, rejected design for cover of *Über das Geistige in der Kunst*, 1910. Opaque paint and bodycolour. 8.7 x 11.1 (3⅜ x 4⅜). Städtische Galerie im Lenbachhaus, Munich. © ADAGP, Paris and DACS, London 2006. **125** Kazimir Malevich, Designs for backcloths of *Victory over the Sun*, 1913. Pencil and gouache on paper. Theatre Museum, Saint Petersburg. **126** Josef Albers, *Variant 4 Greens, 2 Grays*, 1948–55. Oil on masonite, 65.5 x 71.1 (25¹³⁄₁₆ x 28). Solomon R. Guggenheim Museum, New York. Gift, The Josef Albers Foundation, Inc., 1991 91.3884. The Josef and Anni Albers Foundation/VG Bild-Kunst, Bonn and DACS, London 2006. **127** Paul Gauguin, oil paint samples and mixtures with autograph notes, on paper; thought to be verso of *The Breton Cavalry*, 1894. Private Collection. **128** Gauguin's palette, c. 1903. Musée d'Orsay, Paris. Photo © RMN. **129** Clifford Possum Tjapaltjarri, *Water Dreaming at Napperby*, 1983. Acrylic on canvas, 183 x 152 (72 x 59⅞). Flinders University Art Museum, Adelaide. © the estate of the artist licensed by Aboriginal Artists Agency 2006. **130** Ginger Riley Munduwalawala, *Limmen Bight River Country*, 1992. Synthetic polymer paint on canvas, 243.5 x 243.5 x 3.7 (95⅞ x 95⅞ x 1½) (stretcher). Mollie Gowing Acquisition Fund for Contemporary Aboriginal Art 1992. Art Gallery of New South Wales. © the Estate of Ginger Riley Munduwalawala, courtesy of Alcaston Gallery, Melbourne. **131** Albert Namatjira, *Mt Sonder*. Watercolour on paper, 26 x 36.5 (10 x 14½). The Gantner Myer Aboriginal Art Collection, Fine Arts Museums of San Francisco, CA. **132** Bruce Nauman, *White Anger, Red Danger, Yellow Peril, Black Death*, 1985. Neon and glass tubing, 203 x 220 (80 x 86½). Marieluise Hessel Collection on permanent loan to the Centre for Curatorial Studies, Bard College, Annandale-on-Hudson, New York. © ARS, NY and DACS, London 2006. **133** Justinian, *Bishop Maximianus, and attendants*, c. 547. Mosaic from the north wall of the apse, San Vitale, Ravenna. **134** Gospel of St John, Coronation Gospels, f.178v, 8th century AD. Vienna, Weltliche Schatzkammer. Kunsthistorisches Museum, Vienna. **135** National flag of Saudi Arabia. **136** Sergei Eisenstein, scene from *Battleship Potemkin*, 1925. **137** Eugène Delacroix, *Liberty Leading the People*, 1830. Oil on canvas, 260 x 325 (102⅜ x 128). Louvre, Paris. Photo © RMN. **138** Fiona Foley, *Untitled (Aboriginal Flag)*, 1991. Gouache, 18 x 13.2 (7 x 5¼). Collection Parliament House, Canberra. Image courtesy of the artist. Represented in Australia by Niagara Galleries, Melbourne and Andrew Baker Gallery, Brisbane. **139** Jasper Johns, *White Flag*, 1955. Encaustic and collage on canvas, 198.9 x 306.7 (78¼ x 120¾). Collection the artist. © Jasper Johns/VAGA, New York/DACS, London 2006. **140** Key to the Meaning of Colours, from frontispiece of *Man Visible and Invisible* by C. W. Leadbeater, London, 1902. **141** Astral Body of the Developed Man, Pl. XXIII from *Man Visible and Invisible* by C. W. Leadbeater, London, 1902. **142** William Blake, *Albion Rose*, c. 1796. A colour printed etching with hand-drawn additions in ink and watercolour, 27.5 x 20.2 (10⅞ x 8). British Museum, London. **143** Wassily Kandinsky, *Impression III (Concert)*, 1911. Oil on canvas, 77.5 x 100 (30½ x 39⅜). Städtische Galerie im Lenbachhaus, Munich. © ADAGP, Paris and DACS, London 2006. **144** Wassily Kandinsky, Table I from *On the Spiritual in Art*, 1914. **145** Wassily Kandinsky, *Red Oval*, 1920. Oil on canvas, 71.5 x 71.2 (28⅛ x 28¹⁄₁₆). Solomon R. Guggenheim Museum, New York. © ADAGP, Paris and DACS, London 2006. **146** Ivan Kliun, *Untitled*, c. 1917. Oil on paper, 27 x 22.5 (10⅝ x 8¾). Costakis Collection. **147** Ivan Kliun, *Untitled*, 1918. Gouache on paper, 30.8 x 28.8 (12⅛ x 11¼). Costakis Collection. **148** *Definite Affection*, figure 10 from A. Besant and C. W. Leadbeater, *Thought Forms*, 1905. **149** Georges Seurat, final study for *Le Chahut*, 1889. Oil on canvas, 55.6 x 46.7 (21⅞ x 18⅜). Albright-Knox Art Gallery, Buffalo, New York. General Purchase Funds, 1943. **150** Bernardo Buontalenti, engraving after the original design for *Intermezzo III*, 1589. V&A Images/Victoria and Albert Museum. **151** Set design model attributed to Giovanni Niccolò Servandoni, 18th Century. Photo The Art Archive/Château de Chambord/Dagli Orti. **152** Edward Burney, *De Loutherbourg's* Eidophusikon, c. 1782. Watercolour, 19.7 x 27.3 (7¾ x 10¾). British Museum, London. **153** Louis Daguerre, *The Ruins of Holyrood Chapel*, c. 1824. Oil on canvas, 211 x 256.3 x 101). Walker Art Gallery, National Muse Liverpool. **154** 'The Triclinium', from *Le Costume ancien et moderne* by Jules Ferraric c. 1820. Coloured engraving after Alessanc Sanquirico. Bibliothèque des Arts Décorat Paris. Archives Charmet/The Bridgeman A Library. **155** Pietro Gonzaga stage scenery. 172 x 230 (67¾ x 90½). Fondazione Giorgi Cini, Venice. **156** Adolphe Appia, *Die Walkü* 1924. Act II, A wild rocky place. Stadttheat Basel. **157** *Overture to Wagner's* Meistersing A. Besant and C. W. Leadbeater, *Thought Forms*, 1905. **158** Edward Gordon Craig, illustration for the stage set of Henrik Ibse *The Pretenders*, Act 3, Scene 1, 'The Bishop Death', printed on Mould Made Paper, 22.9 8.9 (9 x 3½). Published in *A Production 1926, being designs projected or realized by Edward Gordon Craig, for 'The Pretenders' of Henrik Ib* Oxford University Press, 1930. Reproduce permission of the Edward Gordon Craig Estate. **159** Richard Smith, *Edward Gordon Craig*, 1968. Lithograph on paper, 37.1 x 71. (14¹⁹⁄₁₆ x 28). Tate, London 2006. © Richard Smith. **160** Henri de Toulouse-Lautrec, *Stu for Loïe Fuller*, 1893. Peinture à l'essence on cardboard, 63.2 x 45.3 (24⅞ x 17⅞). Musée Toulouse-Lautrec, Albi. **161** Eugène Delacr *Gluck at the Piano*, 1831. Watercolour and pastel, 22.5 x 17 (8⅞ x 6⅝). Present whereabouts unknown. **162** Alexander Lás *Color-musical performance* (after a watercolc by Matthias Holl), from A. Laszlo, *Color-light music (Die Farblichtmusik)*, Leipzig, 1925. **163** Sergei Eisenstein, still from red sequen from *Ivan the Terrible, Part II*, 1946–58. **164** Sergei Eisenstein, still from blue seque from *Ivan the Terrible, Part II*, 1946–58. **165** Alfred Hitchcock, still from *Marnie*, 196 Photo Universal/The Kobal Collection. **166** Ingmar Bergman, The mourners and Anders Ek at the deathbed, stills from *Cries and Whispers (Viskningar och rop)*, 1972. © 19 AB Svensk Filmindustri. **167** Edvard Munch *By the Deathbed*, 1895. Oil on canvas, 90 x 120.5 (35⅜ x 47½). Rasmus Meyer Samlinge Bergen. © Munch Museum/Munch - Ellingse Group, BONO, Oslo, DACS, London 2006. **168** Jean-Luc Godard, stills from *Pierrot le Fo* 1965. © 1991 Canal+ International/Iberia Fi Société Nouvelle de Cinématographie. **169** Dan Sandin, *Landscape environment from CA* 2003. University of Illinois, Chicago. Court the artist. **170** Amédée Ozenfant, *Le Pot bla* 1925. Oil on canvas, 151.5 x 176.5 (59⅜ x 69½). Centre Georges Pompidou, MNAM, Paris. © ADAGP, Paris and DACS, London 2006. **171** Amédée Ozenfant, *Plan Diagram of Curtain Arrangements for Living Room/Colou Laboratory*, 1937. From *Architectural Review*,

ndex